# THE
# SERIOUS
# JOKE
# BOOK

## George Coote

*The Serious Joke Book*

This edition published in 1998 by Tiger Books
International PLC, 26A York Street, Twickenham,
TW1 3LJ, England

ISBN 1 85501 601 X

Text © G. Coote 1994

Volume © Gap Publishing Pty Ltd 1994
44 Wendell Street, Norman Park,
Queensland 4170, Australia

Printed and bound in the UK by
Cox & Wyman Ltd, Reading, England

# DEDICATION

*To Bonny, my first wife.*

# ACKNOWLEDGEMENTS

WHO told the first joke? Who makes them up?

Are there really any new ones, or are they the same old yarns adapted and re-cycled through generations with only the names changed, not to defend the innocent, but to ensure we dob in the guilty.

I make no claim to the yarns in this book, indeed, I have heard most of them over the years in so many forms and versions it would be impossible to source their origin.

Most have been gathered from fellow travel writers during delays at airports, long flights and longer train rides. Swapping yarns is an affliction of the profession. (I was destined to be a travel writer. My first job was a proof reader for a sky-writing firm. And I hope that didn't go over your head).

I pay tribute to those fellow journos who could always see the funny side of lost luggage, or missing the last flight out of Mozambique, and to those who could still swap eye-watering belly laughs when broke and far from home in dire straits.

# Contents

# INTRODUCTION

EVEN a baby smiles at its father, which is proof that human beings are quick to recognise a joke. From then on, throughout life, any gathering of good folk is better off if it raises a laugh.

A life of journalism and travelling has meant listening to hundreds of speeches, most of them dull. But the speakers remembered were those who had a sense of humour and those who included a few gags. I always remembered the wisecracks and usually forgot the earth-shattering theme of the speech, and if the gags were good I wrote them down. Be it parliament, a municipal council meeting, a court case, a dinner party, a family reunion, a wedding, or even a funeral, these events are all the more memorable, if someone cracks a joke and creates a smile.

The purpose of this book is to make sure there is plenty of ammunition for those who find themselves having to "say a few words" at the rostrum, standing beside the wedding cake, bidding farewell to a retiring colleague at the office, or leaning on the bar holding court at the local.

Given a free choice most people would rather be amused than be on the receiving end of a lecture, and no matter how informative the speech may be it can be improved if peppered with a few gags. It will keep the audience alert, waiting for the next one.

The aim of this book is not to turn speeches into an entire comedy routine. Too many jokes will detract from the purpose of the address, and there are important things to be said at weddings, 21st birthdays or an election speech for local council. The art of public speaking is to select a few anecdotes central to the theme and select a few gags that can be tailored to the topic.

# KEEPING THEM CLEAN

JOKES are known by the company they keep and their tendency to slip below the belt doesn't necessarily rule them out of order. Rude need not be crude, and some of the roughest can be salvaged with different wording to retain the same punchline in an acceptable form. What we are saying here is best illustrated by the limerick, those compact rhymes so often concerned with the bawdy;

> The limerick packs laughs anatomical
> Into space that is quite economical
> But the good ones we've seen
> So rarely are clean
> And the clean ones so seldom are comical.

In this volume we give readers the option;

> If you are ultra-fastidious by far
> And never tell yarns to your Ma
> Here are jokes by the mile
> That will sustain a wide smile
> But don't read any marked (R).

# NOTES ARE ESSENTIAL

PUBLIC speaking is a comparatively simple business if you are properly prepared, but notes are essential. Unless you are an orator of the calibre of Winston Churchill, or have a phenomenal memory, don't try to deliver a speech without notes. Prime ministers don't.

One of the funniest speeches delivered recently was Michael Palin's tribute to George Harrison at a dinner to honour Harrison's financial backing of Handmade Films. Palin, of Monty Python fame, made sure he didn't miss one point of his hilarious monologue by shuffling a sheaf of foolscap notes, held at arm's length because of his long-sightedness. His note-reading was central to his delivery.

Most talks are delivered from completely written speeches, delivered word for word with few, if any, ad-lib departures. With a little practice it can appear to be friendlier and be appreciated as more spontaneous with note cards in one hand and several wisecracks up your sleeve.

The art is delivery and timing. If you have the advantages of a rostrum where your notes can be laid out on the lectern, then it is a comparatively simple matter to prepare well in advance and control the presentation with confidence, especially with a microphone.

Everybody tests a microphone, so turn yours to advantage to gain composure:

"Can you hear me over in that far side? Last time I asked if anybody could hear me in that far corner a bloke stood up and said indeed he could. And he offered to change places with somebody who couldn't!"

Standing before your contemporaries at a less formal office farewell, with no microphone, is a little more difficult but there is usually a semblance of order at these functions and there is at least the expectation of an address. Small prompt cards that can be shuffled in your hand is the most practical way to tackle this gathering.

The third, and most difficult arena for "public speaking" is the club, the pub, or around the dinner table where there is no order, and where contributing rather than dominating the conversation is a fine art. It takes a certain amount of confidence to embark on a lengthy yarn and expect to hold attention while you construct the plot to the punchline. Interjections, distractions and the waiter bringing the soup can cripple a good story unless the teller can cope with the interruption, anticipate the waiter's arrival, or suddenly stop the yarn at a high point of the teller's choosing. When the waiter leaves he shouldn't have to say, "Now where was I?" It is much more satisfying to have his listeners chase him for the rest of the yarn with someone eagerly asking "C'mon, what happened next?"

One-liners are the ideal tin-openers to tap the conversation with strangers around the table. Just raise your glass and say: "You can tell the happy motorcyclists by the insects on their teeth." And just leave it at that. Listen for the appropriate break in the conversation and say: "Oh I heartily agree. I was only saying the same thing to my wife in the bath last night." These are throw-away lines to test the water, and there are two pages of these profound statements in this volume. Your kind of humour will either be quickly embraced, or totally ignored.

A trick to hold attention in the rough and tumble of the bar or dinner table is to introduce your story with an off-beat opening line that will grab their attention.

"Did you hear about the one-armed Irish publican called Jock McTavish who took his first holiday abroad after pulling right-handed beers for 30 years?"

This story about the publican's trip to the Canary Islands is a top yarn and appears in the Travel section of this book. The "one-armed publican called Jock" has nothing to do with the thrust of the yarn but the introduction enables the construction of the story to continue. The listeners wait for the relevance of an Irishman called Jock and are led down a different trail to the punchline.

## SALTING THE TALE

THE art of making an implausible story believable is to salt it along the way.

For example, did you hear about the woman who complained that passing trains rocked her bed so much she couldn't sleep?

"Unbelievable," is what the estate agent said, too, but the woman, who had just taken a lease on the flat near the railway line, insisted it was true and demanded the estate agent come around.

As he was shown in he noticed a mouse trap with a fish in it. "What's that?" he enquired.

"Oh, I'll talk to you about the rising damp later. Right now there is a train due and I want you to experience the vibrations."

They entered the bedroom. It was quiet. "I can't believe passing trains rock the bed," he said.

"Shakes the living daylights out of it," she persisted, looking at her watch. She heard a distant train whistle.

"Here's the five-thirty-five. Quick, lie down on the bed yourself," she said, and she climbed on to the other side.

That's when her husband came in. "What do you think you are doing?" he roared, glaring at the estate agent stretched out on the eiderdown.

"Would you believe, waiting for a train?" he ventured.

Remember, this book provides the raw material presented here in cold type. A little acting, timing and delivery will greatly enhance their reception to your audience. Delivering the appropriate gag at the right time is what it is all about, and when one joke follows another on the same topic, then it's a double-whammy. A series of yarns on the same theme raises those belly laughs that are good for the soul.

So if these cold pages make you smile, then imagine the effect when they are delivered as repartee.

The categories are designed to cover every occasion from births to funerals, including bonking (which actually comes before births).

If it is your responsibility to farewell a retiring office colleague, toast the happy couple, propose the toast at the coming of age party or make a presentation, there are anecdotes in this book suitable for adapting to your guest of honour... or the victim of your address.

Select some, tinker with them and enjoy them yourself, and before taking centre stage remember the ABC and the XYZ of public speaking. ABC is Always Be Cheerful, and XYZ is Examine Your Zipper.

## A WEDDING

LET'S take a wedding anniversary as an example. It depends on how formal the function is, and how well everybody knows each other, but if you have drawn the short straw to "say a few words" then do some serious research on the couple for the proper tribute which needs to be said, and cobble in as many of these one-liners you judge the gathering will appreciate.

Ladies and gentlemen, in-laws and outlaws, friends and foe ... it has befallen my lot to say a few words on behalf of you all and to toast Bill and Mabel who have been married 30 years today.

Mabel tells me that includes ten years of wedded bliss. And Bill reminds us all that the sentence for manslaughter is only 25 years. But they both agree, that the reason they have stuck together so long is that neither will take custody of the kids. I can well remember the day they had to get ... sorry, the day they got married. Bill has always remembered it too. Unlike most husbands who forget these anniversaries, their wedding day never slipped Bill's memory. It was the day Arsenal thrashed Liverpool.

And of course Mabel was not the street-wise matron she is today. Bill says she was so naive when he married her she thought intercourse was a ticket to the races.

Although it was a big wedding with family and friends from both sides, I am reliably informed that Bill and Mabel still sat up all night waiting for their sexual relations to arrive. It was also the night Bill exploded the myth about oysters. He tells me he had a dozen on his wedding night but only eleven of them worked.

Marriage is a marvellous institution. No family should be without it. (Or, marriage is a marvellous institution, but who wants to live in an institution?) Bill tells me that marriage is a matter of give and take, and that he gives and Mabel takes. And Mabel says they have stopped giving each other anniversary presents long ago, now they shake hands each year and call it quits.

Those who miss out on marriage miss a great deal in life. It reminds me of a bishop I know, right in this very town, who was touched with compassion when he saw an elderly couple standing together in the queue at the Op Shop sale. He thought to himself, "They have shared a lifetime together, through thick and thin, and now here they are, fallen upon hard times, in their twilight years." He went up to them and asked if they would like to spend a week's holiday at Bishop's Retreat in the mountains and packed them off in his chauffeured limousine before they could express their thanks. It was a month later when the bishop saw the old man in the Op Shop again, standing alone this time.

"Did you enjoy the holiday? Did you enjoy the food?" he asked.

"Oh, everything was tops," said the old-timer. "But tell me yer grace, who was that old-boiler I had to share the room with?"

And so, ladies and gentlemen, back to the topic in hand. Could we have two minutes silence ... oops, sorry. Could we all raise our glasses and drink to the long and happy health of our dear friends, Bill and Mabel.

## THE ANNUAL MEETING

ANOTHER example is the reunion, the annual general meeting, the yearly bunfight or social gathering. Whether

7

it is pompously formal or loosely ad hoc, somebody has to say a few words:

Gentlemen. Excellent to see such a roll-up tonight. It has befallen my lot to give you a short address. Here it is: 29 Bay Street.

Since last we met we've passed a lot of water under the bridge. We have an apology. Smithers can't get bail.

New members will be delighted to know that our president is a man of substance, a pillar of society who needs no introduction. So he won't get one.

We have the treasurer's report from Sticky Fingers Smithers who has cooked the books to show we have a healthy bank balance. As already stated, Sticky can't be here tonight. He is helping the police with some enquiries.

We should move a vote of thanks to our honorary president who slaves all day over a hot secretary on behalf of us all. And it should be said that his dedication to the club is such that in pursuit of its well-being he never leaves a turn unstoned.

And let's pay tribute to our committee. As you all know, half the members of most committees are hopeless layabouts while the other half do all the work, but with our committee it is completely the reverse.

## GET THE PUNCHLINE STRAIGHT

MANY people who enjoy a good joke lament that they cannot remember them. Those that can remember them, vaguely, lose the plot and lack the confidence to relate them.

The key to it all is to remember the punchline, get it straight, and store it in your mind with a recall word.

A stock of jokes, as this book sets out to supply, will provide the flexibility to match the repartee around the table, especially when you are halfway into the yarn and the resident smart alec (every function has one) interjects with: "Don't tell me its the white horse joke!"

"Wrong, again," you lie, and change direction for horse joke number two, three or four. Style is important.

## HOW TO USE THIS BOOK

MOST jokes can be reconstructed and adapted to suit all occasions.

Take this bland example of three politicians who died on the same day and arrived at the Devil's reception centre simultaneously.

"Ah, a Tory MP," said the Devil. "We've been waiting for you," and he took him to a dungeon where a terrible witch was the only occupant. The MP was pushed into the dingy cell and as the door clanged behind him the Devil's voice over the PA system boomed: "Tory MP, this is your punishment!"

Next was a Labor MP. "We've been waiting for you, too," and taking him to another dungeon which contained yet another horrible witch, he was given a push and, as the door clanged behind him, the Devil's voice over the PA system boomed: "Labor MP, this is your punishment!"

The third polly was the prime minister. "Ah, we have certainly been waiting for you," said the Devil and he was led to another dungeon. Inside, through soft lights, the PM could see Miss Lottzabazooma reclining naked on a satin couch. He was given a shove and, as the door clanged shut behind him, the Devil's voice over the PA system boomed: "Miss Lottzabazooma, this is your punishment!"

Consider how much better that story would be if you used the names of well-known politicians who fitted the bill.

Better still, personalise the same story by including

those around your table; Tom, Dick and Harry. And set up the guest of honour (Harry in this case) by saving him for the last dungeon.

First, Tom gets berated by the Devil over the sins for which he is notorious: "being late for your own wedding, never arriving at a golf match on time, and for collecting parking tickets."

Dick gets thrown into his cell for "telling those boring jokes, ad nauseum and for giving worthless racing tips to close friends" and Harry gets a similar drubbing listing his "in-house" personality traits that your listeners readily recognise. Involving your friends in the joke makes it far more humourous.

So run an astute eye over the "raw material" listed here and consider their modification to different professions and new situations.

IN a Serious Joke Book the funniest jokes are not necessarily upfront. In alphabetical order we are obliged to start, like we all began, with accidents.

## ACCIDENTS
See CARS, MOTORING, DRIVERS.

THE young woman was giving details of the accident to the police and denied she was speeding.

"What gear were you in?" asked the cop.

"An apricot yellow two-piece with chartreuse picture hat," she said.

\* \* \*

TEN per cent of all accidents are caused by drivers affected by alcohol. Which is another way of saying that 90 per cent of accidents are caused by non-drinkers.

\* \* \*

THERE was a knock on the door and Fred found himself being asked to become a Jehovah's Witness.

"I didn't even see the bloomin' accident," he said.

\* \* \*

THE woman at the cocktail party was intent on making the acquaintance of the young medical officer.

"Do you deal with many accidents?" she asked.

"I really don't know," he replied.

"But you are a doctor, what do you mean you don't know?"

"How could I," he said, "My field is obstetrics."

\* \* \*

WHEN Harry arrived at the pub his mates noticed he was on crutches, his face was bruised and there was plaster over his eye. "I must have had one too many when I left here last night," he explained.

His mates said they thought he had been quite sober. "As maybe," said Harry, "but after I left the pub, I turned up High Street, did the roundabout on the corner three times, came back on the wrong side of the road, crossed the median strip and crashed right into the front door of this pub.

"Lucky I wasn't in my bloomin' car!"

\* \* \*

"HOW did this accident happen, sir?"

"My wife fell asleep in the back seat."

\* \* \*

"HOW did this accident happen, sir?"

"Well, the sign said, STOP, LOOK AND LISTEN, and while I was doing that a bloody train ran over me."

\* \* \*

SAID the cop: "Have you ever had an accident, Missus?"

"Well, I met my husband at a service station."

\* \* \*

THE wife told the police that although she had broken the umbrella over her husband's head it was an accident. "If I had known the umbrella would break I would have used a golf club," she said.

\* \* \*

FRED had just parked his old car when a cop came and asked him if he had reported the accident.

\* \* \*

FIVE Hells Angels walked into the bar, ordered their drinks and suggested the lone drinker at the end of the bar should pay. When he refused they punched him up and threw him out of the pub.

"He wasn't much of a fighter," said one of the bikies to the barman.

"He is not much of a driver either," said the barman, "He has just had an accident and driven his truck over five motorbikes."

*     *     *

AFTER a terrible accident at the factory, where Fred fell into the upholstery machine, he is now fully recovered.

*     *     *

THE cop pushed through the crowd at the scene of the accident to see a blonde and a young man having passionate sex on the nature strip.

He quickly put a stop to it and demanded to know what was going on.

"It's all my fault," she said. "He was thrown from his car in the accident and I was giving him mouth to mouth resuscitation, and, well, we both got carried away."

*     *     *

HE was sitting at the bar knocking back double Scotches. As fast as the barman could place them in front of him he scoffed them down in one gulp.

"It's the only way I've been able to drink them since my accident," he explained to a friendly enquirer.

"What sort of accident?" asked his new friend.

"Shocking," he replied. "I knocked one over with my elbow."

## ACCOUNTANTS
See FINANCE

MY old Dad said I'd never make an accountant.

"There are three kinds of people in this world, son," he said. "Those who can count, and those who can't!"

A CHARTERED accountant is an undertaker who has had a charisma bypass.

*　　*　　*

THE chartered accountant went into the pub after work and ordered a pot of beer. As the publican pushed it across the bar the accountant said: "Do you think you could get a nip of whisky in that?"

"Certainly, sir," said the publican.

"In that case," said the accountant, "perhaps you'd just top it up with beer!"

*　　*　　*

THEY say Adam was the first accountant, after he turned a leaf and made an entry.

*　　*　　*

HE thought the new office girl was as beautiful as an Income Tax Refund.

*　　*　　*

HE told his wife he was changing their accountant.

"He's too shy and retiring," he explained.

"Is that a reason to sack him?" she asked

"Yes. He's $200,000 shy and that's why he's retiring."

*　　*　　*

ON his retirement after 35 years as Chief Accountant the company presented him with a silver-bound ledger book, framed and mounted on a little pedestal.

He looked at the trophy and said, "Well at least it has finally settled a concern of mine. I almost chose a career as a gynaecologist."

*　　*　　*

THE executive director visited the company's accountant who was sick in hospital. "John," he said, "the board decided to send you a Get Well Card and I would like you to know it was a majority decision."

*　　*　　*

THE partners in the accountancy firm crossed the road to their local bar for their usual afterwork drink.

"Oh, I forgot to lock the safe," said one.

"It's okay," said his partner. "We're both here aren't we?"

# ADVERTISEMENTS

PLACED in the personal column: "Fred, please do not come home. All is forgiven."

\* \* \*

GIRL wanted for petrol pump attendant.

\* \* \*

MAN wanted to wash dishes, and two waitresses.

\* \* \*

ACCOMMODATION, suit two girls willing to share room or young man.

\* \* \*

ACCOMMODATION: Honeymoon suite, sleeps three.

\* \* \*

STRADIVARIUS violin for sale. Almost new.

\* \* \*

"PHOTOGRAPHER setting up own business needs model, as sleeping or active partner."

\* \* \*

LOST dog. Has three legs, blind in left eye, right ear missing, broken tail, no teeth, recently castrated. Answers to Lucky.

\* \* \*

A SALESMAN was staying overnight in a country town where the only excitement was watching the spin-dry in the laundromat. Out of sheer boredom he opened the Gideon Bible provided in all motel rooms. On the fly-leaf was a message: If thou art bored and lonely and desireth some warm comfort, ring Susie, 58-6683.

\* \* \*

WONDERFUL opportunity for woman to join fishing partners. Must have own boat. Must be able to cook, wash and gut fish. Please send photo of boat.

# ALCOHOLICS

ALCOHOLICS Anonymous is a place where you drink in secret.

* * *

THERE is a new organisation called AAAA.
 It is for people being driven to drink.

* * *

THE vicar was invited to address the Alcoholics Anonymous meeting. "I have lived in this town all my life," he said sternly. "There are 95 hotels and I can honestly say I have never been in one of them."
 "Which one is that?" said a voice from the rear.

* * *

HE bought one of those audio tapes that help you to stop drinking while you're sleeping. It worked. He hasn't had a drink in his sleep since.

* * *

"ALCOHOL is your trouble," said the judge. "Alcohol alone is responsible for your present predicament."
 "Thank you, judge," said the drunk. "Everyone else says it's my fault."

* * *

THE wife sought some advice from the doctor about her alcoholic husband.
 "Has he tried Alcoholics Anonymous?" asked the Doc.
 "I expect so. He'll drink anything," she replied.

* * *

CHAP was walking home when an alcoholic stepped in front of him with a gun in one hand and a bottle in the other. Pointing the gun at his victim the drunk thrust the bottle forward and said, "Take a drink of this."
 The unfortunate man took a swig then spat it out. "It's awful," he gasped.
 "I know," said the drunk. "Now you hold the gun on me while I take a swallow."

THEY were in the Mexican army on curfew duty. "You patrol this side of the street, and I will patrol the other," said Pedro to his mate.

They hadn't gone very far when a shot rang out and Pedro ran across the street to discover his mate with a smoking gun and a dead man on the footpath.

"Why did you shoot him?" demanded Pedro. "The curfew is not in force for another half hour?"

"I know that," said his mate. "But I know where this hombre lives and there is no way he would have got home in time."

\*　　\*　　\*

THE difference between being a drunk and being an alcoholic is that the drunk doesn't have to bother attending all those boring meetings.

\*　　\*　　\*

AN alcoholic is somebody you don't like, but drinks as much as you.

\*　　\*　　\*

AN alcoholic believes a teetotaller is someone who practices moderation to excess, and abstinence is okay provided you do it in moderation.

\*　　\*　　\*

FRED joined Alcoholics Unanimous. "There are no arguments," he explained.

\*　　\*　　\*

THE drunk asked a passer-by if he knew the way to Alcoholics Anonymous.

"Why," he said, "do you want to join?"

"No, I want to resign."

\*　　\*　　\*

FRED stumbled into the AA meeting and knocked over a few chairs.

The secretary frowned: "Oh, we were so happy last night when you turned up sober."

"Well, tonight it's my turn to be happy," said Fred.

THE doctor noticed that the chronic alcoholic could not hold his hands out straight. They shook violently.

"How much have you been drinking lately?" he asked.

"Hardly any," said the drunk. "I spill most of it!"

*　　*　　*

SHE answered a knock on the door. "I am collecting for the Home for Alcoholics," said the caller.

"Well come back around nine o'clock," she said. "My husband will be home then, and you can have him."

*　　*　　*

HE preached moderation in all things. "First, I never drink whisky without water. Second. I never drink water without whisky."

## ANIMALS

THERE is a big difference between buffaloes and bisons.

For a start, you can't wash your hands in a buffalo.

*　　*　　*

WHERE would you find a turtle with no legs?

Exactly where you left him.

*　　*　　*

THE bi-sexual donkey had a hee in the morning and a haw at night.

*　　*　　*

THE suicidal seal flip-flopped into the pub and asked for a Canadian Club on the rocks.

*　　*　　*

A BLOKE went to the pub with a giraffe. They drank all afternoon. By six o'clock the giraffe collapsed in an ungainly heap on the floor and his drinking partner staggered towards the door.

"Hey," said the barman, "Don't go and leave that lyin' on the floor."

The man turned and said, "It's not a lion. It's a giraffe!"

LEO the Lion was swaggering down the jungle path confronting each animal in turn: "Who's the king of the jungle?" he asked Gerald the giraffe.

"You are, of course," said Gerald.

"Who's the king of the jungle?" he asked Harold the hyena.

"You are, of course."

The answers were the same until he confronted Jumbo the elephant. "Who's the king of the jungle?" he asked, blocking Jumbo's path.

With a blast from his trumpet the elephant picked the lion up in his trunk, threw him in the air, caught him, dashed him against a tree then flung him over his shoulder.

"Alright," said Leo dusting himself off. "You don't have to get nasty just because you don't know the answer!"

\* \* \*

LEO the lion was drinking from a stream with his bottom in the air, just as a big chimp was passing. From the chimp's viewpoint it looked like Lily the lion so he crept up for a quiet slap and tickle.

The lion let out a mighty roar and the chimp, realising his mistake, took off like greased lightning. He sped through the jungle with the lion in hot pursuit.

The chimp dashed into a hunter's camp, quickly donned a safari suit, slapped on a pith helmet, dived into a chair, grabbed a copy of The Times and hid behind it as if was reading. The lion screeched into the clearing and as soon as the dust settled asked the "hunter", "Have you seen a chimp dash past here?"

"Not the chimp that dated the lion down by the stream?"

"Hell," said the lion, "don't tell me it's in the papers already."

\* \* \*

THE visitor was admiring the family's pet pig.

"Yes, he's an amazing animal," said the farmer. "Once

he raised the alarm and saved the house from burning down. Another time he saved young Johnny from drowning and pulled him out of the dam ..."

"That's incredible," said the visitor, "but tell me, why does he have one leg missing?"

"Well," said the proud farmer, "you don't eat a pig like that all at once!"

*　　*　　*

ONE zebra got to thinking. "Hey, Zeke," he said to his mate, "are we white with black stripes, or black with white stripes?"

Zeke didn't know and they pondered this problem for a week before asking the king of the jungle.

"Hey Leo, are we white with black stripes, or black with white stripes?"

Leo didn't know but he directed them up to the top of a mountain. "Ask God," he said.

They spent a day sitting on top of the mountain shouting: "Hey God. Are we white with black stripes or black with white stripes?"

It wasn't until sunset that the booming voice of God bellowed out: "You are what you are."

Next day Leo asked them the result. "You are what you are. That's what God said. What the heck does that mean?"

Leo thought this over for a while and then gave his verdict: "It means you are white with black stripes. Otherwise he would have said 'Yo is what yo is'."

# ANNIVERSARIES

ON their golden anniversary he said there was nothing he wouldn't do for his wife and there was nothing she wouldn't do for him.

"And that's how it's been for the past 50 years," he added. "We've done nothing for each other."

*　　*　　*

"I'M afraid I can't make the darts match tomorrow night,

Fred. I promised to take Thingummy out for our silver anniversary."

* * *

FOR 22 years Harry and his wife were deliriously happy. Then they met each other.

* * *

HE asked how they should celebrate their 25th anniversary.

She suggested two minutes' silence.

* * *

HE was telling his mate how he and his wife spent their 25th anniversary. "We left town on the same train, went to the same hotel, managed to get the same room. But this time it was me who went to the bathroom and cried!"

* * *

ON quiet nights, when he is alone, Fred runs their wedding video backwards, just to watch himself walk out of the church a free man.

* * *

IT was their 40th wedding anniversary and Rachael took Izzi to an upmarket part of town and proudly showed him a block of flats. "It's ours, Izzi, we own it," she said.

"But how?" he asked.

"You remember all these years how I charged you $10 each time we made love?" said Rachael. "Well, I saved all that money and bought this block of flats."

"Oh, Rachael, if only I had known, I would have given you all my business."

* * *

THERE'S not much difference between a toilet seat and an anniversary. Men usually miss them both.

# ARMY

THE old diggers were renewing old acquaintances at the Anzac reunion. "Was it you or your brother who got killed in New Guinea?"

A SIGNAL from HQ circulated along the front line declared that there was a $10 bounty for anyone who shot one of the enemy.

Next day at a forward observation post Paddy whispered to Mick, "Psst. There's two hunnerd t'ousand dollars creeping up my side of the hill!"

\* \* \*

THE new rookie looked a trifle uncomfortable when the brigadier stopped in front of him.

"Aren't you happy, man?" asked the officer.

The rookie nervously agreed he was happy.

"And what were you in civvy street?"

"A bloody sight happier," said the rooky.

\* \* \*

CALLED up for national service the young man was being examined by an army doctor.

"Just give me a gun, I'll show 'em," said the lad. "If they shoot off my hands I'll work the trigger with my arms. If they shoot off my arms then I'll do it with my legs. If they shoot off my legs, then b'jeezus I'll pull the trigger with my teeth."

"Good show, that's the spirit," said the doctor.

"Hang on," said the lad. "Don't you think I'm a little crazy?"

\* \* \*

A TOUGH drill sergeant ordered his men to hold up their left legs. One recruit mistakenly held up his right leg, thus placing it beside his neighbour's left.

"Alright, alright," roared the sergeant. "Who's the wise guy holding up both legs?"

\* \* \*

THE sergeant major had been lecturing the new recruits on their duties for the past two hours and suddenly noticed that Private Murphy was dozing.

"Now then, Murphy!" he roared. "Why should a soldier be ready to die for his country?"

Paddy scratched his head for a moment. "You're damned right sir. Why should he?"

*     *     *

THE court martial decreed that the deserter be taken to Boot Hill where he would be shot. It was a grim and rainy day and at dawn the firing squad arrived to escort the condemned man a mile or more to his execution.

He grumbled all the way. "Fancy having to march all this way in this terrible weather just to be shot," he lamented.

"Yeah, but think of us," said one of his guards. "We've got to march back again."

*     *     *

THE tough sergeant major knew that he was unpopular with the ranks and while carpeting a soldier who was due for discharge said: "I've heard it said that when I die some of you blokes are coming back to piddle on my grave. I suppose you will be among them?"

"Not me, sarge," said the soldier. "Once I get out of this army I've promised myself I will never stand in long queues again."

*     *     *

AS the sergeant major approached the camp he was challenged by the new recruit on sentry duty.

"That's not bad Private Smithers," said the officer, "but the expression is 'Friend or Foe' not 'Goodies or Baddies'!"

*     *     *

A PARTICULARLY unpopular sergeant major popped his head up above the trench and a sniper's bullet whizzed within one centimetre of his ear.

"Paddy! Get out and get that sniper," he roared to private Kelly.

Kelly was the regiment's best scout and within ten minutes he was back, the enemy sniper, with raised hands, walking before him.

Then Paddy began to punch hell out of his prisoner.

23

"Hey go easy," said his mates. "What's that for?"

"It's for missing the bloody sar'major," said Paddy.

*   *   *

THE navy recruiting officer looked the applicant up and down. "Can you swim?" he said.

"Why," said the prospective sailor, "don't you have any boats?"

*   *   *

THE visitor breasted the Returned Servicemen's Bar and asked for a double Scotch.

"That'll be eight-dollars-fifty," said the bartender.

"Hell," said the visitor. "If you had have charged like that at Gallipoli we would have won."

*   *   *

THERE was once a discreet brigadier
Fond of his ten thousand a year
But when he heard the guns rattle
Said: "Sounds like a battle!"
And quietly slipped to the rear.

*   *   *

THE C.O. had just welcomed the young army officer, shown him around the camp and was outlining the recreational facilities.

"On Mondays we have a snooker tournament, a jolly good show with the winner taking the jackpot."

"I'm afraid I don't play snooker sir," said the officer.

"Well, on Tuesdays we have a darts match," continued the C.O., "and first to make 301 wins the drinks."

"I'm afraid I don't like gambling or playing darts, sir."

"Really?" said the C.O. "Well, on Wednesday nights a few girls come up from the village for a dance and a bit of hanky panky and..."

"Sorry sir," said the officer. "I have no time for women."

"Good God, man," said the C.O. "You're not gay are you?"

"Certainly not sir," said the officer.

"Oh dear," said the C.O., "then you are not going to like Thursday and Friday nights much either."

# ARTS

FRED is a bit of an artist. He doesn't understand women, but he knows what he likes.

*     *     *

SALVADOR Dali took Picasso aside and said, "Excuse me friend, could I have a word in your eyeball?"

*     *     *

AN artist's model is a girl who shows the painter where to draw the line.

*     *     *

THE model got off the couch and came to inspect the painting. She blushed and said, "Oh Mr Renaldo. You've been looking."

*     *     *

AN artist and his model were smooching on the sofa when they heard a car arrive. "Quick, it's my wife," cried the artist. "Get your clothes off and pretend we're working."

*     *     *

THE mayor had officially opened the one-man art show and was browsing along the paintings when he stopped with a start in front of a picture of a woman reclining nude on a couch.

"That's my wife," he cried. "You scoundrel. You have had my wife up here posing nude in your studio."

The artist, a little terrified, said it wasn't the case at all. "I painted it from memory," he said.

*     *     *

A SOCIALITE approached a prominent portrait artist and asked if he would paint her in the nude.

"Sure," he said, "but I'll have to keep my socks on otherwise I'll have nowhere to stick my brushes."

*     *     *

THE artist said: "I only paint what I see."

The critic said: "Then you should never paint in that condition."

FRED's Dad was an artist. He was always drawing corks.

*     *     *

"MY art is becoming internationally acclaimed. One of these days I will be immoral."

"Don't you mean immortal?"

"I know what I mean."

*     *     *

"DID you sell any of your paintings at the art show?"

"No, but I am encouraged," he replied. "Somebody stole one."

*     *     *

"MUM, what is pop-art?"

"Why do you ask, son?"

"Well, it's what Dad says when he's going to pop-art for a quickie down the pub."

*     *     *

A BLOKE cleaning out his attic discovered an old violin and an oil painting. Thinking they might be valuable he took them to an art dealer.

"Well, that's a Stradivarius," mused the dealer, "and this here is a Rembrandt."

"Then, are they valuable?" he asked hopefully.

"Not really," said the dealer. "Stradivarius was a hopeless painter, and look at Rembrandt's violin. You'd never get a tune out of it."

*     *     *

SALVADOR Dali was robbed while on a visit to New York, but he managed to get a good look at the offender and was able to provide the police with a rough sketch of the felon.

For the next two weeks New York police searched for a man with a head like a horse, a fried egg on his forehead and a sword in his mouth.

# ASTROLOGY

A FAMOUS astrologer was quite entranced by the baby in the pram. "Beautiful," she said, "absolutely beautiful," and beaming at the proud mother she said, "Do you happen to know what sign she was conceived under?"

"Yes," blushed the young mum. "It said 'Keep off the Grass'!"

*     *     *

IT has got to the stage where people who introduce themselves now add their birthsigns.

"Hi, I'm Bill Moloney, Sagittarius."

"Hi, I'm John Spriggs, Cancer."

"Hi, I'm Joe Bloggs, bladder infection."

*     *     *

"WHAT sign were you born under?"

"I think it was a red and green flashing Neon.

## ATHEISTS

AN atheist is a man with no invisible means of support.

*     *     *

FRED was an atheist, but he gave it up. He said there were no holidays.

*     *     *

GRAFFITI. "Thank God I'm an Atheist."

*     *     *

IF God is good
  Why do his peoples
  Put lightning rods
  On top of steeples?

*     *     *

ROSES are red
  Violets are bluish
  If it wasn't for Jesus
  We'd all be Jewish

27

# B

## BACHELORS

A BACHELOR is a man who comes to work every morning, from a different direction.

*     *     *

AFTER his check-up the doctor told Barry the bachelor he was getting on in years and his lifestyle of wine, women and song would have to change.

"In fact, you will have to give up the first two," said the doc, "but you can sing as much as you like."

*     *     *

THE bachelor finished his meal and placed his tip on the table. The waiter took one look at the 15 cents and said: "Thank you for your generosity. You can always tell the character of a diner by the way he tips."

"Oh, really," he said. "What do these five-cent coins tell you about me?"

"Well, you put the three coins in a row," said the waiter. "That tells me you are tidy for starters. The first coin tells me you are frugal and the second coin tells me you are a bachelor."

"That's true," said the diner, impressed. "And what does the third coin tell you?"

"That tells me your father was a bachelor too."

FRED is safe now that he has joined Bachelors Anonymous.

Each time he feels like getting married the club sends round a woman in hair-curlers to nag him for a while.

*     *     *

MANY a poor husband was once a rich bachelor.

*     *     *

HE had so much fun at the bachelor party he postponed the wedding.

## BARBERS

THE sign on the barber shop read: Haircuts, while you wait!

*     *     *

HIS hair was neatly departed in the middle.

*     *     *

HE asked the barber if he had something to stop falling hair. The barber sold him a net.

*     *     *

WHEN one barber cuts another's hair, which one does the talking?

*     *     *

"HOW do you like your hair cut, sir?"
    "Off."

*     *     *

"JUST a shave please, I haven't time to listen to a haircut."

*     *     *

"DO you shave yourself all the time?"
    "No. I often stop for food."

*     *     *

THE barber was late for work. While shaving that morning he talked himself into a shampoo and hair tint.

*     *     *

EVERY time the nation's economic recession gets worse,

29

the local barber puts up his prices. He says longer faces take more time to shave.

* * *

THE customer noticed the barber's dirty hands and complained about it.

"Can't help it if nobody has been in for a shampoo yet," he replied.

* * *

THE boss demanded to know where he had been.

"I've been for a haircut."

"You can't have your hair cut in office time?"

"Why not? It grows in office time."

"Not all of it," said the boss.

"So I didn't get it all cut off," he replied.

* * *

THE sign said: "Beatles' Style Cut Here."

So he went in and was aghast to be shorn almost bald.

"That's not how the Beatles have their hair cut," he protested.

"It will be if they come here," said the barber.

* * *

TWO business acquaintances were seated side by side in the hairdresser's. One barber asked his client if he would like some French toilet water on his hair.

The man declined. "No way, the wife would think I'd been in a French brothel."

The second barber asked the same question to his client who responded: "Sure, I'll have some. My wife has never been in a French brothel."

* * *

FRED had just retired and was about to go on a world trip. He popped in to Bob the Barber's for a short back and sides on the eve of his departure.

"Be sure to come and tell me all about it when you come home," said Bob after he had finished the cut.

Two months later Fred was back in the chair again

relating the highlights. "I even went to see the Pope at St Peter's" he said.

"Wow," said Bob.

"And what's more, the Pope came over and spoke to me."

"That's unbelievable," said Bob, still clipping away. "What did the Pope say?"

"He said, 'Where the hell did you get a haircut like that'!"

\* \* \*

FLIRTY Fred popped into the hotel's barber shop for a haircut and while waiting for the barber to strop his razor he was enjoying a manicure from the very shapely blonde assistant and took the chance to chat her up.

"What time do you knock off," he leered out the side of his mouth.

"About six," she said.

"What about coming up for a drink?"

"I'm married," she said. "What would I say to my husband?"

"Just tell him straight. Tell him you are going out tonight," said Fred.

"You tell him," she said. "That's him stropping the razor."

\* \* \*

A MAN entered the barber's saloon and asked, "How long will you be?"

"About an hour," replied the barber.

"Okay, I'll come back," said the man who then left.

He didn't return until the next day when he entered the doorway again and asked, "How long will you be?"

The barber had six customers waiting and said, about an hour or more.

"Okay, I'll come back."

When the prospective customer did this every day of the week and never returned as he always promised the barber became intrigued and asked his apprentice to follow him.

"Tell me where he goes," he said.

The apprentice was back in five minutes. "He goes straight round to your place," he told the barber.

\* \* \*

THE bald man was astounded to be charged $15 for a cut and trim.

"That's more than you charge for people with a full head of hair," he complained.

"Yeah," said the barber. "A treasure hunt costs more."

\* \* \*

IF barristers can be de-barred, and ministers be de-frocked, can a barber be dis-tressed?

\* \* \*

HARRY Cox was looking for his brother Bob. He couldn't find him in his usual haunts or in the pub. Thinking he might be having a haircut Harry went to the barber's shop.

"Bob Cox in here?" he asked.

"Sorry sir," said the barber. "We only do shaves and haircuts."

\* \* \*

(R) THE barber broke his leg in a skiing accident.

Now he can only cut hair on crutches.

# BEAUTY

HIS wife used to have a nice firm chin. But now the firm has taken on a couple of partners.

\* \* \*

SHE said: "Will you love me when I'm old and grey?"

"Why not," he said. "I've loved you when you were blonde, henna, brunette and blue."

\* \* \*

IT'S no use making your mind up to stay in if your wife has made her face up to go out.

\* \* \*

SHE was wearing a faint perfume. One sniff and you fainted.

WHEN she came down the stairs he said: "My word, you look lovely. That must have taken quite some time."

      \*     \*     \*

BEAUTY comes from within ... from within bottles, jars, tubes, phials, compacts...

      \*     \*     \*

"DOES your sister still make up jokes?"
  "Yes, she still works at the beauty parlour."

      \*     \*     \*

SHE approached the hairdresser.
  "What do you have for grey hair?"
  "The greatest respect, madam."

      \*     \*     \*

THE better a woman looks, the longer a man does.

## BEDS

MORE than one-third of our lives are spent in bed. Most of us were begotten in a bed, and born in a bed and we will probably die in a bed. In between these important events the bed is an essential accessory for play and rest; and no joke book should be without a bed section, and no bed should be without a joke section.

      \*     \*     \*

A BED is where one good turn can get all the blankets.

      \*     \*     \*

BEDS cause hangovers. Statistics prove that drunks will go to bed happy, and wake up feeling terrible.

      \*     \*     \*

WHEN he was in bed he was terrified that somebody might be underneath it. When he got underneath it he was terrified that somebody might be on top of the bed.

The psychiatrist told him he had bed phobia and was treating him at $100 a visit.

After a year of treatment, and the loss of a small

fortune, he told the psychiatrist he wasn't coming back again.

"I had a talk to the barman and he solved my problem," he said.

"Oh, and what did he do?" enquired the psychiatrist.

"He came round and sawed the legs off my bed!"

## BETS

"REMEMBER I bet a tenner I'd beat my drink problem?"
"Yeah."
"Well now I've got a gambling problem."

* * *

CARRYING his bat nervously he walked on to the ground for his first match with the seniors. A spectator called to him: "I've got a bet on you."

"That's nice of you," he said modestly, "I'll probably get a duck."

"That's what I bet."

* * *

THE argument at the bar was on religion.
"And I betcha a tenner you don't know the Lord's Prayer."
"You're on."
"Okay, say it"
"Now I lay me down to sleep..."
"Gawd. Here's the money. I didn't think you knew it."

* * *

THE Elderly Citizens' Club now has a community bus and each Sunday they go off on a mystery tour. To make it interesting the oldies dob in 50 cents in a sweep to guess the mystery destination. Bert the driver has won it three times in a row.

* * *

A PUNTER would bank $500 every Monday morning so regularly that finally the bank manager's curiosity got the better of him. Where did he get the money?

"I am a punter," explained the customer, "but I only bet on sure things."

Intrigued, the banker pressed him for an example of a sure thing.

"No worries," said the punter. "I'll bet you $500 that you've got red jocks. That's a sure bet for a start."

The banker could hardly believe his ears, and slapping the money on the counter he said "You're on."

"Okay, drop your trousers so I can check," said the punter.

"Not here," said the banker, "come into my office."

Once inside the banker said, "There you are, they are definitely not red."

"Not good enough," said the punter, "they look red to me, but I'm colour-blind. D'yer mind if your accountant checks the colour?"

The accountant was called in and immediately fainted.

"What's up with him?" asked the manager.

"Oh, I bet him $1000 I'd get you to drop your dacks before 10 this morning."

## BIRDS

MY wife does bird imitations. She watches me like a hawk.

\*　　\*　　\*

A BIRD in the hand is better than two in a photograph.

\*　　\*　　\*

A BIRD in the hand is useless when you have to blow your nose.

\*　　\*　　\*

HE was responsible for feeding the pelicans at the zoo. It wasn't much of a job but it filled the bill.

\*　　\*　　\*

AT the Stork Club. "Do any deliveries today?"

"No, but I frightened hell out of a few secretaries."

\*　　\*　　\*

"NEXT!" roared the theatrical agent, and when Bert

shuffled in self-consciously before him he muttered, "Well, what do you do?"

"I do bird impressions," said Bert.

"Not another one," said the agent without raising his eyes from documents on his desk. "Get on with it then."

So Bert flapped his arms, dropped a deposit on the window ledge and flew off into the blue sky yonder.

## BIRTHS and BIRTHDAYS

SHE'S just turned 32, but the way she's turned it, makes her 23.

\* \* \*

A husband who forgets his wife's birthday will get something to remember her by.

\* \* \*

WHEN a man has a birthday he takes a day off. When a woman has a birthday she takes a year off.

\* \* \*

SHE was born in the year of our lord only knows.

\* \* \*

I WAS so surprised by my birth, I was speechless for a year and a half.

\* \* \*

IN what State were you born?
   In the nude.

\* \* \*

SHE was looking forward to her 30th birthday. But she was looking in the wrong direction.

\* \* \*

"HAVE you known your wife long?"
   "Yes. Ever since we were the same age."

\* \* \*

LIFE is full of complications. Even when you are born there is a string attached.

"MY mother was disappointed when I was born."
  "Why, did she want a girl?"
  "No. She wanted a divorce."

* * *

"THE stork brought a little peach,"
  The nurse said with an air.
  "I'm bloomin' glad," the father said,
  "He didn't bring a pear!"

* * *

ANOTHER candle on the cake
  Well that's no cause to pout
  Be glad you still have wind enough
  To blow the damn thing out

* * *

THE best way to remember your wife's birthday is to forget it once.

* * *

SHE: "I hate to think about my 30th birthday."
  He: "Why? What happened?"

* * *

IT'S terrible to grow old alone. My wife hasn't had a birthday for three years.

* * *

SHE'S celebrating the second anniversary of her 16th birthday.

* * *

YOU'RE getting old when the only thing you don't want for your birthday is to be reminded of it.

* * *

IT was a brave husband who whispered to his mate, "I'm so glad she was born in winter. The birthday candles heat up the house. If it was in summer she'd need a fire permit."

* * *

IT was one of those cruises so well patronised by the elderly when a sprightly old geezer approached a spinster reclining on a deck chair.

37

"Guess how old I am," he said.

She looked him up and down for a moment, then put her hand up the leg of his shorts. She grabbed his crown jewels, felt their weight, moved them gently from side to side and then declared with authority: "You are 83 and seven months."

"That's amazing," said the old codger, "how do you know?"

"Because you told me yesterday you silly old fool," she replied.

## BOASTERS

WHEN the sliding door opened in the confessional box he started: "Father, I had sex with a pair of lovely 18-year-old nymphomaniac twins five times last week."

"What kind of Catholic are you?" demanded the priest.

"I am not a Catholic," he replied.

"Then why are you telling me this?"

"I am telling everyone!"

\* \* \*

"DO you think I am conceited?" he asked his girlfriend.

"No. What makes you ask, darling?" she said.

"Well, most blokes as handsome as me usually are."

\* \* \*

HE had told her how he won the best and fairest award in his football club, all the details of his life, his training and the goals he scored and his philosophy on life.

Finally he said, "But that's enough about me. Let's talk about you. Tell me, what did you think of my performance in Saturday's game?"

\* \* \*

THE old gent was getting sick and tired of Young Turk boasting of his sexual conquests.

"Listen," he said. "I am 87 and I make love nearly every night of the week."

The young bloke said he didn't believe him.

"True," said the old geezer. "I nearly made it Monday, I nearly made it Tuesday, ... "

\* \* \*

YOUNG Father Murphy phoned the bishop to say he was ill and couldn't celebrate mass. As soon as he heard the bishop say he could get a replacement the young priest grabbed his golf clubs and was one of the first on the course.

St Peter saw this and nudged God. "Look at Father Murphy. Lied to say he was ill, and look at him down there. He has got to be punished."

"Okay," said God, and they watched as the priest pulled out a number one wood, swung a mighty stroke and belted the ball straight up the fairway, narrowly between two bunkers onto the green to roll slowly in for one.

St Peter was aghast. "I thought you were going to punish him."

"I have," said God. "Who can he boast to?"

# BONKS
(R)...

LET's face it, there is a lot of bonking going on. It is the reason we all got here, so we can hardly avoid it as a classification for jokes, especially when most jokes are about pre-bonking, trying to get a bonk, actual bonking and post bonking.

\* \* \*

HE'S bi-sexual, which means if he can't get it, he buys it.

\* \* \*

CHARLIE said he once went without sex for 12 years. "Wasn't even bothered by it," he said. "Then I had my 13th birthday."

\* \* \*

FRED said he gave up sex and booze at the same time once. "It was the worst half hour of my life!" he said.

WHEN Paddy walked into the pub it caused a snigger among his mates at the bar. "Boy, the joke was on you last night, Paddy," they said. "You left your bedroom light on and the blind was up. You put on a great show with your missus."

"Well, the joke's on you lot," countered Paddy. "I wasn't home last night."

*　　*　　*

A HOUSEWIFE was asked by her neighbour how she happened to have so many home appliances around the house.

"Bonking," she replied. "I charge my husband $10 for a bonk. In fact, I have a scale of charges. It costs him 50 cents for a fondle."

Her neighbour thought this was a wonderful proposition and said she would introduce the same scale of fees.

A month later they met again. "By the way, are you making any money," asked the first housewife.

"Afraid not," said the neighbour. "I charge him 50 cents for a fondle and pretty soon I have to get out of bed to lend him another 50 cents, and by then I don't mind paying him ten."

*　　*　　*

FRED was complaining to his doctor that his wife had lost interest in sex. The doc explained that it was a matter of preparation. "Next time you come home from work, bring a bunch of flowers, give her a big kiss, then sweep her off her feet and carry her to the bedroom. You will be surprised."

On Fred's next visit he asked if it worked. "Yes, she was indeed surprised. And so were all the members of her bridge club."

*　　*　　*

FRED was leaning on the bar recounting the most recent tragedy in the neighbourhood. "Ernie came home and found his wife in bed with the bloke next door. He got his gun and shot them both."

"Well, it could of been worse," said his listener.

"What d'yer mean," said Fred, "what could be worse than that?"

"Well, if Ernie had come home early the night before I'd be dead by now."

* * *

THE pretty fraulein approached the Aussie tourist in the Munich beer hall and invited him home. She gave him a nice meal and took him to bed.

In the morning, after a hearty breakfast, he was about to leave and made a little speech about the outstanding hospitality he had received.

"Ja, the speech is nice, but what about marks," she said.

"Bloody oath, nine out of ten I reckon," he said.

* * *

IT was their 50th wedding anniversary and Rachael took Izzi to the city and proudly showed him a block of flats. "It's ours, Izzi, we own it," she said.

"But how did you?" he said.

"You remember all these years I used to charge you $10 for a tumble in bed," said Rachael. "Well I saved all that money and bought that block of flats."

"Oh Rachael. If only I had known, I would have given you all my business!"

* * *

DAVE and Mable checked over their meagre finances and realised times were tough. "I've got an idea," said Dave. "Every time we have a bit of nookie in bed I will pay you a dollar. It will be a means of saving with pleasure."

Two months later they needed some extra funds and busted open the cash box. Dave was amazed to see the bundle of notes which included fives, tens and twenties.

"Mabel, where did you get all this money. Each time we did it I only gave you a dollar."

"Listen Dave," she said, "not everyone is as stingy as you."

* * *

OLD Dad and Mum overheard the above episode with Dave and Mabel. Convinced there was money to be made he suggested Mum should try her luck on the street.

Mum returned that evening, emptied her handbag on the kitchen table and out tumbled the cash which included fives, tens and twenties. It added up to $75 and 50 cents.

"What lousy cheapskate gave you the 50 cents?" demanded Dad.

"They all did," said Mum.

* * *

"MRS Smith," queried the doctor. "Do you smoke after intercourse?"

"I've never looked," she replied.

* * *

THE couple were laying on the bed naked, smoking a post coital cigarette.

After a while she said, "Mother always told me to be good. Was I?"

* * *

MRS Murphy, the young mother of triplets, was being congratulated by her neighbour, Mrs Kelly.

"Yes, 'tis a wonderful thing indade," said the proud Mum, "and you know the doctor says it only happens once in a hundred t'ousand times."

"Heavens," said Mrs Kelly in astonishment, "whinever did yer foind time to do yer housework?"

* * *

CHAP suffering from laringitis could hardly talk with his sore throat, so he went to the clinic after hours.

The door was opened by the doctor's pretty young wife.

"Is the doctor in," he whispered.

"No," she whispered. "Come on in."

42

CHAP walking along the beach one evening in the dark stepped on a bloke's bottom. And a girl's voice said "Thank you!"

* * *

HE was telling his mate that he and his wife had discovered a new way of making love; back to back.

"That would be nigh impossible wouldn't it?"

"Oh we have another couple in to help us," he explained.

* * *

BOB, Jane, Mary and Bill had been friends for years. The two couples went on a camping trip and pitched their tents close together. While sitting around the camp fire they got to talking about the current trend of swinging couples and ventured far enough to suggest they try it.

"Haven't had so much fun for years," said Bob later. "Do you think the girls are having as much fun as we are?"

* * *

ONE night the husband came home early from afternoon shift and found the lodger in bed with his wife.

"What's the meaning of this?" he cried. "It's a fine way to repay our hospitality. After all we've done for you... and stop doing that while I'm talking to you!"

* * *

HE came home from the pub fairly late and his wife met him at the front door. "We've had a burglar," she sobbed.

"Did he get anything?" he said in alarm.

"He sure did," she said. "I thought it was you!"

* * *

IT was Friday night and Barbie had just finished preparing the evening meal for her husband John when there was a knock on the door. She opened it and was surprised to see her husband's best mate, Freddie.

"John's scored some overtime," said Fred. "He told me to tell you he won't be home until eleven-thirty."

A long chat on the doorstep resulted in Barbie inviting Freddie inside. "In fact, you might as well eat some of this food I have prepared."

Freddie was in like Flynn. And after the food, and half a bottle of good red, began chatting up Barbie about the good old days when they used to go together, before she was married. In fact, he soon got to the point. "Give us a kiss for old time's sake?" he said.

"No, I'm an honest married woman," she said.

"Okay," said Fred. "Give us a kiss for old time's sake... and twenty dollars," and with that he slammed the note on the table.

Barbie looked at the money. Well, she used to kiss him for nothing once. No harm in a kiss. So she gave him a quick peck and scooped up the cash.

Freddie had another drink and began praising Barbie's figure. "You're still in great shape," he said looking at her blouse. "Give us a quick look ... for fifty dollars."

And with that he dropped fifty on the table.

He used to do more than looking once, for nothing, thought Barbie. A quick flash shouldn't hurt anybody. So a quick flash it was, and again she scooped up the money.

To cut a long story short there was a bit more chit-chat and $200 dropped on the table, followed by a quick adjournment to the bedroom.

Indeed it was eleven-thirty when John arrived home that night and Barbie got out of bed to make him a cup of tea.

"Did Freddie call round?" he asked.

Barbie nodded.

"Did he bring my pay?"

*　　*　　*

A PLUMBER one night feeling free
Was plumbing his girl by the sea

44

Said the maid, "Quick, stop plumbing,
I fear someone's coming."
Said the plumber, still plumbing, "It's me."

## BOOBS

THE old man was the only other occupant of the train compartment and he looked like a kindly grandfather so the young mother had no qualms about breast-feeding her baby.

"What a lovely child," said the old man. "What do you feed him on?"

"Just milk and orange juice," she said.

The old man thought about this for a moment. "Which one is the orange juice?" he said.

\* \* \*

AFTER three years in a seminary three priests were assigned to parishes in Tottenham. At the railway station the clerk in the ticket box proved to be a buxom young woman with a deep cleavage. It brought the three of them out in a sweat.

"Three tickets to Titterton," stammered the first before retiring in embarrassment.

"Here, I'll have a go," said the second, and approaching the window stuttered: "Three titties to Tockerton."

"You are making a shocking mess of it," said the third, snatching the money and getting a grip on himself. He sternly approached the buxom wench and said: "Three tickets to Tottenham, Miss, and unless you dress more demurely St Finger will point his Peter at you."

\* \* \*

THE two gossips noticed young Mrs Lottzabazooma in the park.

"Is that hussy breast-feeding again, right out in public?"

"It's her right enough," said the other sticky-nose. "And look, the boy's at least 16, and not even her son.

WORRIED about her daughter's cough her mother took her to the doctor who proceeded to examine her chest.

"Big breaths," he said.

"Yeath," she replied. "And I'm only thixteen."

\* \* \*

THE long legged blonde arrived at the wedding in a topless frock.

"You can't come in," declared the verger.

"I've got a divine right," she said.

"Your left's not bad either, but you can't come in this church without a hat."

\* \* \*

A MOUSE dashed up a girl's leg, under her frock and came to rest in the crevice of two ample bosoms.

"You are obviously a Titmouse," she said.

"No I'm not," he replied. "I'm a Mickey Mouse, but I overshot the mark."

\* \* \*

A BUXOM young Miss from Valetta
Loved to parade in a sweater
Three reasons she had
To keep warm was not bad
But the other two reasons were better.

\* \* \*

ON a maiden a man once begat
Fine triplets named Mat, Pat and Tat
It was fun in the breeding
But when came time for feeding
She found she had no tit for Tat.

# BOOKS

"EXCUSE me Miss," he said. "I'm writing a phone book. Could I have your number?"

\* \* \*

THERE'S a new dictionary published for the showbiz

world listing all the actors and actesses. It's called "Who's Whose."

* * *

A BLOKE lent me a book on memory training last week. I want to return it, but I can't remember his name.

* * *

BY the time a man learns to read women like a book, he's too old to start a library.

* * *

HE said to the librarian, "I'd like a book. Something very deep."

"What about 20,000 Leagues Under the Sea?"

* * *

MY wife's preference is chequebooks. Once she starts one she can't put it down until its finished.

* * *

"I READ your new book," said the snobbish critic to the author. "Who wrote it for you?"

"Who read it for you?" he replied.

* * *

CRITIC: "What do you consider your best work of fiction?"

Author: "My last Income Tax Return."

* * *

DOOR to door salesman was selling leather bound dictionaries for a mere $5.

"What's the catch?" asked the householder.

"Oh, it's got all the words alright, but they are not in alphabetical order."

* * *

A BLOKE who was run over by the mobile library began to groan and moan. The librarian jumped out of the vehicle, bent down and said, "SSShhhhh!"

* * *

HAVE you noticed how every prominent politician, even former prime ministers, decide to write books when they

47

retire? It would have been better for the country if they had read one.

## BROTHELS
(R)...

"IT'S a business doing pleasure with you," said the hooker accepting her fee.

\* \* \*

THE old chap toddled into the house of ill repute and the madam told him it would cost $100. He was quite surprised. "You're putting me on," he said.

"That will be an extra $10," said the madam.

\* \* \*

THE old bloke made it shakily into the Blue Light Brothel. The receptionist looked him over and noting his age said, "Just a moment, Pops, I had better call the Madam."

After a whispered conference the Madam nodded agreement and said to the old gent, "Sorry love, we think you've had it."

"Oh, then how much do I owe you?" he said reaching for his wallet.

\* \* \*

WHILE playing in the street two young boys noticed that only men were calling at the house with the red light and that after a short conversation which appeared to consist of "$30 for a short time," these men would disappear inside, only to emerge later looking satisfied and contented.

The boys decided to give it a go and pooling their resources they knocked on the door.

"We've only got $3," they said to the madam, "so can we just have a short time?"

The madam took them in, took their money, knocked their heads together, kicked them in the backside and threw them back on to the street.

As the lads got to their feet one said, "Gee, I'm glad we only had three dollars. I couldn't stand thirty dollars' worth of that!"

*　　*　　*

IZZY Cohen had just taken his trousers off and was about to get into bed with Tiger Lil when there was a hell of a commotion downstairs. The cops had raided the house.

He just managed to grab his clothes, climb through the window, slide down the drain pipe and dash into the bar next door where he met his friend Sam.

He related his narrow escape, which had effectively dampened his ardour. "But listen Sam," he said. "As soon as the cops disappear, whip up to the first floor and give Tiger Lil a bang. It's paid for."

# BUSES

CONDUCTOR: "Full fare for the kid, he's five."

Mother: "How could he be five, I've only been married three years!"

Conductor: "Look lady, I take fares, not confessions."

*　　*　　*

A WOMAN rushed into the hardware store and said: "A mousetrap please, and hurry because I have a bus to catch."

"Sorry, lady," said the shop-keeper. "None of the mousetraps we've got are big enough."

*　　*　　*

THE bus was so crowded even the young men couldn't get seats.

*　　*　　*

THE busline has a timetable, but it is against the rules to leave on time. It would upset the entire schedule.

*　　*　　*

THE arrogant bus driver was always telling people where to get off.

THE drunk on the bus told the ticket inspector that he had bought a ticket, but couldn't find it.

"It's okay," said the inspector, "I'm sure you have paid."

"It's not okay at all," insisted the drunk, still searching his pockets. "Without my ticket I don't know where I'm going."

* * *

A COPPER arrested a bloke for smoking on a bus.

"Can't you see that sign which says No Smoking?" said the cop.

"No, and I can't read anyway," said the bloke, who appeared to have three too many.

"What's your name?" demanded the cop, but all he got was a mumbled reply.

"Write it down," said the cop handing him his notebook.

The drunk scribbled something illegible.

"What's that?" said the cop.

"I don't know," said the bloke, "I told you I can't read!"

* * *

PADDY, his wife and their seven kids were waiting at the bus-stop when they were joined by a blind man. When the bus arrived it was almost full and the conductor said only eight could board.

"Okay Teresa," said Paddy to his wife, "you take the kids on board and me and the blind man will walk."

Without giving the blind man an option in the matter Paddy helped his family scramble aboard and the bus took off.

He and the blind man then set off walking down the road and all went well until the constant tap-tap-tap of the blind man's cane began to irritate Paddy.

"Tap-tap-tap, that damned tapping is driving me crazy. Can't you put a bit of rubber on the end of it," he complained irritably.

The blindman was quick to respond. "If you had've

stuck a bit of rubber on your own stick we would be on that bloomin' bus."

## BUSINESS

"HOW'S business?"

"Looking up."

"You mean it's flat on its back."

* * *

"PRICES subject to change, according to customer's attitude."

* * *

AT the board meeting: "All those in favour say Aye. All those against, resign."

* * *

YOUNG Moishe was learning economics and asked his father about the ethics of business.

"Ethics?" repeated his father. "You ask me about ethics? Well, my lovely boy, let me put it this way. A lady comes in and buys a garment for $95 and she pays with a $100 note. She is very excited about the garment and as she leaves with the parcel under her arm I notice she has left her $5 change on the counter.

"Now here my son comes in the big question of ethics. Do I tell my partner or not?"

* * *

AN art critic interviewing the famous contemporary artist asked why he tolerated the sexual escapades of his young wife.

"I would rather a 20% interest in a going concern, than 100% in a bankruptcy," he said.

* * *

PLOTKIN met Rozenbloom on the street and said, "Tell me, Mr Rozenbloom, we bump into each other often on this street, we meet at the synagogue and we meet at the market. So why is it you never ask me how's business?"

"Okay Plotkin. How's business?"

"Oi voi, don't ask!"

* * *

IN a small school in Dublin the teacher told the class she would give 50 pence to whoever could name the holiest man in history.

One hand went up like a shot, that of little Izzie Cohen. "That would be St Patrick, Miss."

Teacher handed over the money and said, "Izzy, how come the only boy to know the answer is Jewish?"

To which Izzy replied, "In my heart of hearts I know it was Moses, but business is business."

* * *

THE landlord of a pub in Carlton was a fanatical Blues supporter and even had a large sign in the bar which read: "No Collingwood supporters served in this pub."

One day a bloke wearing a black and white scarf breasted the bar. "I know you don't serve Collingwood supporters, but I'm desperate for a drink and I'll pay $5 for a pot."

The publican thought this over, then decided to serve the beer.

It was gulped down in one draught.

"Same again," said the Magpie fan, "in fact I'll have two," and he slapped a tenner on the bar.

When he asked for a third the barman said tentatively, "That's another fiver?"

"That's okay," he said, pushing $20 across the bar, "I'll have a couple for the road." When the drinker had gone the publican put up a new sign: "Only Collingwood fans served here."

(N.B. Use your own local football teams and colours.)

* * *

WHEN the wife went on a dirty week-end and her rich lover bought her a fur coat worth $10,000, the problem was, how to bring it home.

After lengthy thought she pawned it. She then told

her husband that while driving to the airport, on the trip to see her mother, a woman had hailed her cab and begged a ride. She said the young woman only had minutes to catch a plane that would take her to a betrothed wedding in Istanbul which would make her rich. She had no money, except a pawn ticket which she insisted should be payment for the ride.

With this tale the wife urged her husband to redeem the ticket for her.

He did so and presented his wife with a pair of binoculars, which were ideal for viewing the new fur coat her husband's secretary was wearing at the races next day.

* * *

MOISHE had started in the second-hand trade but was now one of the richest businessmen in the city. As his Rolls Royce stopped in front of the Ritz one night an old school mate who had fallen on hard times was waiting for him.

"Hey Moishe, remember me?"

"Eddie Rozenbloom, of course I do. Haven't seen you in years. How's business?"

"Moishe," says Eddie. "I've hit a bad patch. In fact I was wondering if you could let me have five dollars for a bed."

"Sure Eddie. Bring it around in the morning!"

* * *

TWO Jewish gentlemen were seated together on a plane. They had been in the air for 30 minutes when the younger man asked the other if he had the time.

There was no answer. "Can you tell me the time please?"

Again there was no answer and the younger man detected some kind of deliberate resistance.

The aircraft was on its descent path when the older man quickly looked at his watch and said it was ten past three.

53

There was silence for a while before the young man said. "Why didn't you tell me the time earlier?"

"Well, you know what it is like on flights. People get talking to each other. We could become friendly, especially when we are both Jewish. I would be obliged to invite you home. I have a lovely daughter and you are a young man, quite handsome. Romance could blossom and before long you could be asking for her hand in marriage. And to put it bluntly, I don't want no son-in-law who hasn't got a watch."

\* \* \*

WHEN Abe met Isaac he said: "I hear your store was robbed last night. Lose much?"

Isaac replied: "A little, but it could have been much worse. Yesterday I just marked down the entire stock by 20 per cent."

\* \* \*

"SO your opening sale has just closed, what now?"

"So now we open the closing sale."

\* \* \*

HE walked into the pawnbroker's shop in Russell St, Melbourne and asked for the loan of $20. "Where's your collateral?" asked the pawnbroker.

He indicated the Rolls Royce parked out front. "Right there," he said, "and here are the keys and ownership documents."

He got his $20 and was off. Three days later he returned to claim the car with a crisp $20 in his hand. He received the keys and was charged $5 interest.

He was about to leave when curiosity got the better of the pawnbroker. "Pardon me, but why should a man like you need the loan of $20?"

The businessman replied, "Oh I don't really. I'm down from *Sydney* to do some business, and where else can you park a car for a few days for $5?"

(N.B. You can replace 'Melbourne' and 'Sydney' with cities relevant to your situation.)

IT was three in the morning and the worried husband was pacing up and down the bedroom floor to the consternation of his wife who found it very difficult to sleep.

"What's wrong?" she asked.

"I'm sick to death with worry," he said. "We owe a thousand dollars on the mortgage tomorrow and we haven't got a cent," he said.

The wife got out of bed, looked up the phone book and dialed a number. When the bank manager answered, obviously still dazed from a deep sleep she said. "There is no way my husband can pay, so you will be a thousand dollars short tomorrow."

She hung up and said, "Now come to bed and let him worry about it."

*     *     *

IT was three in the morning when a busker began playing his banjo outside the bedroom window of a wealthy tycoon.

Eventually the window was opened. "What do you think you are doing waking me up in the middle of the night?"

"Listen, mate," said the busker. "I don't tell you how to run your business, so don't tell me how to run mine!"

# C

## CAMELS

ANGUS was delighted to find himself a girl at the pub who appeared to be no drain on the pocket. When he asked could he get her a glass of wine she said no, she didn't drink.

When he asked if she would like a cigarette she said no, she didn't smoke.

"What about a packet of crisps?"

"No, I'm not hungry," she said.

"A game of pool?"

"No, I don't play," she said.

"Then can I take you home?" asked Angus, who was delighted when she said yes.

When they arrived at her house she opened the front door, and there, lying in the hallway was a dead camel.

"Well," said the young woman, "I didn't say I was tidy, did I?"


## CARS
See ACCIDENTS, MOTORING, DRIVERS

WHEN it comes to used cars, it's hard to drive a bargain.

★   ★   ★

USED cars are alright, as far as they go.

56

SHE was trying to get a new car for her husband, but nobody would swap.

* * *

HE had a stereo system in his car for years. His wife in the front and her mother in the back.

* * *

FRED got behind in his car payments and, in an effort to shame him into paying the hire-purchase company wrote: "What would your neighbours think if we came and repossessed your car?"

He wrote back: "Dear Sirs. I took the matter up with my neighbours and they all reckon it would be a lousy trick."

* * *

"THIS car," said the salesman, "runs so smoothly you can't feel it, so quietly you can't hear it, so perfectly you can't smell it and so fast you can't see it."

Fred considered this for a moment. "Then how the hell do we know it's there?"

* * *

FRED listened to all the motoring advertisements and is now having a terrible time with his car. He bought a carburettor which saved 30% on petrol, an exhaust system which saved 50% on fuel and a set of spark plugs which saved 25%. Now every time he goes for a drive his fuel tank overflows.

* * *

WHEN it comes to petrol consumption some cars perform better than others. "But Fred's car is the best I've ever heard of," said Barney.

He explained: "Fred told me he met a blonde at the pub on Friday night and drove her home, hours and hours away. And he said he went all that way for nothing!"

* * *

FRED phoned the car yard and asked for the dealer who had sold him the car just two days before.

"You said this car had only one owner, a little old lady who drove it to church each Sunday?"

"That's right," said the salesman.

"Well, can I have her address," said Fred. "I have just cleaned out the glove box and there is a bottle of whisky, a packet of condoms and a bikini top she might be looking for."

# CATS

THEIR cat was called Ben Hur.

It had originally been called Ben, until it had kittens.

\* \* \*

THE music professor entered the spinster's home to hear the strains of classical music delicately performed on the piano, but he got the shock of his life when he entered the drawing room and saw that it was a large black tom cat at the keyboard.

"Taught himself," said Miss Haversham proudly.

"That's amazing," said the professor.

"Wrote that particular piece himself, too," she said.

"Astounding," marvelled the prof listening to the chords and nuances of the minuette.

"Marvellous," he said. "Have you had it orchestrated?"

The cat dived out the window and hasn't been seen since.

\* \* \*

WHEN he saw a lovely gold watch as the centrepiece of a window display, set on a velvet cushion with gold chain around it, he decided immediately it was to be the ideal present for his wife's 50th birthday.

"I'd like to buy that watch in the window," he told the shopkeeper.

"It's not for sale," was the reply.

And against the man's pleading to sell him the watch the shopkeeper said, "Look mate, I don't sell watches. I de-sex tomcats."

"Well, what are the watches in the window for?"

"What would you want me to put in the window?" replied the shopkeeper.

* * *

THE youngster ran to his mum crying. "Dad just drowned our cat," he blubbered.

"Maybe he had to do it," she said.

"No he didn't. He promised me I could."

* * *

"STOP pulling the cat's tail, Johnny."

"I'm not. 'I'm just holding it. It's the cat that's doing the pulling."

* * *

THE elderly spinster had called the vet because her cat seemed to be off her food. He made a quick examination and pronounced that the cat was pregnant.

"Impossible," said the spinster. "Moggie never goes out. I feed her in here. She has had no contact with stray cats of any kind."

Just then a battered old Ginger Tom wandered out from behind the couch.

"There's the culprit," said the vet.

"Preposterous," said the spinster, "That's Moggie's brother."

* * *

HER tom cat was out every night ranting, wailing and impregnating all the other cats in the neighbourhood. It never spent a night at home.

So she took him to the vet and had him fixed.

Now he is still out every night, acting as a consultant.

* * *

WHEN Paddy's cat died he asked the priest to say requiem mass. "No way. What d'yer think the church is coming to?" said the priest.

Paddy asked the Anglican vicar to bury his cat and got the same response.

The priest met Paddy next day. "Are you still fussing about that cat?" he said.

"Yes," said Paddy. "I even asked the Jewish Rabbi if he would bury him for $500, but he refused too."

The priest's face lit up. "Why didn't you say he was a Catholic cat?" he said.

## CENSUS

A COW-COCKY was filling in the census form. In answer to the question, "Length of residence in Australia," he wrote: "Thirty feet, ten inches, with a verandah front and two sides."

\* \* \*

THE census taker told the mayor of the little bush town that he was puzzled about the town's population. For the past five years he had been on the job the population was the same, 1,503. "Must be something wrong."

"No," said the mayor. "It's always been 1,503."

"But don't you have babies?"

"Yep," said the mayor, "and everytime we do some bloke has to leave town."

\* \* \*

A CENSUS official was assisting a farmer's wife to fill in her forms. "How many children have you got?" he asked.

"Six," she replied. "Three sets of twins."

"How very extraordinary," said the census man. "Twins every time."

"Oh no," she said with a blush. "Not every time. Hundreds of times, nothing."

\* \* \*

SHE told the census taker she had five children, and he was astounded to learn that they were all born two years apart, and all on August 12.

"What's your husband's profession?" he asked.

"Precision grinder," she replied.

YOUNG woman answered the door for the census taker and told him her husband had died five years ago.

The official noted this down, then asked if she had any children.

"Yes, three," she said. "Aged one, two and five."

The official queried this. "Didn't you say your husband was dead?"

"Yes. He is but I'm not!"

\* \* \*

CENSUS taker went next door where the woman told him she had four children. "But I am definitely not having any more."

"Why?" said the official.

"Because I read in a magazine that every fifth child born in the world is Chinese."

## CHOOKS

CHOOKS are the only things you can eat before they are born and after they are dead.

\* \* \*

WAITER: "Those are the best eggs we've had for years."

Diner: "Well, bring me some you haven't had for so long."

\* \* \*

PADDY crept around the back of the country parish presbytery and stole one of the priest's chooks, then promptly went to confession.

"I stole a chook, father," he began. "I know it was wrong and I am sorry. Can I give it to you for penance?"

"Certainly not," said the priest. "Return it to the person you stole it from."

"I've offered it to him, but he says he doesn't want it," said Paddy.

"In that case you might as well keep it and say ten Hail Marys," said the priest.

THE young wife wanted to impress her husband that she was a good cook, so she rang him to ask if he could bring home a live chicken.

He bought the chook at the market and then realised his car was being serviced and would not be available for another two hours.

He decided to pass the time by going to a movie, and hid the chook by stuffing it down the front of his trousers.

Once in the theatre he became absorbed in the movie and was oblivious to the fact that the chook had stuck its head out of his fly.

Two women were sitting next to him and one nudged the other. "You should see what's sticking out of this bloke's pants."

Her friend was blase, "Seen one, seen 'em all", she said, not bothering to take her eyes off the screen.

"Yeah, but this one is eating my pop corn!"

*　　*　　*

FEELING guilty about running over what appeared to be a prize rooster, the travelling salesman stopped his car and approached the nearby farmhouse and knocked on the door.

He told the farmer's wife he would like to replace it.

"Please yourself, luv," she said. "The chooks are around the back!"

*　　*　　*

"TWO of our chooks have stopped layin'," said the farmer to his wife.

"How do yer know?"

"Cos I just run over them with the tractor."

*　　*　　*

SHE was stocking up for her hobby farm and ordered a dozen chooks, and a dozen roosters.

"Madam, you only need one rooster," he pointed out.

She gave him a stern look. "Evidently you don't know what it is like to be overlooked."

A FARMER was having his lunch on the front porch when a squawking chicken dashed around the corner with a rooster in hot pursuit. As the chooks dashed down the porch a few crumbs of bread fell from the farmer's sandwich and the rooster stopped to gobble them up while the hen got away.

"Strewth!" exclaimed the farmer, "I hope I never get that hungry."

* * *

WHEN the shire president arrived at the country town all the neighbouring chooks gathered in the main street. They heard he was to lay a foundation stone and they didn't want to miss it.

* * *

THE local vet was in the middle of a complicated operation when the phone rang. It was Farmer Brown's wife who wanted to know how long she should leave a rooster with her chooks.

"Just a minute," said the vet turning back to his operation. The woman thanked him and hung up.

* * *

THE old rooster had been king of the chook house for years and he intended to keep it that way, so when yet another young cock was tossed into the yard by Farmer Brown it was time for some quick negotiation.

"There are 40 hens here, buster, and I am not going to fight you for them. We will need all our strength. So let's decide it with a race. Three times around the perimeter of the yard gets the lot."

The young rooster looked at the stringy old geezer. "I don't think you could make it twice around, Pops."

"Then give me a start," said the old rooster and he was off and running with a three metre break. The old farmer was sitting on his porch when the roosters came in sight; the old one in front desperately hanging on to his lead, the young one flat-out and gaining slowly.

The farmer reached for his shotgun, took aim and shot the young rooster dead.

"Y'know, Martha," he said to his wife, "it's funny, but that's the third queer rooster I have had to shoot this month!"

## CHRISTMAS

GO to church this Sunday and avoid the Christmas rush.

* * *

A COUPLE of fattened turkeys were chatting in the chook house.

"Tell me, Cyril," said one, "do you believe in Santa Claus?"

* * *

ONLY 25 shoplifting days to Christmas!

* * *

WHY wasn't Christ born in Australia?

Well, where would you find three wise men, or a virgin?

* * *

ACTUALLY there were four wise men. On the way to Bethlehem one of them said he knew a short cut.

* * *

THE rich kid kept pestering his father that he wanted a Mickey Mouse outfit for Christmas.

So his old man bought him the NSW State Cabinet.

(N.B. Change 'NSW State Cabinet' to any political institution in the news.)

* * *

DON'T give me a watch for Christmas. I've already got one. And I can assure you a man with one watch knows what time it is, while a man with two watches would never be sure.

* * *

IN the department store at Christmas the little boy had been waiting patiently in the queue to meet Santa. When his turn came Santa picked him up, sat him on his knee and said: "Ho, ho, ho, little boy. And what would you like for Christmas?"

The little tyke jumped down and kicked Santa fair in the shins. "I just told you yesterday you silly old goat."

* * *

THE kid said: "What's Christmas, Dad?"

So Dad took him to a department store where he met Santa Claus and saw the toy department. "That's Christmas, son!"

Little Isaac said to his father, Moishe, "What's Christmas, Dad?"

Moishe took the lad to a vast and empty warehouse. "That's Christmas, son!"

## CLAIRVOYANTS
### (AND THINGS SUPERNATURAL)

THE annual general meeting of the Clairvoyants' Society is postponed, due to unforeseen circumstances?

* * *

DURING World War Two, Adolph Hitler consulted his clairvoyant to find out how long he would live and on what day he would die.

The clairvoyant looked into the crystal ball and said "Mein Fuhrer, I have a vision that you will die on a Jewish holiday."

Hitler flew into a rage. "Which Jewish holiday?" he screamed.

"Mein Fuhrer, any day you die will be a Jewish holiday."

* * *

A MAN visited the fortune teller at the circus and sat down in front of her crystal ball. He was a sceptic.

"I see you are the father of two children," she began.

"Ha! That's what you think," replied the man, "I'm the father of three children."

"That's what you think," smiled the fortune teller.

FRED sat silently while she looked into the crystal ball. Suddenly she threw her head back and began roaring with laughter. She shook with mirth until Fred leaned across and punched her in the nose.

It was the first time he had struck a happy medium.

*     *     *

"WHY do you call your father-in-law the Exorcist?"

"Because every visit he rids our house of spirits."

*     *     *

THE two drunks at the bar were having a philosophical discussion on reincarnation.

"And how long have you believed in reincarnation?" said one.

"Ever since I was a frog," said the other.

*     *     *

THE Olde English Pub was called the Black Cat. Legend had it that it was named after the favourite moggy of the first innkeeper on that site. The cat had met its death when a runaway stage coach had run over it, cutting off its tail.

And for the past two hundred years its ghost appeared each time the pub changed hands.

Thus it was that the new licencee, up late cooking the books, was confronted by the ghostly apparition of the cat, carrying its tail in its paw.

"My soul won't rest until my tail is restored," moaned the ghost. "Can you help me?"

The publican put down his pen. "I'm afraid it can't be done," he said, "I am not allowed to retail spirits after ten-thirty."

## CLUBS

IT was Groucho Marx who declared: "Any club which would admit me as a member isn't worth joining."

*     *     *

THE club president was delivering his annual report and

was praising the committee. "Unlike other clubs where half the committee does all the work and the other half are hopeless, here, it is completely the reverse!"

* * *

HE heard the club was looking for a treasurer.

"But didn't they take on a new treasurer just a month ago?"

"Yes. That's the one they are looking for!"

* * *

"I SAY, old chap, who is Fonsonby talking to?"

"He is talking to himself."

"Then why is he shouting?"

"He's deaf!"

* * *

THE oldtimers were lamenting that the club had gone to the pack. "Noisy lot, all on the make," said one. "All corduroy trousers, thin moustaches and crew-cut hair. And the women are just as bad."

* * *

THE doorman to the swank club saw a limousine stop at the kerb. In his haste to get out and open the door he tripped on the step and went head-first into the gutter.

The manager rushed out and picked him up. "That's enough of that, James. People will think you're a member."

* * *

WHEN Sam walked into his poker club it caused a snigger among his mates at the bar. "Boy, the joke was on you last night, Sam," they said. "You left your bedroom light on and the blind was up. You put on a great show with your missus."

"Well, the joke happens to be on you lot," Sam retorted. "I wasn't home last night!"

## CONMEN

HE took a young lady home to his flat, offered her a Scotch and sofa, and she reclined.

THE judge fixed him with a beady eye: "How could you take money from people who trusted you?"

"Because it just doesn't work with people who don't trust you," the conman replied.

* * *

"GOOD Evening," said the barman. "What's your pleasure?"

"A Scotch and a box of matches," said Con.

He sinks the drink and puts ten cents on the counter, explaining that the money is for the matches. "I didn't really want a drink, but when you invited me so nicely, well..."

The barman said he was only being polite and when Con refuses to pay he is ordered out and barred from the pub.

A week later Con returns and the barman shouts: "Hey you. I told you last week you were barred from this hotel."

"I've never been here before," said Con. "You must have me mixed up with somebody else."

"Then you must have a double," said the barman.

"Thanks," said Con, "and a box of matches."

* * *

AS Con walked into the pub he asked his friend: "What's your great ambition in life?"

"To own a pub," said his mate. "What's yours?"

"A double brandy, thanks," said Con.

* * *

TWO conmen in an English pub called the publican over and asked him to settle an argument. "Are there two pints in a quart, or four?" asked one.

"There are two pints in a quart," confirmed the publican.

They moved back along the bar to where they had been drinking and soon the barmaid asked for their order.

68

"Two pints please Miss, and they are on the house."

When the barmaid appeared to doubt her boss would dispense free beer, one of the lads called out to the publican at the other end of the bar: "You did say two pints, didn't you?"

"That's right," shouted the publican. "Two pints."

\* \* \*

THE blind man had his hand out. "Can you spare a dollar?"

She looked at him suspiciously. "Why, I'm sure you can see out of one eye."

"Well, fifty cents then?"

\* \* \*

SHE stopped at the next blind man and dropped all her small change into his cup with a clunk.

"God bless you lady," he said. "I knew you was kind hearted the moment I saw you turn the corner."

\* \* \*

SHE intended the 50-cent piece to drop into his hat, but she missed and it clinked on to the pavement. In a swift movement the blindman scooped it up.

"How did you see that?" she said. "I thought you were blind."

"No, I'm not blind," he said. "It's my mate that's blind, and I am filling in for him while he's at the movies."

\* \* \*

HE was propped up against *Young & Jacksons* on crutches with his head bandaged and one arm in a sling. In the other hand he held his hat outstretched.

"You poor man," she said, dropping a fiver in the hat. "But think how much worse it would be if you were blind."

"You're dead right, lady" he said. "When I was blind I kept getting foreign coins."

\* \* \*

WHILE leaning on the bar, Ron the Con said, "D'yer want to buy a watch, Fred?"

"Let's see it," said Fred.

"Shh," said Ron, "the bloke next to you is wearing it."

*     *     *

THE gangling lad from the bush was amazed to learn that his new friend, Larry the Lounge Lizard was 100 years old.

"I'm surprised. You look very healthy," said the lad.

Old Larry gritted his teeth bravely, "Trouble is," he said, pushing his glass forward, "thirst doesn't show on the outside."

*     *     *

BACK on the farm from his first visit to the city, Dave proudly showed the family a large, sparkling diamond ring.

"Is it the real thing?" they gasped in amazement.

"It had better be," mumbled Dave, "otherwise I've been done out of a tenner."

*     *     *

RON the Con walked into the pub and ordered a pie and sauce. As it was served to him he told the barman he had changed his mind. He pushed the pie back and said he would have a beer instead.

When it came to payment Ron said he owed nothing. He had swapped the pie for the beer.

"But you didn't pay for the pie," argued the barman.

"And I didn't eat the pie. You've still got it," said Ron.

A little bamboozled, the barman said, "Here is a dollar. Go over the road to the pub opposite and pull the same stunt."

Ron pocketed the money. As he reached the door he said, "I might as well tell you. The publican over the road gave me $2 to pull the same stunt here."

*     *     *

THEY had dined well and after the wine Con reminded Ron it was his turn to take care of the bill. Ron called the manager and asked for an interview in his office.

"We have been doing a survey on the prevalence of those people who order large meals and then declare they have no money. What do you do?"

The manager said there was nothing much that could be done. "It only means notoriety, bad publicity and costly litigation if we prosecute. We usually bring them into this office and give them a good kick in the backside."

Ron bent over and said: "In that case can you take for two?"

*　　　*　　　*

AS the train left the station the conman sized up the old prospector sitting opposite. When they got to talking the conman proposed they play a game to pass the time.

"What kind of game?"

"General knowledge quiz. You look like a man of the world," said the conman. "We each ask the other a question, and if one can't answer he pays the other a dollar."

The old geezer thought this over for a minute. "Yeah, I like a quiz. But I don't like the even money bit."

"What do you mean?"

"Well, I've spent most of my life in the bush. I'm just a simple man, whereas you look like a city-slicker to me. So I suggest that if you can't answer my questions, then it costs you a dollar, but if I can't answer yours, then you should let me off with 50 cents."

The conman was sure he was on a winner. "Okay, I pay 50 cents to your dollar."

"Then here's the first question," said the old geezer. "What's got five legs and flies backwards?"

"Don't know," said the conman slapping down a dollar.

"My question now, and I'm interested to know exactly what does have five legs and flies backwards?"

"Blowed if I know. Here's your 50 cents," said the old man.

# CONUNDRUMS

IF you weigh a whale at a weigh-weigh station, where do you weigh a pie? Somewhere over the rainbow, weigh up pie!

\* \* \*

FRED was a keen one for conundrums, so when the barman presented one he listened intently.

The barman said: "My mother had a child. It wasn't my brother and it wasn't my sister. Who was it?"

Fred scratched his head and admitted he was beat.

"It was me," declared the barman triumphantly.

Fred thought it was a good one and couldn't wait to relate it to his wife. In fact he woke her up to tell it.

"My mother had a child. It wasn't my brother and it wasn't my sister. Who was it?"

His sleepy wife said she didn't have a clue.

"Easy," said Fred. "It was Harry the barman down at the pub."

\* \* \*

"WHAT'S the difference between a tram and a taxi?" he said.

"I give in, I don't know," she said.

"Good, then we'll take the tram."

\* \* \*

WHAT did Mrs Quasimodo give Quasi for Christmas?

A Wok! She thought it would help her iron his shirts.


# COURTING
See ENGAGEMENTS

"I DON'T believe we've met. I'm Mr Right."

\* \* \*

"I AM writing a phone book. Could I have your number Miss?"

"LET'S get married, or something."
"Let's get married, or nothing."

*  *  *

OUT on her first date her mother's words were ringing in her ears: "Say no to everything he suggests."

So after dinner and a couple of drinks he said: "Do you mind if we fool around in bed?"

*  *  *

IT was their second date and after a few drinks in the cock-tail lounge he thought the time was right. He leaned over and whispered in her ear, "How about coming away with me for the week-end to a little cabin I have in the snow?"

She replied: "I suspect my anticipation of your pro-clivities in the esoteric aspects of sexual behaviour pre-clude such an erotic confrontation."

He scratched his head, "I don't get it."

"Exactly," she replied.

*  *  *

"I WILL go to the end of the world for you," he said.

"Yes, but will you stay there," she yawned.

*  *  *

HE said it was love at first sight.

Then why didn't he marry her?

Because he took a second look.

*  *  *

FRED'S been turned down so many times he is like the hot page in a naughty novel.

*  *  *

"I'VE heard plenty about your love-making."

*  *  *

"AM I the first man you've ever made love to, dearest?" he asked.

She studied him for a moment. "You could be," she said, "there is something familiar about your face."

*  *  *

THE ardent suitor was urging his girlfriend to live with

him. "It will be exactly like the real thing only we won't have the expense of getting married. And then if we find later that we have made a mistake, then we won't have the cost of the divorce."

"Yes," she said. "But what do we do with the mistake?"

*     *     *

HE had been watching the blonde at the other end of the bar for some time before he got sufficient courage to approach her.

"Would you like a Harvey Wallbanger?" he asked.

"Love one," she said. "But let's have a drink first."

*     *     *

HE snuggled up to her and said: "I'm yours for the asking."

She snuggled back and said: "I'm asking fifty bucks!"

*     *     *

IT was love at first sight and they had taken the big step and slept together for the first time. They were still in bed when the phone rang next morning.

He reached out and picked up the receiver, listened for a moment, then gave her a shake.

"It's for a Miss Sheila Kelly," he said. "Is that you?"

*     *     *

THE stern father took the lad aside when he had brought his daughter home. "I'd like a word," he said.

"If you are going to see our Ethel regularly I hope you know the difference between right and wrong."

The young man gulped. "But surely you yourself have brought her up to know what's right?"

"Indeed we have," said the father.

"Well, I've taken care of the other side, so everything's fine."

*     *     *

WHEN Myrtle finally brought a bloke home her parents were relieved that this might be the Mr Right that would take her off their hands. But when they took a closer look they took Myrtle aside.

"He's not exactly a young man," whispered Mum to her daughter. "He's fat, he's bald and he's pretty old isn't he?"

"There's no need to whisper, Mum," said Myrtle, "he's stone deaf too."

## CROCODILES

PADDY O'Reilly was walking up High St with a crocodile on a lead when a concerned policeman stopped him.

"Where are you going with that beast?" asked the cop.

"I am taking him to the zoo," replied Paddy, which satisfied the cop.

Next day the same cop saw the same Paddy with the same crocodile on the same lead.

"I thought you were taking that thing to the zoo?" said the cop.

"Aye, I did, and he liked it. Today I'm taking him to the pictures."

\* \* \*

PADDY took his crocodile into a pub and said: "Do you serve Catholics?"

The barman said he did.

"Well, Oi'l be having a pot of stout, and two catholics for my crocodile!"

\* \* \*

TARZAN was coming home after a hard day's work and turned the bend in the river just in time to see a crocodile taking one of his kids.

He rushed in and told Jane, but she was more intent on taking Tarzan to bed. "Don't worry about it," she said. "We've got plenty of kids. Let's go to bed and make another one."

The following evening after a hard day's work Tarzan staggered home just in time to see a crocodile taking another kid.

"Oh, don't worry," said Jane. "Come to bed and we'll make another one."

"Listen," said an angry Tarzan, "I'm not working all day and making love all night just to feed the damned crocodiles!"

## CRICKET

IT was the club's social dance and the young debutante had trouble dancing with her awkward partner.

"Sorry," he said, "I'm a little stiff from bowling."

"I don't care where you come from," she said, "just keep off my feet."

\* \* \*

FRED'S wife rang the cricket club.

"Sorry, he has just walked to the crease. He is about to bat. Shall I ask him to ring you back?"

"No. I'll hang on," she said.

\* \* \*

THE club's best batsman was on the phone to his captain trying to explain why he couldn't play next day.

"No, I can't let you off the game," said the captain who was made of stern stuff. "If I did, then I would have to do the same for any other player whose wife dies."

\* \* \*

THE famous test player began his career with the Werribbee Wanderers so the social committee sent him a telegram asking if he would make a guest appearance for $100.

The cricketer sent back a telegram: "Will accept, but double the offer or count me out."

The committee's immediate reply was: "1, 2, 3, 4, 5, 6, 7, 8, 9, 10."

\* \* \*

EVENTUALLY they got Allan Border as guest player at the Werribbee Wanderers testimonial fund raiser and indeed there was a large crowd at the ground.

Ned, the club's fast bowler, had never faced a test cricketer before and he felt the tension as he hurled down his first ball.

To Ned's surprise the off stump went flying. Clean bowled. "No ball," roared the umpire, and then took Ned aside. "Slow down you idiot. They've come to see Border bat, not you bowl."

\* \* \*

TWO fans settled down at the MCG when one realised he had left his wallet in his mate's Mercedes. He returned from the car park 15 minutes later, pale and shaken.

"I've got bad news, Bob. A truck has crashed into your car and the impact set it on fire. It's totally destroyed."

"And have I got some bad news for you," said Bob to his mate. "Border is out for a duck."

\* \* \*

FRED's wife snuggled up beside him in bed and whispered: "Remember the Saturday you proposed to me. My word you were bold then."

"No way," said Fred. "I was caught."

\* \* \*

"SO, you had a hard time trying to explain the test match to your wife?"

"Yes, especially when she found out I wasn't there."

\* \* \*

THE cricketer was getting a medical. "I dunno, Doc," he said. "My fielding is very bad lately. I can't bowl like I used to and everytime I go in to bat I get a duck lately."

"Why don't you try some other sport?" said the doctor.

"I can't," he said. "I'm captain of the Australian Eleven."

\* \* \*

THE cricket fan was trying to interest his girlfriend in the game and took her to the Saturday match.

Pointing out a promising batsman he said, "It won't be long before that bloke will be our best man."

"Oh Frederick," she gushed, "this is so sudden."

THE visiting church team was surprised to see no scoring facilities at the sports ground. "Don't worry about that," said the bush captain, a well-muscled shearer, "we keep the scores in our heads, and if there is any dispute we settle the argument behind the shearing shed after the game."

\* \* \*

"THAT was very sporting of you to cheer our team for winning the match," said the church captain to the Patchywollock host. "By the way, where's the umpire?"

"He's in the dam," was the reply.

\* \* \*

THE Devil challenged St Peter to a cricket match. "Remember," said St Peter, "we have all the good cricketers up here." "Yes," said the Devil, "but we've got all the umpires down here."

\* \* \*

THEY take their cricket seriously in the bush. A stranger at the Patchywollock v. Wonga Creek game was cheering the batsman's play and at the same time applauding the bowler and fieldsmen.

This bothered one local shearer.

"Do you come from Patchywollock?"

"No," said the stranger.

"From Wonga Creek then?"

"No," said the stranger.

"Well in that case mind you own bloody business and keep your trap shut."

\* \* \*

THE batsman was describing his big hit.

"I gave it everything I had. The ball went into the sky and hit a passing duck."

"Hit a duck? Was it wild?"

"It was ruddy-well livid."

\* \* \*

THE boys were playing cricket in the backyard with a shiny new ball. It attracted the interest of their father.

"Where did you get the ball?" he asked.

"We found it," chorused the kids.

"Are you sure it was lost?"

"Of course it was lost. We watched them looking for it."

* * *

THE bush town's cricket match was stopped when the ball was hit clear over the fence. While players from both sides searched in the long grass they were watched by an idle lad sitting against the fence.

"Did you see a cricket ball come over?" one of the cricketers asked him.

"No I didn't," said the lad, "but I have brought this fairly new one from home that I could sell you."

* * *

FRED was always bragging. "I walked out of the Gabba last Saturday," he said, "and a crowd of 30 or more clamoured around me for my autograph."

"Come off it, Fred."

"Fair dinkum. If you don't believe me, ask Allan Border. He was standing right beside me."

* * *

FRED was trying to join the local team.

"Have you had any experience?" asked the captain.

"Well, I think I once played with Don Bradman."

"Really?"

"Yes," said Fred, "he told me after the game who he was. He said if I was a batsman, he was Don Bradman."

* * *

THERE is a man in Wycheproof who has devised a game that in some aspects is similar to cricket.

What he doesn't know, is that the Australian Eleven has been playing it for years.

* * *

TWO old boys were bragging in the bar at Lords.

"What was your highest score," said one.

"One hundred and fifty," said the other.

"Well, mine was one hundred and fifty-five," said the first smuggly. "And what was the highest number of wickets you got?" he continued.

"Oh no. You go first this time."

\* \* \*

NED was building up record averages as the club's fast bowler, but he was a little worried when he learned that his father-in-law was to umpire the day's match.

Ned hurled the first ball down at terrific pace and caught the batsman LBW.

"Owzat!" he yelled.

"Not out," said the umpire.

The second ball came down like a missile, snicked the bat and was caught by the wicket-keeper.

"Owzat!" roared Ned.

"Not out," said the umpire.

With the wildest fury he could muster the third ball screamed down the wicket, hit the middle stump and snapped it in half, sending wickets and bails in the air.

"Ruddy-well nearly got him that time," said Ned.

\* \* \*

AFTER a series of bad decisions from the umpire, Ned approached him and said: "If I called you a stupid old goat who didn't know the first thing about cricket what would you do?"

"I would report you and you would be fined," said the umpire.

"What if I didn't say it, and just thought it?"

"Well, nothing could be done about it."

"Okay," said Ned, "then we'll just leave it at that, then, eh?"

\* \* \*

ON the train Fred couldn't keep his eyes off the old codger sitting in the opposite corner with one of his boots glued to his ear. He was listening with intense concentration.

Fred's curiosity finally got the better of him. He leaned across and said: "What's going on?"

The old man motioned him to be silent and continued listening until Fred pulled the boot away and asked again.

"If you must know," grunted the old man, "I'm listening to the test match."

"Here, give me a go," said Fred snatching the boot and putting it to his ear.

He listened for a while. "I can't hear a thing," he said.

"No, and you won't either," grinned the old man. "They just stopped for tea."

\*     \*     \*

THE big shearer's cook was batting in the annual bush grudge match and had survived three appeals for obvious LBW.

The next delivery hit the middle stump and sent the bails flying.

"Owzat?" they roared.

"Not out," said the umpire.

"What kind of a damned decision is that?" cried the bowler. "He's been out four times already."

The umpire was adamant. "I say he stays. We've only got a nine-gallon keg and he's the best guzzler in the whole district"

\*     \*     \*

AN expectant father rang the hospital to see how his wife was progressing. By mistake he was connected to the cricket ground.

"How's it going?" he asked.

"Going well," came the answer. "We've got three out and hope to get the rest out before lunch. The last one was a duck!"

# CRICKET INSULTS

"WHY are you looking so down-hearted?"
  "The doctor says I can't play cricket."
  "When did he see you play?"

       \*     \*     \*

CAPTAIN: "It's a pity you didn't take up the game sooner."
  "You mean I'd be better now?"
  "No, you would have given the game up long ago."

       \*     \*     \*

OUT for a duck the angry batsman marched into the pavilion and said, "I've never played so badly before."
  The captain appeared surprised: "You mean, you've played before?"

       \*     \*     \*

"THAT was the best innings I've ever played."
  "Well, you mustn't let that discourage you."

       \*     \*     \*

"ARE your team members good losers?"
  "Good? They're perfect!"


# CRIMINALS

THE prisoner said to the social worker: "Women have been my downfall."
  "What kind of women?"
  "Those who carry handbags."

       \*     \*     \*

HE said his Dad gave him three words of advice on being financially solvent.
  "What were they?"
  "Stick 'em up!"

       \*     \*     \*

A TRAVELLER was walking down a dark street one night when he was stopped by a tramp who said: "Excuse me, Guv. Would you be so kind as to help a poor unfortunate who is hungry and out of work, with no money and no worldly possessions, except for this sawn off shot gun...!"

\* \* \*

THEY were walking arm in arm down High St when she saw a diamond ring in the showcase window. "Oh, it's lovely," she said.

So he heaved a brick through the glass and grabbed it.

A little further on she saw a fur coat on display and implored him to get it for her.

He heaved another brick through the window and snatched it.

Around the corner she stopped at the show window which featured a beautiful Jaguar sports car. "Oh, I'd love that," she said.

"Enough, Myrtle," he said. "Do you think I'm made of bricks?"

## CUSTOMS AGENTS

CUSTOMS officer was inspecting a sweet young thing's suitcase and discovered six pair of French knickers. "What are these for?" he asked.

"Sunday, Monday, Tuesday, Wednesday, Thursday and Friday," she replied.

"And what about Saturday?" he asked.

She replied with a smile and a wink and minced by.

Next was a big German frau who flung her suitcase onto the counter.

"And what are these for?" said the customs officer discovering 12 pair of thick flannel bloomers.

She replied: "January, February, March, April.........."

\* \* \*

CUSTOMS officer at the airport asked Paddy if he had anything to declare.

"No, only this bottle of holy water from Lourdes."

The officer was interested and asked to see it. When

Paddy produced it the officer removed the cork and put his nose to the bottle.

"That's not water," he said grimly. "That's whisky."

"Mother of God!" exclaimed Paddy, "It's another bloomin' miracle!"

*　　*　　*

A MARRIED couple, Freda and Fred, had been successfully smuggling native birds out of Australia to the United States for years.

Freda suggested they could double their earnings by smuggling some American wildlife on the return trips.

"For example," she said. "I've got a squirrel here and I am going to hide it by stuffing it down the front of my pants."

"And this is for you, Fred," she said, handing him a skunk. "That will bring big money in Australia. Stuff it down the front of your trousers."

Fred protested: "What about the smell?"

Freda shrugged her shoulders. "If it dies ... it dies."

# D

## DANCING

DANCING is the perpendicular expression of horizontal desire.

*     *     *

"I DON'T dance, but I'd love to hold you while you do."

*     *     *

DANCING is a physical contact sport.

*     *     *

DON'T miss our next show. Six dancing girls and five beautiful costumes.

*     *     *

"COULD I have the last dance?"
  "You've just had it."

*     *     *

HE: "Doesn't this dance make you long for another?"
  She: "Yes, but he couldn't come tonight."

*     *     *

A GIRL is something you look damned silly dancing without.

*     *     *

THE clergyman had delivered a fiery sermon against the evils of dancing and made it clear that he was opposed to any kind of dancing. After the congregation had filed out he was approached by a young dancing enthusiast. "Just what's wrong with dancing?" he asked.

"Well, for one thing," said the minister, "it's the close touching of the bodies."

"Not so," protested the parishioner, "it is all in the mind of those who look at it with the wrong attitude."

"Then let's suppose," argued the minister, "that you came home from work and found me holding your wife in that manner. What would you think?"

"I'd think that you'd better be dancing," was the reply.

\* \* \*

AT a country dance a young couple were pressed together, dancing cheek to cheek. She whispered in his ear, "Come out to the car."

He declined, saying the tune being played was one of his favourite numbers, but she persisted and pleaded for him to come out to the car.

He finally agreed. When they left the hall it was pitch black outside so he produced a torch from his pocket to light the way to the car.

She said: "Did you have that torch in your pocket all night?"

"Yes," he said.

"Well let's go back to the dance," she said.

\* \* \*

FRED was asked how he got his black eye.

"I was teaching my girlfriend the tango when her father came in. How was I to know he was stone deaf?"

\* \* \*

THE debutante at the country ball
  Knows that pride goes before a fall
  So when she trips the light fantastic
  She always wears good strong elastic.

# DEATH
See FUNERALS

DEATH is nature's way of telling you to slow down.

"SO Old Smithy is dead. Did he leave his wife much?"
  "Nearly every night."

* * *

"WHAT's the death rate around here?"
  "Same as any place. One death per person."

* * *

AS Woody Allen said: "It is not that I'm afraid to die. I just don't want to be around when it happens."

* * *

WHILE on holiday, Fred bought the local paper, and browsing through the death notices he was intrigued to see that everyone had died in alphabetical order.

* * *

HE died a natural death. He was hit by a car.

* * *

"DOC, I'm afraid I'm going to die."
  "Nonsense! That's the last thing you'll do."

* * *

THE clock and watchmaker millionaire died recently. They reckon it will take years to wind up his estate.

* * *

"HEY Mum, how did Dad know the exact date he was going to die?"
  "The judge told him."

* * *

THE relatives gathered around to hear the solicitor read Fred's short will:
  "Being of sound mind I spent the lot before I carked it."

* * *

SHE was complaining to her neighbour. She had made constant trips to the city, three times to the insurance office, twice to the probate office, hundreds of papers and documents to sort through. "I sometimes wish Fred hadn't died," she said.

SHE was ebbing fast and she raised herself on one elbow and beckoned her John to come closer. "On the day of the funeral," she gasped, "it would please me if you would ride in the same coach as mother."

"Okay" he said grudgingly, "but you know it will completely spoil my day."

* * *

OLD Jake was on his death bed. He raised himself on one elbow and beckoned his wife closer.

"Emily," he gasped. "You were with me through the Great Depression."

She nodded.

"Emily, you were with me through the worst droughts in the fifties."

She nodded.

"And you were with me when we lost the farm in the bush fires. Now here you are again, by my side when I'm about to cark it."

She nodded.

"You know Emily," he said, "I'm beginning to think you've been bringing me bad luck."

* * *

DYING at sea can have its complications. The captain informed the first mate that the passenger in Cabin 25 had died and ordered him to arrange for a burial at sea.

An hour later the mate came onto the bridge and reported that the matter relating to Cabin 27 had been attended to.

"What," said the captain aghast. "I said Cabin 25. Didn't the man tell you he wasn't dead?"

"Yes, Cap'n," said the mate, "but he was a Pommie and you know what lying bastards they are."

* * *

HERE snug in her grave
My wife do lie

Now she's at rest
And so am I.

* * *

UNDERNEATH this pile of stones
  Lies the remains of Harry Jones
  His name was Smith
  It was not Jones
  But Jones was put
  To rhyme with stones.

# DEFINITIONS

AUTOMATIC SHIFT: When the driver moves closer to his girlfriend.

AUTOBIOGRAPHY: The car's logbook.

APEX: The female of the gorilla species.

ADVERTISEMENT: Something that makes you think you've longed for it for years, but never heard of it before.

ALIMONY: A mistake by two people paid for by one.

ABSENTEE: A missing golfing accessory.

ANTI-FREEZE: When you don't talk to your uncle's wife.

ADAMANT: The very first insect.

ADIEU: Hymie Finklestein.

ADORN: What comes after the darkest hour.

AROMATIC: An automatic longbow.

ARTFUL: A painting exhibition.

AWE-STRUCK: Being hit with a paddle.

AVAIL: Helpful for ugly women.

ALPHABET: Not quite the complete wager.

ABUNDANCE: A local hop usually staged in a barn.

ACME: Pimples on the face running towards the top.

BURLESQUE SHOW: Where attendance falls off if nothing else does.

BADMINTON: The reason the lamb tasted off.

BORN EXECUTIVE: A bloke whose father owns the company.

**BRAZIER:** Something to warm your hands on.

**BALANCE:** Something you lose if the bank pushes you.

**BARBARIAN:** The man who cuts your hair.

**BOOKCASE:** Litigation about a novel which ensures wide sales.

**BRUSSELS SPROUTS:** A world famous statue found in that city.

**BOXER:** A bloke who stands up for the other fellow's rights.

**CLIMATE:** The best thing to do with a ladder.

**CONDESCENDING:** A Greek parachutist.

**CONSCIENCE:** The thing that aches when everything else feels good.

**COWARD:** A man who thinks with his legs.

**CABBAGE:** The fare you pay a taxi driver.

**DETEST:** The West Indies playing India (cricket).

**ELECTRICIAN:** A switch doctor.

**FASTIDIOUS:** A girl who is fast and hideous.

**FAUCET:** What you have to do if the tap won't turn.

**FETE:** A boring picnic worse than death.

**FLOOSIE:** A sweet girl with the gift of the grab.

**GRANARY:** A home for senior female citizens.

**GALLERY:** A hostel for young women.

**HUMBUG:** A singing cockroach.

**HYACINTH:** A yank greeting a gal called Cynthia.

**IDOLISE:** Eyes that refuse to look at anything.

**INCOME:** What you have to make first, because you can't make it last.

**JEALOUSY:** The friendship one woman shares with another.

**LACTIC:** A grandfather clock which doesn't work.

**MONOLOGUE:** A discussion between man and wife.

**MARCONI:** The first man to send a message through a length of spaghetti without it touching the sides.

**NONDESCRIPT:** A television play.

**ODIOUS:** Not very good poetry.

PARENTS: Couples who practise the Rhythm Method.

PEDESTRIAN: A motorist with teenage sons.

RACIAL DISPUTE: When the course judge calls for a photo.

REFLECTION: What a girl looks at, but is not given to.

SAGE: A bloke who knows his onions.

STALEMATE: A husband who has lost his ardour.

SNUFF: Sufficient unto the day.

SONATA: A song sung by Frank.

# DENTISTS

A MAN and his wife rushed into the dentist's surgery and offered double the going rate if he would pull a tooth immediately.

"We are in a hurry to get to the airport," explained the husband. "We are running late and there is not time for that anaesthetic stuff. Just rip it out."

The dentist said it would be painful.

"To hell with the pain. Just rip it out," he insisted.

"Very well," said the dentist. "You certainly have courage. Now which tooth is it?"

The man turned to his wife. "Hop up into the chair, Myrtle and show him."

*     *     *

"GOOD grief, you've got the biggest cavity I've ever seen," said the dentist. "You've got the biggest cavity I've ever seen."

"Okay," said the patient, "you don't have to repeat it."

"I didn't" said the dentist, "that was the echo!"

*     *     *

SHE thought the Tooth Fairy was a Gay Dentist.

*     *     *

"I DON'T know which is worse," said the sweet young thing settling into the dentist's chair, "having a tooth pulled, or having a baby."

"Well make up your mind," said the dentist, "so that I can fix the chair in the appropriate position!"

* * *

"SATISFACTION Guaranteed, or your teeth refunded."

* * *

THE wharfie was built like the proverbial outhouse and as he settled in the chair he gripped the dentist by his short and curlies.

"We're not going to hurt each other, are we?" he said.

* * *

"WHY are you screaming?" said the dentist. "I haven't started drilling yet."

"I know, but you're standing on my feet," said the patient.

* * *

A DESPERATE looking gangster settled into the chair after telling the dentist he needed a tooth pulled out.

"Which one is it?"

"That's for you to find out," growled the tough guy. "I ain't no stool pigeon."

* * *

A FARMER who had an abiding fear of dentists asked his neighbour what the new bloke was like. "Did that new dentist stop the pain in your tooth?" he asked.

"Well put it this way," said his mate. "You remember last week when I stepped on that rake, got cracked on the head by the handle, fell backwards, and sat on that rabbit trap?"

"Yeah."

"Well that was the first time since I visited that new dentist that the pain in my jaw didn't bother me."

* * *

NERVOUS patient: "This will be the first tooth I've lost."

Nervous Dentist: "That's a co-incidence. This will be the first tooth I've pulled."

"WHAT was it like having all your teeth out?"
"Terrible. I'll never do it again."

## DESERT ISLANDS

"THE most important thing we have in common," he said as they staggered ashore on the desert island, "is that I'm a man and you're a woman."

                \*       \*       \*

A FOOTBALL star fell overboard from a cruise ship and finally drifted ashore on a tropical island. He was eventually revived by a beautiful native girl.

She took him to her hut where she supplied him with food.

Then she produced a bottle of Scotch from a crate which had also drifted onto the beach.

Then she said: "Would you like to play with me?"

The footballer was frankly astonished. "Don't tell me you've got a football too?"

                \*       \*       \*

AN Englishman, an Australian and an Irishman had been marooned on a desert island for 15 years. One day the Aussie saw a bottle floating past and waded in to the sea to retrieve it. When he pulled the cork a Geni appeared.

"Oh what a relief to get out," he said. "I've been stuck in there for a thousand years, and the rules say you three blokes have got one wish each."

The three mates could not believe their eyes, but the genie insisted he was real, and so were the wishes. "But remember, it's just one each."

The Englishman was sceptical, but said he would give it a try. "I wish I was back on the Old Kent Road in London town," he laughed. In a blinding flash he disappeared.

"I wish I was back in the Members' Stand at Flemington Races," said the Aussie quickly. Another flash and he was gone.

The Irishman thought hard, screwed his face in thought but couldn't make up his mind. "Oh, I wish my mates were back here to help me!"

# DIPLOMACY

DIPLOMACY is when you make your in-laws feel at home, when you wish they were.

\* \* \*

YOUNG bloke had just become engaged and met his fiancee's mother for the first time. "How old do you think I am?" she asked the lad.

"Well," he said after a moment's thought, "I am wondering whether to make you ten years younger to fit with your looks and figure, or ten years older on account of your wise intelligence."

\* \* \*

"LOOK at that ugly old bag over there," said one drinker to his mate, "got a face like the back of a bus."

"That's my wife," replied the other cooly.

"Got great legs," said the first.

\* \* \*

THE white missionary had lived with the Bullabukanki tribe for 18 months when the chief took him aside and said the reverend was in big heaps of trouble.

"Yesterday a white baby was born to my sister, and you are the only white man in this village," said the chief sharpening his axe.

The missionary broke out in a sweat. "Look, old man, I know it looks bad, but see your flock of sheep down by the river?"

"Yeah, I see them," said the chief.

"Well can you see the black sheep in the flock. There is only one and ... "

"Okay, okay," said the chief, "I'll keep quiet if you'll keep quiet."

# DIVORCE

SHE told the lawyer: "I want a divorce."

"On what grounds?" he said.

"Bigamy," she replied. "He can't have his Kate and Edith too."

*     *     *

HARRY mumbled a few words in church and found himself married. A few years later he mumbled a few words in his sleep and found himself divorced.

*     *     *

SHE was given a divorce because the judge found her husband had flat feet. They were always in the wrong flat.

*     *     *

SHE says maintenance is the best policy. That's a man's cash surrender value.

*     *     *

THEY had to admit she was a great housekeeper. Divorced three husbands and kept the house each time.

*     *     *

SHE was suing for divorce. She told the judge that every time she and her husband drove past one of his girl-friends, he made her duck her head.

*     *     *

HE left his wife because of another woman. Her mother.

*     *     *

JUDGE: "I have taken all factors into account and decided to award your wife $150 a week."

Defendant: "That's real decent of you, yer honour. Why, I might throw in a few dollars myself."

*     *     *

FRED was leaning on the bar and confided in Bill that he was going to get a divorce.

"The wife hasn't spoken to me in five months. Not a word," he said.

Bill pondered this and said "Don't be too hasty, Fred. Wives like that are damned hard to find."

* * *

HE said his father was very disappointed when he was born.

"Why, did he want a girl?"

"No, he wanted a divorce."

* * *

THE pretty young wife was suing for divorce.

"On what grounds?" asked her solicitor. "You've got to have grounds".

"But we do," she assured him. "Yes, we have large grounds, a 20 hectare block."

"No, no," he said. "Do you have a grudge?"

"Yes, we have a double garage because we have two cars."

"No, no," said the solicitor, near exasperation. "Does he beat you up?"

"Never," she said. "I'm always up at six, and he sleeps in till ten sometimes."

The solicitor finally grabbed her by the shoulders. "Reasons!" he shouted. "What are your reasons?"

"Oh, we don't seem to be able to communicate," she said.

* * *

FREE at last, ain't life grand
  I've just divorced my old man.
  I laughed til I cried at the judge's decision
  He gave him the kids
  And none were his'n.


## DOCTORS
See HOSPITAL

THE doctor felt the patient's thin purse and admitted there was nothing he could do.

MOST doctors can decide on the treatment you need just by feeling your wallet, but throughout history the medical profession has never ceased to produce an endless supply of doctor jokes. Here are but a few:

\* \* \*

DOCTOR to new patient: "First I need to study your medical history. Do you pay your medical bills promptly?"

\* \* \*

"I WILL examine you for twenty dollars."
  "Go ahead, Doc. If you find it you can have it."

\* \* \*

WHAT'S the use of consulting a doctor about a cold when he gives you a heart attack with the bill?

\* \* \*

"I THINK I've got amnesia, Doc."
  "Okay, then I will ask for my fee in advance."

\* \* \*

THE doctor finally discovered a cure for amnesia, but forgot what it was.

\* \* \*

"DOCTOR, I have a small, embarrassing wart."
  "Divorce him."

\* \* \*

PATIENT: "Aren't these pills habit-forming?"
  Doctor: "Rubbish, I've been taking them for years."

\* \* \*

"DOCTOR, I've got Parkinson's disease, and I think he's got mine."

\* \* \*

"ARE you taking the medicine regularly?"
  "No, Doc. I tasted it and decided I'd rather keep coughing."

\* \* \*

"WELL Doc, how do I stand?"
  "I don't know. It's a damned miracle."

PATIENT: "I'm having trouble breathing, Doc."

Doctor: "Well I'll soon put a stop to that."

\* \* \*

THE woman marched into the doctor's surgery dragging her young son along by the ear. "Doc. I just want to ask you one question. Can a a boy of twelve take out his own appendix?"

"Most certainly not madam," said the surgeon.

She belted her son across the head. "Hear that, Nigel. Now put it back at once."

\* \* \*

AFTER a lengthy examination the doctor came out of the surgery and said to the patient's wife, "I don't like the look of your husband."

"Neither do I, but he's nice to the kids," she said.

\* \* \*

THE doctor told his patient he had better sit down. He had two items of bad news. "First, I am sorry to say you have a sexually transmitted disease," said the doc.

"Oh, that's terrible," said his patient. "How will I explain it to the family?"

"And you also have Alzheimer's Disease," added the doc. "Oh, no! A double calamity, what a shock," lamented the patient. "Er, what was that first thing you said I had?"

\* \* \*

HE parked his sportscar outside the clinic and bounced in without an appointment. "I just want to thank the doctor for his treatment," he said.

"But, you're not a patient of mine are you?" said the Doc.

"No, but my late Uncle Harry was."

\* \* \*

"THE doctor told me to take these pills for the rest of my life."

"So, what's the problem?"

"He only gave me half a dozen."

"THE doctor gave me two weeks to live."

"Goodness, what did you say?"

"I told him I'd take the first two weeks in December."

\*     \*     \*

MURPHY was given two weeks to live. He decided to take one week in January and the other in March.

\*     \*     \*

O'REILLY was given six months to live. But when he said he couldn't pay his bill the doctor gave him another six months.

\*     \*     \*

A BUSINESSMAN went for his annual medical. The grim-faced doctor said he had better sit down because he had some bad news. "To put it bluntly, you've got ten hours to live," he said.

"No, I can't believe it," said the businessman, "I want a second opinion."

"Well, you've got a nasty disposition, too," said the Doc (no, that's not the joke).

The businessman hurried to another clinic and was given the same distressing diagnosis. "You have nine hours to live."

Finally accepting the inevitable he got into his car and drove home. "Edna my darling," he said looking at his watch, "I have about eight hours to live."

As soon as his wife grasped the gravity of the situation she said, "Ralph, your slightest wish is my command. What would you like?"

He thought for a moment and said: "To bed!"

They were at it for an hour, and after a short rest she said, "What now, Ralph?"

He thought for a second. "Let's do it again!"

She compliantly agreed and after another hour she asked if he would like anything else.

Ralph said he was ready for a third.

"Oh for goodness sake," she cried. "It's okay for you, but I've got to get up in the morning!"

★　　★　　★

THE doctor had given Fred the dreadful news that he had contracted cancer and only had six months to live, so why was Fred telling everyone he was dying from AIDS.

"It's like this Doc," he explained. "I don't want anyone fooling around with my wife after I'm gone."

★　　★　　★

THE doctor told him he had good news and bad news. Which did he want first. The patient opted for the bad news first and the doc told him he had three weeks to live. "Hell, what's the good news then?" he asked.

The doctor leaned close and whispered, "See that blonde nurse there. I'm taking her out tonight!"

★　　★　　★

THE Doc told his patient he had some bad news, and some very bad news.

"What's the bad news?"

"You've only got two weeks to live."

"What news can be worse than that?" cried the patient.

"I should have told you a fortnight ago."

★　　★　　★

THE doctor had finished his examination and with a smile on his face said: "Mrs Jones, I have some very good news for you."

"Miss Jones," she corrected.

The doctor wiped the smile off his face. "Miss Jones, I have some very bad news for you!"

★　　★　　★

"IT'S my nerves," she said. "Please doctor you have to give me something for my nerves."

The doctor reached for a packet of pills. "Take these, they are $10 a packet."

She said: "I'll give you $7 for them."

Doctor: "There's nothing wrong with your nerve, lady."

*100*

THE farmer's wife, the mother of ten kids, called in to tell the doctor cheerfully that she won't be coming back as an expectant mother any more now that she had her birth control appliance.

The doctor was puzzled because she indicated that her "appliance" was an ordinary hearing aid.

"Before I had it," she explained, "we would get into bed at night and my husband would say "Will we put out the light and go to sleep, or what?"

"And I would say 'What'?"

*    *    *

OLD Fred was having his annual check-up.

"Well, old man," said the doctor tactfully, "you are getting on in years and I suggest you play it safe and give up half your sex life."

Fred thought this over for a moment, then asked which half he was supposed to give up. "Talking about it? Or thinking about it?"

*    *    *

THE doctor checked his patient over and with a puzzled frown said: "I can't really tell what the trouble is. I think it must be due to drinking."

"I understand Doc. I'll come back when you're sober!"

*    *    *

THE doctor was explaining to Paddy O'Leary how nature adjusted some physical disabilities. "For example, if a man is blind he develops a keen sense of hearing and touch. If he is stone deaf, then he develops his other senses..."

"Oi know what you mean," said Paddy. "Oi've noticed that if a bloke has one short leg, then the other one is always a bit longer."

*    *    *

THE doctor answered the phone to hear an excited voice say: "Quick, send an ambulance. My wife Bridget is about to have a baby!"

"Calm down," said the Doc. "Is this her first baby?"

"No, this is her husband, Pat speaking!"

*     *     *

THE doctor examined the young woman and said with a smile: "You can go home and tell your husband he is going to become a Daddy."

"But doctor, I'm not married."

"Well, you can tell your boyfriend."

"But doctor," she said. "I haven't got a boyfriend. I have never been out with a man."

The doctor walked over to the window and looked into the night sky. "Last time this happened there was a big star in the east," he said.

*     *     *

FRED complained to his doctor that his wife had lost interest in sex. The doc counselled him that it was a matter of preparation.

"Next time you come home from the office, bring a bunch of flowers, greet her with a big kiss, sweep her off her feet and carry her upstairs to the bedroom. You will be surprised."

On Fred's next visit he asked if it had worked. "Yes, indeed she was surprised," said Fred, "and so were all the members of her bridge club."

*     *     *

PADDY went to the doctor. He had two burnt ears.

"The phone rang when I was ironing, didn't it," said Paddy explaining.

"But what about the other ear?" asked the doctor.

"Well I had to phone you for an appointment, didn't I!"

*     *     *

A MARRIED couple visited the doctor who specialised in sex therapy. Romance had gone out of their lives, they said. Sex wasn't interesting anymore.

The doc listened to their nightly routine of evening meal, television and the same old missionary position.

"No wonder it's dull," he said. "You have made it monotonous, even the same time every night. What you have got to do is make it spontaneous. Do it when the mood takes you." And he gave them a pep talk on spontaneity.

A week later they came back, all smiles.

"We did what you suggested," said the husband. "Half way through a candle-lit dinner I felt randy. Ethel said she did too, so I leant over and ripped off her blouse, then pulled her down to the floor and we made love under the table. It was ecstatic spontaneity," he said.

And Ethel added, "But they said we could never go back to that restaurant again!"

\* \* \*

"MY brother swallowed a box of fire crackers."

"Is he alright?"

"Don't know. We haven't heard the last report."

\* \* \*

THE aging playboy was having his annual medical check.

"Sex?" asked the doctor.

"Infrequently," came the reply.

"Hmmm," said the doctor, "is that one word or two?"

\* \* \*

FEELING run-down and listless, Fred visited the doctor for advice. The medic examined him and solemnly announced: "The remedy is simple. Whatever it is you are doing, stop it!"

\* \* \*

THE notorious casanova went to the doctor to complain of impotence.

The medic was astonished. "You of all people," he said. "Why, you have a reputation as long as my arm."

The patient replied, "What's the good of a reputation if it won't stand up?"

\* \* \*

PENSIONER couple wanted the doctor to check the way

they make love. He watched and said it is the way most people did it. They came back next day and asked him to check again. Doc approved.

When they arrived the third day the doctor asked what the heck was going on.

The old man finally explained: "I can't take her to the old men's home. We can't go to her place. We can't afford a motel room on the pension. So we do it here and get a 75% rebate on Medicare."

\* \* \*

PADDY was angry, and his wife was obviously pregnant, when the doctor finally called.

"Look at this," said Paddy indicating his wife's condition. "I've been away at sea for a year and look at this. How do yer explain it?"

"Simple," said the doctor. "That's a vindictive pregnancy. Somebody has had it in for you while you have been away!"

# DO-GOODERS

THE social welfare officer was making an annual inspection of the asylum when he noticed a chap out in the garden who seemed to enjoy a contented composure.

"Oh no, I'm not like that lot in there," said the gardener. "They have all lost their marbles."

Indeed the official couldn't help notice the garden neatly divided into rows of vegetables and flowers and in further conversation learned that the gardener had not only built his own shed but the aerial on the roof was part of his short-wave radio system he had also built. "I write books on that computer, and I paint in oils in my spare time," he told the inspector.

The official was amazed. "You shouldn't be here in this institution," he said, "it's a crime."

"That's what I've been telling them for years," said

the gardener. "My papers were lost in a complicated change of solicitors and I have been unable to get a proper legal clearance," he said.

"Well I am going to do something about this first thing tomorrow morning," said the official turning to leave.

He had taken three steps when the gardener stooped, picked up a red brick, threw it and hit the official square on the back of his head knocking him to the ground.

"You won't forget, will you?" he asked.

## DOGS

THE dog entered the bar, sat up on a stool and ordered a gin and tonic. The barman served him, the dog swallowed the drink, left some money on the bar and left.

"That's extraordinary," said a drinker who had watched the whole thing.

"Yes," said the barman. "He usually has a brandy."

*      *      *

"LOST Dog," said the newspaper notice, "Has three legs, blind in left eye, large scar on throat, right ear missing, tail broken in two places, no teeth, recently castrated, answers to Lucky."

*      *      *

FRED said his dog Deefer could read.

He said he proved it the other day when the dog walked up to a "Wet Paint" sign, inspected it carefully, then followed the instructions.

*      *      *

MY dog's so obedient
   He does as he's bid
   The park bench said "Wet Paint"
   And that's what he did!

*      *      *

FRED put some Spot remover on his dog. Now he's gone.

"IS that an obedient dog, Fred?"

"Too right. I only have to say 'attack', and he has one."

* * *

SID the Spiv said his greyhound could run like greased lightning. "He is so fast on the track that on every third lap he has to jump over himself."

* * *

ONE drover was surprised to see his mate playing poker with his sheepdog. "I know kelpies are intelligent," he said, "but that one's a ripper."

"Ar, he's not that good," drawled his mate, throwing down another card. "Every time he gets a good hand he wags his tail!"

* * *

LEANING on the bar the drover said: "I am a man of simple tastes. I'm happy with a bottle of whisky, a tin of biscuits and a dog."

"Why the dog?" asked a listener.

"Hell, somebody has got to eat the biscuits!"

* * *

WHEN the publican spotted the little dog being brought into the pub he loudly declared it was not allowed.

"But you don't understand," said the drinker, "I'm blind and that's my guide dog."

"What?" roared the publican. "That's a Chihuahua."

"Well I'll be blowed," said the drinker, "they told me it was a Labrador."

* * *

MERV took his mongrel dog to a flea circus and the clever mutt stole the show.

* * *

WHEN drover Bill retired he set about fulfilling his dream of riding with the gentry at the hunt club. He was told that his scruffy horse barely met the equestrian standards, and not to come back until he had his own hound.

Not to be deterred, Bill fronted up for the Saturday

hunt with his trusty mount and his faithful greyhound. He was grudgingly accepted, but he failed to tell the officials that his greyhound bitch was on heat. Ten minutes after the chase started the Master of Foxhounds turned to his companion and said: "Which way are they headed?"

"West," was the reply.

"And where's the fox?"

"At the moment he's running seventh but gaining ground rapidly!"

* * *

"DID you say your dog's bark was worse than his bite?"

"Yes."

"Well for goodness sake don't let him bark. He's just bitten me."

* * *

THE salesman was bailed up by a ferocious dog. Finally its mistress came out and said: "It's okay. You know the old saying, a barking dog never bites."

The worried salesman replied: "I know it, you know it, but does that bloomin' dog know it?"

* * *

WHEN Mrs Moloney met Mrs Murphy at the market she noticed that her friend had a puppy under her arm.

"That's a nice pup," said Mrs Moloney.

"Yes, I got it for Murphy," said her friend.

"Lucky you. I wish I could swap Moloney for one!"

* * *

A MAN was sitting on the bank of the river having his lunch when a lady of 'the blue rinse set' came along the path with her pet poodle.

The yapping dog showed a lot of interest in the man's sandwich.

"Shall I throw him a bit?"

She nodded her approval.

So the man picked up the dog and threw it in the river.

IT was during the Great Depression and the drover had hit on hard times. Not to put too fine a point on it, he was starving. He looked at his faithful kelpie, Rufus, and with a tear in his eye said, "Sorry old-timer, it's you or me." And with that painful decision, Rufus ended up in the camp pot.

It was the first meal the drover had had for three weeks. And as he leant back against a stringybark, licking his lips after the satisfying meal he looked at the bones piled up on his plate.

"Pity Rufus is not here," he mused. "He would have loved those scraps!"

\* \* \*

"SORRY, Sir, dogs are not allowed in this restaurant," said the waiter.

"But this is a talking dog," said its owner.

"If that dog can talk I will give you both a free meal," said the sceptical waiter.

"Right then Rover," said the owner to his pooch, "what's on the top of this building?"

Rover growled: "R-r-r-roof!"

"Now I'll ask one," said the waiter."Who is the greatest footballer in the league?"

"R-r-r-roof," repeated Rover.

The waiter kicked them both out on the footpath, and as they walked away Rover said: "Who should I have said?"

\* \* \*

WORD had got around, and at the next pub the barman said, "Is it true that your dog can talk?"

"No," said the old man, "and if he tells you he can, he's a bloomin' liar."

\* \* \*

THE old-timer wandered into the pub with his dog and a tame goanna which he placed on top of the piano. The dog climbed up on the seat and began to play the piano while the goanna sang a number of popular songs.

The drinkers were amazed and the publican rewarded the old-timer with a beer and said, "That's a great act. You are wasting your time travelling around the Outback pubs."

"They are not as good as you think," confessed the old-timer. "The goanna is tone deaf and can't sing a note. The dog is a ventriloquist."

\* \* \*

"I THINK your dog likes me Gladys. He hasn't taken his eyes off me all night."

"That's because you are eating off his plate!"

\* \* \*

WE have a fine watch dog. So far he has watched somebody steal our car, watched the garage burn down and watched a bloke pinch the lawn mower.

\* \* \*

THE Buddhist knocked on the vicar's door with the sad news: "My carma has just run over your dogma."

\* \* \*

"I DON'T want you to bring your dog into the house. It's full of fleas," she said.

"Fido, stay out of the house. It's full of fleas."

\* \* \*

I HAD a dog called Carpenter. He used to do little jobs around the house.

I had a dog called Mechanic. Give him a kick in the nuts and he would make a bolt for the door.

But I rue the day I called my third dog Sex. It got me into a lot of trouble. When I went to the town hall to register him I said to the clerk, "I would like a licence for Sex."

He said, "I wouldn't mind one myself."

When I got married I asked the vicar if we could have Sex at the wedding. He said okay as long as it didn't interrupt the ceremony.

When I booked into the hotel for our honeymoon I asked the receptionist if he had a room for Sex. "They all are," he said.

My wife and I were always fighting over Sex. Finally it caused our divorce. I told the judge I had Sex before marriage. "Didn't we all," he said. One night he slipped his lead and ran off. I was in the park when a cop asked me what I was doing. "I am looking for Sex," I said. My case comes up next Monday.

\* \* \*

"I HAD to shoot my dog yesterday."

"Was he mad?"

"Well, he wasn't too pleased about it."

\* \* \*

IT was winter and the regulars in the country pub were gathered around the fireplace when Pete the Punter entered the bar with a mongrel dog called Ralph.

He loudly announced to one and all that this dog understood every command he could give it. "Never gets it wrong," he said.

There were drovers who owned top dogs around the bar and they looked askance at the mangy dog which was supposed to be so obedient.

Pete said he wasn't talking about simple commands like "sit," "stay," and "all that rubbish."

"I'm talking about a five-word sentence, and instant obedience," said Pete.

This was too much for the sceptics and they soon collected $100 to prove him wrong. Pete matched it, put the money on the bar, picked up the dog, threw it on the blazing fire and roared: "Ralph, get off that fire!"

\* \* \*

A COUPLE of dogs met on the street. "What's your name?" said one.

"I'm not sure. I think it's Down Boy."

"HOW much did that terrier set you back, Fred?"

"Six hundred dollars ... he's half bull and half foxie."

"Which half is bull?"

"The part about the six hundred dollars."

* * *

THE grocer was alarmed to learn that Mrs Jones' weekly order of a dozen cans of pet food was being fed to her husband. "Oh he doesn't know the difference," she said. "He even likes it."

"But it could kill him," protested the grocer.

Mrs Jones took no heed, but a month later she entered the shop wearing a black armband.

"I told you so," said the grocer. "I told you that dog food would kill him."

"Oh no, it wasn't the dog food," she said. "We were going home the other evening when he sat on the tramline to scratch himself and got bowled over!"

* * *

A FLEA had spent the evening in the pub. At closing time he hopped out and landed flat on his face.

"Who the hell moved my dog," he said.

* * *

THE spectators at the local cricket match were surprised to see that the next batsman was a fox terrier. The dog shaped up at the crease and began hitting balls for sixers.

"That's amazing," said one of the spectators.

"Yes, he's good, but he is still a disappointment to his parents. They wanted him to play football."

* * *

THE movie buff settled into his seat and was surprised to see a man in front with his arm around a large dog which seemed to be enjoying the movie. The dog was growling at the villain and giving excited yelps each time the hero escaped.

The movie buff was fascinated. "Excuse me," he said,

tapping the chap on the shoulder. "Your dog is amazing. I just can't get over it."

"Frankly, he has surprised me too," said the owner. "He hated the book."

*     *     *

"DOES your dog bite?" enquired the friendly chap of the bulldog sitting beside Paddy.

"No," said Paddy.

The friendly chap extended a hand to pat the dog and nearly had it bitten off.

"I thought you said your dog didn't bite," the man said in alarm.

"That's not my dog," said Paddy.

*     *     *

AN expensive poodle fell into a river and was having difficulty staying afloat. In fact it was drowning. Isaac Goldstein dived in, brought the dog to shore, gave it mouth to mouth resuscitation and revived it.

""That was wonderful," said the grateful owner. "Are you a vet?"

"Of course I'm a vet," replied Goldstein. "I'm a bloody soaking."

## DRIVERS
See ACCIDENTS, MOTORING, CARS

THE model driver, of course, is the one who has just seen the car in front pulled up by the police.

*     *     *

IF your wife insists on learning to drive, don't stand in her way.

*     *     *

"HAS your wife learned to drive yet, Fred?"

"Only in an advisory capacity."

*     *     *

"HOW's the wife's driving lessons going, Fred?"

"Improving. The roads are starting to turn when she does."

* * *

REMEMBER when the police didn't hide behind trees on the side of busy roads with radar guns, but took their chances out in the traffic like everybody else?

* * *

WHEN she drove the car up to the toll gate the keeper said: "That will be $5 for the car and $2.50 for the passenger."

Martha replied: "The car's yours for a fiver, but I won't take less than three dollars for my old man."

* * *

TWO men struggled into the pub dragging their mate between them. When they reached the bar they let him go and he collapsed in a heap on the floor.

"Two beers please," said one of those still on their feet.

The barman looked down at the crumpled heap on the floor. "What about him?"

"Oh, no more for him. He's driving."

* * *

FOLLOWING the sound advice to take a rest when sleepy, a motorist pulled over, stopped the car on the side of the road, settled down and closed his eyes.

He was just drifting off when a jogger rapped on the window and asked for the time. Bleary-eyed he reached for his watch and announced that it was 6 am.

Sleeping at last he was soon awakened by another jogger rapping on the window asking if he had the time.

"It's six-fifteen," he said grumpily. At this rate he wasn't to get any sleep so he wrote a note and stuck it on the window for all passing joggers to see. It read "I do not have the time."

Again he settled down for his badly needed nap, but only for a few minutes before there was another rap on the window.

"Hey mate," said yet another jogger, "it's seven o'clock!"

# DROVERS

DROVERS are the strong silent type and don't usually waste words. One night at the camp fire beside the river, Frank said: "There's a bloke down near the river bank."

"Getting fish is he?" said his mate.

"No."

"Gettin' rabbits then?"

"No."

"Well what's he gettin?"

"He's gettin' drowned," said Frank.

★ ★ ★

IT was the time of the great drought thoughout Australia and Dan the drover decided to move his mob south. He had them grazing in the Derwent Valley when a Tasmanian farmer asked where he had come from.

"Three thousand kilometres from the back o' Bourke," drawled Dan. "We were on the road for three months."

"Crikey," said the local. "How did you get that mob across Bass Strait?"

"Ah, we didn't come that way," Dan explained.

# DRINKERS

DRINKERS' Motto: Conserve water, always dilute it.

★ ★ ★

HE drinks to forget, but he has forgotten why.

★ ★ ★

HE believed the best way to pull himself out of trouble was with a corkscrew.

★ ★ ★

SHE said one glass was enough
    Or two at the most
    "Three and you're under the table
    Four and you're under the host."

## DRUNKS
See ALCOHOLICS

ABSTINENCE is a good thing, but it should always be practised in moderation.

* * *

THE difference between an Australian wedding and an Australian funeral, is one less drunk.

* * *

"AFTER three whiskies my husband turns into a most disgusting beast, but after the fourth I pass out altogether."

* * *

DRUNK, to barman: "Has Paddy been in tonight?"
   "Yes, he popped in about an hour ago."
   Drunk: "Was I with him?"

* * *

"TELL me, why do you swig your drinks so fast?"
   "Because I once had one stolen."

* * *

"THE doctor told me I would have to limit my drinking to one each day. I'm now up to April 10, 2005."

"TERRIBLE beer they serve in this pub."
   "Yes, I'll be glad when I've had enough."

* * *

BRUCE the Boozer has finally given up drink, for the sake of his wife and kidneys.

* * *

"I'VE got no sympathy for a man who spends every night drinking," she said sternly.
   "If I could spend every night drinking I wouldn't need your sympathy," he replied.

* * *

"I JUST got twenty bucks off Merv."
   "Off Merv? I always thought he was tight."
   "He was."

THE barman looked up to see a green rat, a pink elephant and a yellow snake wander into the pub together.

"You're too early fellas. He hasn't had his third pot yet."

\* \* \*

HE suffers from alcoholic constipation. He can't pass a pub!

\* \* \*

HE suffers from alcholic rheumatism.

He gets stiff in most joints.

\* \* \*

A LARGE woman at a social function was startled to find herself seized and embraced by a man who was slightly under the weather. But the man quickly released her and apologised.

"Excuse me. I'm so sorry," he mumbled, "I thought for a moment you were my wife." The woman quickly recovered from her surprise and snarled: "Fancy having a drunken slob like you for a husband, you clumsy, gross disgusting beast."

"Crickey," he slurred, "you not only look like her, you sound like her too!"

\* \* \*

DENIS went to the doctor because his hands kept shaking.

The doctor checked him over and said, "Do you drink much?"

"No," said Denis, "I spill most of it."

\* \* \*

THE town drunk received an inheritance and was able to fulfill his dream and build a houseboat and retire. He named his boat Cirrhosis of the River.

\* \* \*

"I THOUGHT you said you get drunk after one whisky."

"Yes, and I do. Usually it's the fifteenth."

"THEN what will we drink to?"
   "What about three in the morning?"

* * *

HE said the reason he likes whisky is because it makes you see double and feel single. "But I always know when I've had enough. That's when I fall over."

* * *

"THERE is indeed an evil worsht than drink."
   "Whatsh that then?"
   "Thirsht, that's what."

* * *

THE drunk approached the policeman.
   "Offisher, can you tell me where I am?"
   "You are on the corner of Main St and Chester Avenue."
   "Forget the details. What town is it?"

* * *

PASSING a cemetery late at night a drunk saw a sign: "Ring the bell for caretaker."
   He did, and a sleepy voice growled: "What do yer want?"
   "I want ter know why you can't ring the bloomin' bell yerself?"

* * *

"DRINKING makes you look beautiful, darling."
   "But I haven't been drinking."
   "No, but I have."

* * *

WOMAN looking under the table in a hotel saw Fred lying there. "Oh, I'm sorry," she said. "I was looking for a lady's husband."
   "Well I'm one, luv," said Fred. "Crawl under."

* * *

IF your friend has had too much to drink, never fill him with coffee or you will have a wide-awake drunk on your hands.

PAT and Mick staggered out of the pub together but soon lost each other. Pat approached a policeman.

"Offisher," he said, "have you seen a fella wandering about without me?"

*   *   *

BRUCE went to the doctor for a check-up.

"It's quite obvious to me," said the Doc, "that alcohol is entirely responsible for your poor physical shape."

"Well I'm glad to hear that," said Bruce. "The wife keeps insisting it's my fault."

*   *   *

"WHY do you keep coming home three parts sloshed?" demanded his wife.

"Because I keep running out of money!"

*   *   *

FRED had been celebrating for most of the night before he staggered to the bar and loudly proclaimed: "Drinks for everybody, and have one yourself, barman."

There was a rush to the bar and after everybody was served the barman said to Fred, "That will be $57.80."

"But I haven't any money," said Fred quietly.

With that the barman grabbed him by the shirtfront, punched him several times and threw him out on the street.

A few minutes later Fred returned through the swinging doors, staggered up to the bar and loudly proclaimed: "Drinks for everybody, except you, barman, you get bloomin' nasty when you drink!"

*   *   *

THEY were leaning on the bar in a deep philosophical discussion. "Do you know that ten per cent of all road accidents are caused by drinking drivers?"

"Which means," said his mate, "that the other 90 per cent are caused by teetotallers."

*   *   *

AN old Scot on his death bed called his best friend, Jock,

to his side. "I bin saving a bottle of whisky, and when I'm gone I want you to sprinkle it on my grave. Will you do that, Jock?"

"Och Aye, but would ye mind if I pass it through my kidneys first?"

\* \* \*

THE pub had just closed and Paddy was taking a short cut through the cemetery when he fell into a newly-dug hole which the grave-diggers had left uncovered. Paddy made a valiant attempt to get out but couldn't make it. He gave up, pulled a bottle from his hip pocket and decided to settle in the corner until morning.

Half an hour later another drunk fell into the hole.

"You'll never get out, lad," said Paddy.

But he did, in one mighty leap.

\* \* \*

WHISKY kills more people than bullets.

That's because bullets don't drink.

\* \* \*

FRED was having trouble with a drinking problem and swore that he would correct it with willpower. He had decided to walk straight past the pub without going in.

As he approached it he kept repeating to himself, "You can do it. You can do it."

The pressure was tough, but Fred persevered, right past he went.

Fifty metres past and he congratulated himself, "I knew you could do it. You were great. Let's go back and I'll buy you a drink."

\* \* \*

PADDY entered the pub at lunchtime. "Was I in here last night?" he asked the barman.

"Yes," was the reply.

"Was I drunk?"

"Yes, very drunk."

"And did I spend much money," pressed Paddy.

"Yes, about twenty dollars," said the barman.

"Thank goodness. I thought I lost it!"

* * *

IRISH publican: "I'm sorry gents, but the bar won't be open for another hour. But would you loike a drink while you are waiting?"

* * *

TWO drunks were about to board the train when they saw the sign: "Dogs must be carried."

"Hold it," said one. "Where are we gonna get a dog at this time of night?"

* * *

WIFE: "Why do you drink liquor?"

Husband: "What do you suggest I do with it?"

* * *

THE sergeant answered the phone in the police station. The voice at the other end was slow and slurred.

"I wanna report a theft, offisher. I've been robbed. Shum dirty crook has shtolen things from my car."

"What kind of things?" asked the sergeant.

"My shteering wheel, brakes, dashboard, accellerator... the bloody lot's gone."

The sergeant humored him for a moment, and said he would investigate. "Bloody drunks," he said when he hung up.

Five minutes later the phone rang again.

"Cancel that report. It's all right. Yers can stop lookin," said the same voice. "My mishtake. I got inter the back seat!"

* * *

THE cops had been instructed to clean up the neighbourhood so it was dead easy when one drunk staggered towards a constable and said: "Excuse me offisher, what time is it?"

The cop replied, "One o'clock," and hit him once over the head with his baton.

"Crikey," said the drunk, "I'm glad I didn't ask you an hour ago."

*     *     *

THE drinker was sobbing into his beer. "What's up, mate?" asked the barman.

"I can't remember the name of the girl I am trying to forget."

*     *     *

SAID the drunk as he staggered into the kitchen. "Am I home darling?"

# DUMB

SHE thought an aperitif was a set of dentures.

HE thought alter ego was a conceited priest.

SHE thought intercourse was a ticket to the races.

HE thought VAT 69 was the Pope's phone number.

SHE thought a bigamist was a thick Italian fog.

HE thought fidelity was unadulterated boredom.

SHE thought Good Friday did Robinson Crusoe's housework.

HE thought Robinson Crusoe was a world famous tenor.

SHE thought a Norwegian fjord was a Scandinavian car.

HE thought manual labour was a Spanish waiter.

SHE thought Chou En-lai was Chinese for breakfast in bed.

HE thought a brassiere was something you warm your hands on.

SHE thought Au Pair was a living bra.

HE thought polyunsaturated was a parrot in a raincoat.

SHE thought awe-struck was being hit by a paddle.

HE thought a bulletin was a can of pressed beef.

SHE thought climate was the only thing you could do with a ladder.

HE thought hyacinth was a greeting for anybody called Cynthia.

SHE thought an optimist was a hope addict.

HE thought odious was not very good poetry.

SHE thought an operetta was a girl who works at the telephone exchange.

HE thought Yoko Ono was Japanese for one egg please.

SHE thought a transistor was a nun in men's clothes.

HE thought grammar was the woman who married grandpa.

SHE thought Joan of Arc was Noah's wife.

HE thought a lieutenant commander was the lieutenant's wife.

SHE thought pregnant was the past tense of virgin.

HE thought a polygon was a dead parrot.

SHE thought the tooth fairy was a gay dentist.

HE thought the landed gentry were tricked into marriage.

SHE thought blue serge was a sad Russian.

HE thought a cross section of the public were taxpayers.

SHE thought a crowbar was where the girls hung out for a drink.

HE thought Badminton was why the lamb tasted awful.

SHE thought good housekeeping was the name of a magazine.

SHE thought a penal colony was an all-male nudist camp.

HE thought Karl Marx was the brother of Chico and Harpo.

SHE thought Columbine is the wife of the guy who discovered America.

HE thought that where there is life there's opium.

SHE thought Kosher is Jewish bacon.

HE thought myxomatosis was wiping out Rabbis.

SHE thought a meadow lark was a party in a paddock.

HE thought the Union Jack was something you got at the Trades Hall.

SHE thought hypocrisy was a Greek philosopher.

HE thought vice-versa was a rude poem.

SHE thought a teetotaller was the scorekeeper at golf.

\* \* \*

DUMB Doris said she was thin, and her friend Wendy was thin, but there was a girl in the office who was as thin as the two of them, put together.

\* \* \*

SOME blokes are three bricks short of a load, not the full two-bob, or two sandwiches short of a picnic.

\* \* \*

THE small outback community was getting a lecture on first aid and how to stop bleeding.

"Of course you all know what a corpuscle is," said the instructor.

"Most of us do," said the chairman, "but you'd better explain it for the sake of those who have never been in one."

# E

## ECONOMY

IT is a recession when your friend loses his job. It is a depression when you lose yours. And it is a recovery when Paul Keating loses his. (Or substitute the politician of your choice).

*       *       *

THERE are two types of people. Those with swimming pools and those who can't keep their heads above water.

*       *       *

THE owner of a small business was telling his bank manager that the recession was tough: "Things are so bad that even people who don't pay have stopped buying."

## EDUCATION
### See SCHOOLS, TEACHERS

EDUCATION is what you get from reading the fine print. Experience is what you get from not reading it.

*       *       *

"EDUCATION has failed the younger generation," said the businessman. "Our survey shows that as many as 40 per cent can't read, another 40 per cent can't write and the other 30 per cent can't add up."

THE teacher pointed to little Solly Cohen and said, "Solly, what's three per cent?"

"You're right, teacher," said Solly shrugging his shoulders, "what is three per cent!"

*       *       *

LITTLE Nigel's mother had been away for a week and asked her son about events during her absence.

"There was a big thunderstorm on Wednesday and I was so scared me and Daddy snuggled up in the same bed."

"Nigel," said the boy's pretty nurse, "you mean Daddy and I."

"No," said the kid. "That was last night. I'm talking about Wednesday."

*       *       *

TWO Australians in London down on their luck saw an advertisement for two footmen. "References essential," it said. "That's okay," said Bruce, "I'll write yours and you can write one for me." Thus they arrived on the estate and offered the duchess two glowing references. "First things first," she said. "Formal wear here means wearing kilts, so drop your trousers while I check your knees."

The lads were a little surprised but they did so. The duchess gave the knees the nod of approval and said, "Okay, now let me see those testimonials."

After they were thrown off the property Bruce said: "With a little more education we would have got that job."

## EGO

THE human body is an interesting phenomenon. A pat on the back can result in a swollen head.

*       *       *

HIS ego was bigger than the Outback.

MOST actors are all ham and ego.

       *     *     *

HE was the kind of chap who had plenty to be modest about.

       *     *     *

HE makes so many enemies, he really needs an enemy agent.

       *     *     *

THERE were so many famous egos at the theatrical awards, I was the only person in the room I'd never heard of.

## ELEPHANTS

WHY have Elephants got Big Ears?
  Because Noddy won't pay the ransom.

       *     *     *

ONE reason elephants drink so much water is that nobody ever offers them anything else.

       *     *     *

AN elephant was drinking from the Zambesi when he noticed a turtle asleep on a log. He ambled over and kicked it clear across the river.
  "What did you do that for?" asked a passing giraffe.
  "Because I recognised it as the same turtle which took a nip out of my trunk 53 years ago."
  "What a memory," exclaimed the giraffe.
  "Yes," said the elephant, "turtle recall."

       *     *     *

"WHO'S the king of the jungle?" called the lion swaggering down the bush trail.
  "Oh, you are," replied the tiger with its tail between its legs.
  "Who's the king of the jungle?" said the lion to the leopard.
  "Oh you are," said the leopard cowering in the grass.

"Who's the king of the jungle?" said the lion to a huge elephant which blocked the jungle path.

Without answering the elephant gathered the lion in his trunk, hurled him in the air, caught him and smashed him against a tree.

"Look," said the lion. "Don't get mad just because you don't know the answer!"

* * *

AN elephant escaped from a circus and no trace had been found until a lady who had never seen an elephant before rang the police. She was panic-stricken.

"There is a weird monster in my back yard," she said. "It is pulling up the cabbages with its tail. But what is worse... I cannot describe what it is doing with them!"

## ENGAGEMENTS
See WEDDINGS, NEWLY-WEDS, MARRIAGE and MARRIEDS

THE suitor had been shown into the lounge room to wait for his date while she got ready, when her little brother came in.

"Is Jean your oldest sister?" he said to make small talk.

"Yep," said the kid.

"And who comes after her?"

"You and two other blokes."

* * *

THE lad has just asked Paddy O'Leary for his daughter's hand in marriage. "Can you support our Teresa in the manner to which she is accustomed?"

"Indeed, sir I can."

"Have you ever seen her eat?" said Paddy.

"Indeed sir, I have."

"But have you ever seen her eat when there's nobody looking?"

I HAVE come to ask for your daughter's hand."

"Okay, take the one that's always in my pocket."

* * *

"SIR, I would like to marry your daughter."

"Okay, leave your name and address and if nothing better turns up we will contact you."

* * *

"SIR, I wish to marry your daughter."

"Do you drink alcohol young man?"

"Thanks all the same, but let's settle this business first."

* * *

"SIR, I wish to marry your daughter."

"Can you support a family?" enquired the prospective father-in-law.

"Yes sir, I can."

"There are eight of us."

* * *

"SIR, I want your daughter for my wife."

"Well I'm not swapping until I've seen your wife."

* * *

THE young man was so nervous when he approached his highly formal prospective father-in-law that he blurted out the words: "I am asking for your daughter's hole in handy matrimony!"

* * *

"IF we did become engaged," she said, "would you give me a ring?"

"Certainly, what's your number?"

* * *

WHEN he proposed she got so excited she insisted on showing the ring to her workmates in the office. She soon returned and threw it at him. Three of her girl-friends had recognised it.

* * *

"YOU have broken it off with Milicent?"

"Yes. She was just a passing fiancée."

"I HAVE been asked to get married hundreds of times," she pouted.

"By whom?"

"My mum and dad," she said.

* * *

"I WONDER if my fiancée loves me?"

"Of course she does. Why should she make you an exception?"

* * *

"NO," she said. "I don't love you, so I won't marry you. But I will be a sister to you."

"That's okay," he said. "How much do you think our father will leave us?"

* * *

"DO you believe in free love, Jack?" she asked.

"Well, I've never sent you an invoice, have I?"

* * *

"FRED," she said, "when we are married I want to share all your worries and troubles and help lighten your burden."

"Forget it, Madge, I've got no worries or troubles."

"But we're not married yet, darling."

## ESTATE AGENTS

A YOUNG Swedish woman was thinking of buying the house. The estate agent was showing her the property. They inspected the lower floor then he said "Now we'll go upstairs and I will show you the bedroom and den."

She looked at him sideways: "And den what?"

* * *

AN auctioneer has no friends. Only nodding acquaintances.

* * *

AFTER I got married I said to my mother-in-law, "My house is your house."

"Three days later she sold it."

SIGN outside a big home: COSTA PLENTI.

*  *  *

HE said Swindle & Wrun had the best salesmen in the business. "They sold me a block of land and when I went to see it I discovered it was five metres under water."

"Well, didn't you go back and complain?"

"Yes, that's the trouble. They then sold me a boat."

*  *  *

HE breasted the bar and announced: "The drinks are on me. I've just sold the house for $100,000."

And as they all placed their orders he added: "Mind you, the council might go bananas when they find out."

*  *  *

TWO country land agents were leaning on the pub's verandah rail looking at the dust storm going by.

"All that country changing hands, and we're not getting a cent commission," grumbled one.

*  *  *

A WOMAN who had just taken a lease on a unit near the railway line rang the estate agent to complain that passing trains rocked her bed so much she was in fear of falling out of it.

The agent came around. "But it's so quiet," he said, "I can't believe that passing trains rock the bed."

"Shakes the living daylights out of it," she persisted, looking at her watch.

She heard a distant train whistle. "Here's the five thirty-five. Lie down on the bed yourself," and she climbed on to the other side.

That's when her husband came in.

"What do you think you are doing?" he roared, glaring at the estate agent.

"Would you believe waiting for a train?" he ventured.

## FAIRYTALES

TWO young women were walking along a country lane when a large green frog jumped out before them and said: "Please dear maidens. One of you kiss me and I will turn into a handsome prince."

One girl quickly scooped up the frog and put it in her handbag.

"Aren't you going to restore him to a prince?" asked her friend.

"No. Princes are a dime a dozen. But a talking frog, now there is potential for making a dollar."

## FAMILIES

FRED can trace his family tree right back to the time when it was his ancestor's address.

\* \* \*

I AM not saying my brothers were fast eaters, but ours was the only house with racing colours on our knives and forks.

\* \* \*

CECIL got in after midnight and his mother wanted to know where he had been.

"I've been out with a boy I know."

"You mean a girl, don't you?" she said.

"Boy or girl, what's the difference?" he said.

"If you don't know the difference, then I guess it's alright," said his relieved mother.

* * *

THE teenage girl got home very late and explained to her mother: "You know how it is, Mum ... "

"Yes, I certainly do. And what is his name?"

* * *

BERT got interested in his ancestors. He looked up his family tree and found most of them still swinging in the branches.

* * *

THE family had gathered around because old Grandpa was dying.

"Is there anything I can do for you?" said his wife.

The old man raised himself on one elbow and peered at a jug of beer on the table.

"I wouldn't mind a swig of that," he gasped.

"Well you can't," snapped his wife. "That's for the wake."

* * *

"MUM, how do lions make love?"

"Don't know, son. All your father's friends are Rotarians."

* * *

"MUM, Dad's going out again.

"Well pour some more petrol on him."

* * *

JUST when your children get old enough, so that you can stand them, they can't stand you.

* * *

CHILDREN should be seen and not had.

* * *

EVERY family should have at least three children. Then if one is a genius the other two can support him.

THEY say children brighten the home. That's because they never turn off the bloody lights.

* * *

SHE took after the mother, who took after the father, who took after the maid.

* * *

ANY one of your friends can become an enemy, given time. But a relative is one from the start.

* * *

SUCCESS is relative. The more success the more relatives.

# FARMS

AT the National Agricultural Conference it was easy to pick the dairy milking champion. He was the bloke who shook hands with everybody, one finger at a time.

* * *

BATTLING Bill had brought his family down from the farm to attend the Royal Show. A prize winning bull was the major exhibit, with an entrance fee of one dollar. Bill asked the attendant if he could get a concession for his family; himself, his wife and 13 kids.

"Hang on a minute," said the attendant, "I'll bring the bloomin' bull out and give him a gawk at you."

* * *

IT was the night of the school concert and all the kids had their poems, songs and recitations at the ready; except little Charlie who had just come down from the country and had started school that day.

"C'mon Charlie," said the teacher. "Surely you can do something for the concert."

It took much cajolling, but finally Charlie agreed to do some farmyard impressions.

The instant applause gave Charlie a boost of confidence and he strode to centre stage. "Farmyard noises," he announced.

Then cupping his hands to his face like a megaphone he yelled at the top of his voice: "Get off that blasted tractor. Shut that blasted gate. Get that blankety bull out of that yard ...!"

*　　*　　*

YOUNG Johnny was late for school again. "And what kept you this time, Johnny?" asked the young mistress in despair for yet another yarn.

"It's the breeding season, Miss, and I had to put the bull to the cows," he said.

"Couldn't your father do that?" she said.

"No," said Johnny, "it's gotta be a bull!"

*　　*　　*

FARMER Murphy met Farmer O'Leary in town. "What did you give to your ailing bull when it had colic?" asked Murphy.

"A good dose of phenyl," said Murphy.

A week later they met in the pub. "What did you say you gave your sick bull?" said O'Leary.

"Phenyl," said Murphy.

"Well I gave phenyl to my bull and it died," said O'Leary.

"So did mine," said Murphy.

*　　*　　*

THE farmer's sons were sent home from the bush school with a note from the teacher complaining that they swore too much. Their father gave them a lecture, a thump in the ear and sent them to bed without dinner.

Next morning when they sat at the table they were asked what they wanted for breakfast.

"I'll have some of those bloody cornflakes," said one, and immediately received a thrashing from his father.

"And what would you like," said the angry father to his second son.

"I don't know. But it won't be those bloody cornflakes, that's for sure."

TWO city slickers attended the Royal Agricultural Show and were impressed with the fine examples of life on the farm. They got absorbed in watching Paddy grooming a large fearsome bull, until he sat quietly on a stool beside it.

"Gee it must be late, what's the time?" said one of the city slickers. Paddy put two hands under the testicles of the bull and lifted them gently. "It's ten past six," he said.

The men were about to leave when the significance of Paddy's uncanny country skill sunk through.

"Did you see that?" said one.

"Amazing," said the other.

They couldn't believe it, and talked it over for awhile before gingerly approaching Paddy again.

"Er, can you tell us the time again, please?"

Paddy, still seated on his stool, gently lifted the bull's balls once more. "It's a quarter-past six," he said.

The city slickers could contain themselves no longer.

"How do you do that?" they asked.

Paddy told them to climb through the rail and bend down near him. "Look, when I lift the bull's balls you can see the town hall clock from here!"

★　　★　　★

FARMER and his son were on a train headed for their first visit to the city when a priest hobbled into their compartment on crutches, with his foot in plaster.

"Slipped in the bathtub," he explained.

When the priest got out at the next station the son said: "What's a bathtub, Dad?"

"I dunno son, I'm not a Catholic."

★　　★　　★

DAVE had come down from the farm for his first visit to the city and was enjoying a beer in a pub when a character sidled up to him and whispered: "How would you like to buy some pornographic material?"

"No use to me, mate," replied Dave. "We haven't got a pornograph."

* * *

A CENSUS official was assisting a farmer's wife to fill in her forms.

"How many children have you got?" he asked.

"Six," she replied. "Three sets of twins."

"How very extraordinary," said the census man. "Twins every time."

"Oh no," said the farmer's wife. "Not every time. Hundreds of times, nothing!"

* * *

THE union rep was checking on the farmer who was suspected of underpaying his employees and was being introduced to the farmhands.

"This is Harry," said the farmer, "he milks the cows, and looks after the dairy and gets $200 a week with room and board."

"And this is Mary. She cooks and does the housework and gets $130 a week with room and board."

"Fair enough so far," said the union rep. "Is there anyone else?"

"Yes," said the farmer. "There's the half-wit. He works fifty hours a week and gets around $15 a week with room and board."

"Ah," said the rep. "I'd like to speak to him."

"You're talking to him right now," said the farmer.

# FARTS

NO less a literary giant than Chaucer gave recognition to the humble fart in his 13th century writing of "The Miller's Tale." Then Jonathan Swift, author of "Gulliver's Travels," wrote in 1731 that the odd fart was notorious for its stifling effect on romance.

Farts are an undeniable part of life. They are often

tried to be denied with euphemisms like flatulence or breaking wind but it never disguises the reality that a fart is a fart.

Rich men, poor men, beggars and thieves, even politicians and bishops pay homage to the old adage: Better to have an empty house than a grumbling tenant.

It can be said that the sign of a consolidated marriage is when either partner can fart without the need to say "excuse me."

\* \* \*

IT's a sign of wedded security
A marriage that's reached its maturity
When neither accuses
Nor offers excuses
For farts that fly with impunity.

\* \* \*

THE Queen was showing the Archbishop of Canterbury around the Royal Stables when one of the stallions close by broke wind in such a loud and gusty manner it couldn't be ignored.

"Oh dear," said the Queen blushing, "how embarassing. I'm frightfully sorry about that."

"It's quite understandable," said the archbishop, and after a moment added, "as a matter of fact, I thought it was the horse."

\* \* \*

THE chubby matron was consulting her doctor and explaining her problem in a timid manner. "What can you do for me, doctor, I have a lot of wind."

The doctor gave her a kite.

\* \* \*

A BUSINESSWOMAN explained to her doctor that she had an unusual complaint. She was always breaking wind, at board meetings, during interviews, in lifts, on the tram. It was impossible to control.

"But at least I am fortunate in two respects," she told

the doctor, "they neither smell nor make a noise. In fact you will be surprised to know it's happened twice since I've been talking to you Doctor."

The doctor reached for his notebook, scribbled a prescription and handed it to her.

She read it. "What? Nasal drops?" she queried.

"Yes," said the Doc. "We'll fix your nose first then we'll have a go at your hearing."

*     *     *

SECOND businesswoman tells the doctor she is suffering from the same problem. The Doc listens to a few extraordinary blow-offs that register 6.2 on the Richter scale then asks her to lower her bloomers and hop up on the couch.

She is alarmed when he reaches for a long pole with a hook on the end of it.

"Goodness, what are you going to do with that," she said.

"First it's necessary to open some of these skylights," he replied.

*     *     *

THE feuding neighbours had decided to patch up their differences over a few drinks. All was going well until one of the blokes broke wind.

"How dare you fart in front of my wife," roared the husband.

"How was I to know it was her turn," replied the other.

*     *     *

LADY Fotheringham suffered from flatulence a great deal and was prone to make certain noises when she got excited while entertaining friends at the manor. She was fortunate in having in her employ a very loyal and discreet butler called James.

Upon hearing these subdued explosions James would instantly say "Excuse me," and promptly leave the room taking the blame with him and saving her ladyship great embarrassment.

But one day James fell ill and was replaced by a butler from the employment service to help out on an important tea party.

In the middle of a conversation with the vicar Lady Fotheringham suffered one of her attacks accompanied by the usual sound effects.

She turned to the new butler and said: "James, stop that!"

"Certainly madam," said the new James, "which way did it go?"

\*       \*       \*

THERE was a young girl from Jakarta
   Who was widely renowned as a farta
   Her deafening reports
   At athletics and sports
   Made her much in demand as a starta.

\*       \*       \*

OVER the years Fred had never attempted to control his bad habit of breaking wind. It sounded like a gale ripping a spinnaker to shreds and often registered 7.3 on the Richter scale. Constant pleas from his wife, Myrtle, to control these thunder claps failed to have effect until one day she threatened to leave him.

"Okay, I'll do my best," he said.

"Not good enough," said Myrtle. "Prove it by refraining from that terrible practice for one whole month," she insisted.

Fred promised. And despite times when he gripped the armchair until his knuckles went white, crossed his legs and grimaced in pain, he never let one go for weeks.

One night he arrived home from the office to find the dining table set with flowers and candles. "What's all this?" he asked.

"It's a month tonight and you've been so good I have cooked one of your favourite dishes as a reward." She then placed a blindfold over his eyes. "I want it to be a surprise," she said.

Fred sat there in silence, and while listening to Myrtle rattling pots in the kitchen he felt a king-sized fart gathering force. He crossed his legs, clenched his fists and the sweat gathered on his brow.

"What the hell," he thought, "the month is up, I've gone the distance and I'm sitting here like a fool with a blindfold on while I can still hear her out in the kitchen. It would be safe to let one rip."

With that he leant to one side, lifted one rump off the chair and with a grin of great relief let it rumble free.

It was just in time for he heard Myrtle's footsteps coming and felt her fumble with the blindfold before ripping it off.

That was the signal for a chorus of "Happy Birthday" from Fred's family all seated around him at the birthday table.


# FASHION

FASHION is something that goes in one era and out the other.

*     *     *

MY ol' Dad was dedicated to fashion. When we were kids he would say: "If you must polish your boots while you are still wearing them, take your socks off. Then if you get some black nugget on your ankles you simply put your socks back on and nobody knows."

*     *     *

AND if it is a formal occasion, do your best to get two matching thongs.

*     *     *

THE tall blonde told the attendant in the fashion store that she wanted a pair of low heels.

"To wear with what, madam?"
"A short, plump, rich stock-broker," she replied.

*    *    *

"HOW do you like the fit, madam?"
"Fit? It's a convulsion."

*    *    *

IT'S not the cost of a strapless gown, it's the upkeep.

*    *    *

THE bride wore a beautiful gownless evening strap.

*    *    *

HER dress looked pretty good considering the shape it was on.

*    *    *

WHEN he criticised the scantiness of her swim suit, she laughed it off.
OR... When he complained that her strapless dress was too daring, she laughed it off.

*    *    *

THE outfit made her look like a million dollars; all wrinkled and green.

*    *    *

"I WANT the dress in the window."
"Well it's in the window."

*    *    *

A TIGHT skirt has never yet stopped a girl's circulation.

*    *    *

"I'D like to see something cheap in a straw hat."
"Here, try this. And the mirror is over there."

*    *    *

"I'D like to buy that hat in the window."
"It's not necessary. We can sell it here over the counter."

*    *    *

SHE said she was a physical education instructor and she wanted a pair of bloomers to wear around her gymnasium.
"How big is your gymnasium," enquired the attendant.

141

SHOPPER: "I'd like to see something in silk stockings."
   Attendant: "You men are all alike."

*     *     *

WHEN he heard that Parisian women would not be wearing dresses much longer this season he decided to go there for his holidays.

*     *     *

HE chooses his own suits, but his wife picks his pockets.

*     *     *

THE latest thing in men's clothing is women.

*     *     *

FATHER: "Why are you wearing my raincoat?"
   Son: "Well you don't want your best suit to get wet, do you?"

*     *     *

SHE was ecstatic over the bargain. "Look at this dress," she said, "I bought it for a ridiculous figure."
   "Yeah, I know," said her husband, "but how much did you pay for it?"

*     *     *

"HOW many shirts does your husband wear a week?" she asked.
   "You mean how many weeks does he wear his shirts," she replied.

*     *     *

ACCORDING to the latest fashion magazine, women will be wearing their legs longer this summer.

*     *     *

HE asked what Mabel's new evening dress looked like.
   He was told: "In a lot of places it looks like Mabel."

*     *     *

"WHENEVER I am down in the dumps, I treat myself to a new hat."
   "We wondered where you got them."

*     *     *

"NO one knows," complained Miss Cox

142

"The pain that it engenders
"Keeping up my bobby-sox
"With ord'nary suspenders."

* * *

HE was a bit old-fashioned and it upset him to see the outrageous dress of some young people in the street.

"Just look at that one?" he barked at a bystander. "Is it a boy or a girl?"

"It's a girl, and she's my daughter," came the reply.

"Oh, I'm sorry," apologised the grump, "I didn't know you were her mother."

"I'm not," snapped the bystander, "I'm her father!"

* * *

MODERN fashions are crazy. Fish-net stockings and forcing feet into those high heel shoes is ridiculous. I've told my father to stop wearing them.

* * *

SOME dresses worn by women
  Are like fences at the zoo
  They safeguard lovely bodies
  But don't obstruct the view.

## FATHERS-IN-LAW
See MOTHERS-IN-LAW

THE old codger was hogging the fireplace, monopolising the telly and stinking the lounge room with his pipe. Finally, it got too much for the young couple and she whispered to her husband, "Look dear, fair's fair. He's been here ever since we were married. It's time your father went home."

"My father. My father," he gasped. "I thought he was yours!"

* * *

"WHEN I see your father coming up the front path," she said to her husband, "I sometimes wish I had loved and lost."

143

WHEN he arrived home his wife had a smug look. "There was a door-knock collection today," she said. "People were collecting for the Old People's Home. So I gave them your father."

*      *      *

MADGE: "I've just got a bottle of whisky for my father-in-law."
   MARY: "That's a good bargain!"

*      *      *

MADGE: "I stuck up for Pops the other night."
   MARY: "Yeah?"
   MADGE: "They said he wasn't fit to eat with pigs. I said he was."

*      *      *

IT took time, but Madge eventually developed an attachment for her father-in-law. It fitted over his mouth.

*      *      *

HER father-in-law once got a job on a farm. He left it after a few weeks. He got tired of standing out in a wheat field with his arms outstretched scaring the crows away. He not only chased the birds off, they even brought back the grain they stole the previous year.

## FATHERS AND SONS

HE was a young father, wheeling the pram through the gardens while the baby was screaming its head off. "Take it easy Jason," he said calmly, "there's nothing to fuss about."

A middle-aged woman noticed his soothing manner and marvelled at the new breed of young husbands.

When the baby screamed even louder she heard him say: "Cool it, Jason, don't get excited, lad, cool it son."

Touched by his gentle manner the woman leaned into the pram and cooed: "There, there Jason, what's bothering you?"

"Excuse me, lady," said the father, "that's Jeremy, I'm Jason."

* * *

FATHER and son were posing for a picture to mark the son's graduation from university. "Stand closer," said the photographer to the father, "and put your hand on his shoulder."

"Wouldn't it be more appropriate," replied the father, "if he put his hand in my pocket?"

* * *

TWO fathers were at the bar of their club sharing their problems. "My son is at college and is always writing home for money. I don't know what he does with it," lamented one.

"My daughter is at college and never asks for money. I wonder where she is getting it," lamented the other.

* * *

HE came home from the office to find his lay-about son asleep in the garden hammock once more. It was time he had a lesson about life.

He shook him awake and said: "You've been out of school for three years, you haven't tried looking for a job. Isn't it time you smartened yourself and studied for a profession?"

"Why?" said the son sleepily.

"So that you can become a businessman like me."

"Why?" persisted the son.

"So you can make a lot of money."

"Why?"

"So you can have enough in the bank."

"Why?"

"So that you can retire and not go to work."

"But I don't go to work now," said the son.

* * *

"WHAT'S a monologue, Dad?"

"That's a conversation with your mother, son."

"WHEN I was your age," said the father to his teenage son, "I would be up at dawn, run ten miles across frosty ground, dive into the sea, run another mile along the beach and sprint all the way home. I would do all that before breakfast and think nothing of it."

The son yawned and said, "I don't think much of it myself."

* * *

IN many fields of endeavour the cleverness or fame of the father often proves the stumbling block for the son.

"Well thank goodness," said Mum, "our Johnny has nothing to fall over."

* * *

TWO fathers were discussing the trials and tribulations of bringing up teenage sons. "I insist on discipline," said one. "I have always insisted on discipline from the day he started to walk."

Just then the boy under discussion entered the room waving a set of car keys in his hand. "Hi Dad. I'm taking the car. I've pulled a bird and I have just raided one of your bottles of Scotch to make sure I'm on a winner. I won't be back tonight."

The visiting father's jaw dropped. "I thought you said you had disciplined him?"

"Of course I have," said the first. "He didn't have to come and tell me, did he?"

* * *

HIS father was sternly insisting that he continue his education to ensure he gained a profession. "Digging holes is the only job you can get where you start at the top," he said.

* * *

TWO old boys met at the club after years apart. "How's your son making out in life?" asked one.

"Oh he's the top car salesman of a nation-wide franchise. Going so well he topped the sales chart and they gave him a brand new Mercedes," said the proud father. "But he gave it away. Can you imagine that, gave it away."

"That's amazing," said the other old chap. "My son's in real estate and development. Clinched the biggest deal this year and they gave him a penthouse, but he gave it away. Can you imagine that?"

Right then a third old boy came in. "How's your son?" they asked him.

"Bit disappointing really," he said. "He's turned out to be a raving homosexual. But still, he's managing quite well. One of his best friends gave him a Mercedes last week, and another gave him a penthouse."

## FEMINISTS

MARRIAGE: It begins as you sink in his arms, and ends with your arms in the sink.

\*     \*     \*

EQUALITY is a myth; women are superior.

\*     \*     \*

WHAT do you call a man who has lost 90 per cent of his brain?

A widower!

\*     \*     \*

IF a woman does household chores for $200 a week, that's domestic science. If she does it for nothing, that's marriage.

\*     \*     \*

COMMON sense would save a significant number of marriages. If women used it, there wouldn't be any.

\*     \*     \*

THE feminists are hailing a miracle birth.

The baby has a dick AND a brain.

\*     \*     \*

SHE said she wouldn't mind having a baby, but unfortunately you have to marry one to get one.

THERE are three kinds of men; the handsome, the caring, and the majority.

* * *

A WOMAN who strives to be like a man lacks ambition.

* * *

THE only problem with women, is men. And the worst thing about men is that all the nice ones are gay.

* * *

SHE said we all have to live with our disappointments. "But why do I have to live with mine?"

* * *

WHEN the boss put the hard word on the lively new girl she had the answer: "No way, bozzo, you've got the words 'liberated' and 'free' mixed up."

* * *

LOVE is the delusion that one man is different from the rest.

* * *

WHEN a woman makes a fool of a man it's usually an improvement.

* * *

IT is said that the wisest of men can become foolish over women; and the most foolish of women is wise to men.

* * *

THE only difference between men and pigs is that when pigs drink they don't make men of themselves.

* * *

MEN are like pigeons. They should never be looked up to.

* * *

THE only thing wives have in common with their husbands is that they were married on the same day.

* * *

SHE wanted a husband and put an advertisement in the personal column. She got a hundred replies saying: "You can have mine!"

WOMEN are called birds because of all the worms they pick up.

* * *

FRED was a window cleaner and he couldn't believe his eyes when he saw a young woman get out of the bath and start drying off, right in front of him.

She was a feminist, and instead of screaming she stared straight back at him in an effort to shame him.

Their eyes locked in confrontation for an interminable minute. Neither would budge.

Finally Fred roared: "What are ya staring at? Haven't ya ever seen a window cleaner before?"

* * *

TWO unattached office girls decided it would make economic sense if they teamed up to take advantage of the twin-share prices on their next holiday. After they booked in to their first hotel room one turned to the other and rested her hand on her shoulder. "There's something I haven't told you about myself," she said. "I'll be frank..."

"Oh no you won't," interrupted her friend, "I'll be Frank."

* * *

THE young couple had a knee-trembler against a paling fence and got so excited they knocked it down.

The commotion aroused the house-holder who grabbed the young man and collected $100 on the spot for repairs to the fence.

Later the young bloke said: "Listen Mabel. You are a feminist and you are always shouting about equal rights. Here's your chance. You owe me $50 for half cost of the fence."

"No way," she said. "It was you who did all the pushing."

## FINANCE
See ACCOUNTANTS

"I WOULD go through anything for you."

"Good. Let's start with your bank account."

THE ship's purser asked the sailor how he had spent his month's pay on shore leave.

"Some went on drink, some on women. And I guess I squandered the rest," was the reply.

* * *

EVERY day a ragged old man with a tray of shoe laces would take up a position at the entrance to a city skyscrapper, and every morning and executive entering the building would drop a dollar in his tray, without taking any laces.

One day the executive dropped his usual dollar and was about to walk away when the old man tapped him on the shoulder. "Excuse me, sir. I don't like to complain, but laces are now $1.50."

* * *

THRIFT is the most admirable virtue of any ancestor.

* * *

COP to bank manager: "Can you describe the missing teller?"

"Yes, he's six foot tall and $100,000 short."

* * *

A YOUNG Jewish lad was learning arithmetic. "What's two-and-two, Father?"

Dad: "Are we buying or selling?"

* * *

WITH the new world order, the USA will, from now on, be known as the IOUSA.

* * *

ALWAYS borrow money from a pessimist. He doesn't expect to get it back.

* * *

MONEY, money, money.
  If a man is always chasing it, he's mercenary.
  If he doesn't chase it, he lacks ambition.
  If he hoards it, he's stingy.

If he spends it, he's a spendthrift.
If he gets it without working, he's a parasite.
If he scrimps and saves, he is wasting his life.

\* \* \*

TREASURER'S report: "Last year we were poised on the edge of a precipice. This year we have made a great leap forward!"

\* \* \*

I HAVE always tried to pay my bills with a smile. But invariably they want money.

\* \* \*

REMEMBER, the darkest hour is just before the pawn.

\* \* \*

"WHAT is your major worry?"
"Money."
"I didn't know you had any."
"I haven't."

\* \* \*

"HEY Fred, lend us twenty bucks until pay day to buy a round of drinks."
"Okay, but when's pay day."
"How should I know. You're the one who's working!"

\* \* \*

"HEY Fred, remember last time when I was broke and you helped me out with twenty bucks and I said I'd never forget you?"
"Yes."
"Well, I'm broke again!"

\* \* \*

MONEY won't help you make friends. But you'll have a better class of enemy.

\* \* \*

THE wealthy financier took a tumble for a blonde and lost his balance at the bank.

\* \* \*

SHE told her banker: "I haven't got much collateral, but will you take one of those promiscuity notes?"

THE manager told the new clerk to count a package of one thousand single dollar notes. He noticed the clerk laboriously counting and heard him reach, "502, 503, 504, 505." Then the clerk threw the package into the drawer and remarked: "If it's right that far, it's probably right all the way."

* * *

THE Prime Minister was on the dais as the parade of military might passed by. First squadrons of jets flew overhead, then lines of tanks, heavy artillery and columns of infantry armed to the teeth. Finally, a group of men in pin-striped suits, awkwardly marching out of step brought up the rear of the parade.

"Is that your Secret Service Mr Minister?" asked a foreign diplomat.

"Hell no. They are our economists. They can cause more damage than the rest put together!"

* * *

THE Chinese businessman pressed the teller to explain why his interest rate had increased two points from the previous day.

"Fluctuations," said the teller.

"And the same to you, ya bloomin' ocker," said the Chinaman.

* * *

A YOUNG accountant was overjoyed to learn that he had won a million dollars in Lotto. He lived with his Mum and Dad and they were equally excited when he broke the news.

"Naturally I want to share my good fortune so I am going to make you a present of $100 each," he told his parents.

There was silence for a moment before the old man spoke.

"Well son, we've done a lot for you," he began. "It was a struggle during the depression, and we never had much money. In fact, we didn't have enough to get legally married."

"What," said the shocked son, "you mean ... I am..."

"Yes, son, and a damned miserable one at that."

* * *

THEY had been down-and-outers all their life, but Bill and Jacko had always managed to share a Lotto ticket, and of course, one day their dream came true. They celebrated with a beer in their local pub and agreed that a million dollars would not change their nature, except for the flash car they had always wanted.

Bill paid for the beers and off they went to the car sales showroom where they shocked the salesman by buying a Rolls Royce each.

Bill produced his cheque book with a flourish and reached for his pen when Jacko said: "No, no, Bill. Fair go. You paid for the beers."

* * *

THE man who writes the bank's advertising is not the same man who makes the loans.

* * *

WHEN Jock McTavish received a letter from the electricity board threatening to cut off the electricity if he didn't pay his long-overdue account he stormed down to the office.

"Look here," he told the manager. "Each month I put all the bills in my hat, give them a good stir, then pull one out and pay it. But if you don't stop hounding me with threatening letters your bill won't even go in the hat next month."

* * *

"DEAR Bank Manager. Stop sending me letters, just because my account is in the red. I didn't pester you with letters when my account was in the black."

* * *

THE owner of the corner shop was adamant. She told Paddy: "I'm sorry, but you can have no more credit. Your bill's already bigger than it should be."

"I know that," retorted Paddy. "As soon as you cut it to the proper amount I'll pay it!"

## FIREFIGHTERS

THERE was a fire at the nurses home. It took the firemen 15 minutes to put it out. It took the nurses three hours to put the firemen out.

\* \* \*

THE phone rang at the fire station and a frantic voice said: "I have just had the front yard landscaped, and there is a new rock-garden which cost me heaps and a flower bed down the side..."

"What's this got to do with the fire station?" yelled the officer.

"Plenty," continued the caller. "The house next door is on fire and I don't want you blokes trampling all over my new garden."

\* \* \*

STATION officer Jones took the call. "There's a house on fire in Centre Rd," said the frantic voice.

"We're right in the middle of a poker game at the moment and I've got a winning hand. Can you throw a bucket of petrol on it and keep it going till we get there?"

\* \* \*

THE Mexican fireman was the proud father of twin boys. He called one Jose and the other Hose B.

\* \* \*

THERE's a bloke who sells Immitation Fire Insurance to people with imitation fireplaces.

\* \* \*

AND we all know why firemen have bigger balls than policemen. They sell more tickets.

\* \* \*

THE firefighter answered the phone to hear Paddy in a panic.

"Quick, there's a fire! There's a fire!"
"Where is it?"
"At my place of course."
"I mean what's the location?"
"It's in the kitchen."
"But how do we get there?"
"Crikey. Haven't you got a fire engine?"

# FISHERMEN

PADDY said that he once cleaned 500 fish in one day.
  "Now that takes guts."

\* \* \*

"I WISH I could afford the time to go fishing."
  "But you are always fishing."
  "Yes, but I wish I could afford it!"

\* \* \*

HE went off for a week's fishing and didn't catch anything until he got home.

\* \* \*

AGAINST his wife's wishes he set off for another week-end. "What's that Dad's carrying?" said their young son.
  "It is called a fishing rod, dear, and it has a worm at both ends."

\* \* \*

ONE dedicated fisherman told his fellow angler that he had a marvellous dream the previous night. "I dreamt I was alone in a boat with Raquel Welch and we were both nude."
  "Well what was good about it," asked his mate.
  "We caught 50 bream and a record sized salmon," he said.

\* \* \*

THE angler from the city settled down on the banks of the river with all his sophisticated gear and tried to make conversation with an old local seated on a nearby log with a line in his hand.

"Do you fish with flies here?"

"Fish with them? I've fished with them, camped with them, and tried to sleep with them," said the old timer.

\* \* \*

TWO fishermen were out in their boat one Sunday morning when they heard the church bells ring in the distance. One said contritely, "You know, we really ought to be in church."

Baiting his hook the second chap replied: "I couldn't have gone today anyway. I've got the wife sick in bed."

\* \* \*

TWO lads from went fishing and got caught in a terrible storm. Night fell and things began to look bad as they were blown to sea at the mercy of the wind. One began to sob and pray: "Oh Lord. I have not been very good in my life. I have drunk to excess, gambled my wages, cheated on my wife. But if you spare my life now I promise faithfully I will …"

"Hang on a minute, Bert," interrupted his friend. "Don't go too far, I think I see a light."

\* \* \*

AN angler's wife asked him for some money. He gave her two fifties, two twenties, three tenners and a fiver. She threw the small one back.

\* \* \*

IT was the worst trout season New Zealand had experienced for years and the disgruntled American tourist held up his single fish.

"I've come half way round the world to catch this one darn fish so I reckon it has cost me at least $10,000."

"Bloomin' lucky you only caught one then," said his guide.

\* \* \*

AT the waterside bar the young fisherman was describing

156

the crayfish he had pulled to the surface. "It was at least a metre long," he said.

His listeners were amazed. "Well, where is it?" they asked.

"Oh, it busted the top of the pot and got away," he said.

An old salt who had been leaning on the bar during this revelation said "I was fishing and my line hooked onto an old ship's lantern on Shipwreck Reef. When I hauled it up the lantern was still burning."

The young man eyed the old salt with suspicion. "Fair go mate, you don't expect us to believe that."

"Well," said the old man, "if you chop half a metre off your crayfish, I will blow the bloomin' candle out!"

★　　★　　★

OH give me the luck to catch a fish
   So big that even I
   When talking of it afterwards
   May have no need to lie.


## FLASHERS

THREE old maids were sitting on a seat in the park when a member of the raincoat brigade flashed at them. Two of the old ladies had a stroke. The third was too slow.

★　　★　　★

IT was so cold the other day that the local flasher was seen describing himself to a woman.

★　　★　　★

FRED the Flasher had been working the riverbank for 30 years and Pete the Perv asked him when he was retiring.

"I have been thinking about it seriously," said Fred. "But I think I will stick it out for another year."

157

# FLOOSIES

SHE has an impediment in her speech. She can't say no.

*   *   *

SHE had always been a gold-digger, so when her husband's partner died she was quick off the mark to arrange a replacement she had groomed for the job.

"Darling," she said, "I have just the right candidate to replace your partner who died yesterday."

"That's alright with me," he replied, "provided you can arrange it with the undertaker."

*   *   *

THE sugar daddy presented his floosy with a beautiful skunk coat. "Amazing," she said, "that such a beautiful coat could come from such a smelly little beast."

"Look," he said, "I don't expect gratitude, but there's no need to get personal."

*   *   *

LIL went out with many men
    And accepted all they gave her
    But she married a man with a will of his own
    Made out in her favour.

*   *   *

FLOOSIE'S toast:
    Here's to the men I've loved
    And here's to the men I've kissed.
    And here's my profound apologies
    To all the men I've missed.

# FOOD AND WINE

EAT, drink and be merry, for tomorrow we diet.

*   *   *

HERE'S a toast to Mum's cooking. And may my wife never know how bad it was.

PEOPLE who like home cooking should stay home.

*  *  *

WINE improves with age. I like it more the older I get.

*  *  *

HOW do you make Liviewitz wine?
  Leave without paying.


## FOOTBALL
See FOOTBALL FANS

THE team was facing defeat. At the final change the coach roared some fight into them. "And you Murphy, it's about time you got ferocious."
  "What's his number?" said Murph.

*  *  *

THE woman reporter asked him: "Are all the champion football players conceited?"
  "I don't really know, but I'm not."

*  *  *

"WHERE does your football team play, Grandpa?"
  "What football team? What are you talking about?"
  "Oh, Dad says that when you kick off we can get a new house!"

*  *  *

THE game was so close that the two football fans would not leave the stand, despite their hunger. "Send that kid for some pies," suggested one. They were $2 each so they gave the kid $6 and told him to get one for himself.
  The kid came back five minutes later and handed back $4. "They only had one pie left," he said.

*  *  *

THE star recruit who had just been transferred for an enormous sum was being interviewed on telly.
  "You appear to be earning more money than the prime minister," said the interviewer.

159

"Only fair," said the football star, "I play a lot better than he does."

*　　*　　*

YOUNG man looking for a job travelled to the country and approached the general store in a small town. The man behind the counter was also the president of the country football league and offered the lad a job immediately. "We need a centre-half forward with courage and a strong set of hands," he said.

"Sorry sir," said the lad. "I don't know a thing about football."

"No worries. We need umpires too."

*　　*　　*

THE player was dashing through with the ball when he was brought down with a blatant trip.

"Free kick," roared the umpire.

"Who to?" shouted one of the players.

"Us," said the Ump.

*　　*　　*

A PSYCHIATRIST has a thriving practice, particularly in the football season. He tried an idea-association test on a patient one day and asked him what came to mind when he thought of something brown, firm and had smooth curves.

"A football," said the patiently immediately.

"Good. And what do you think of when two arms slide around your waist?"

"An illegal tackle," was the instant reply.

"Now picture a pair of firm thighs..."

"A fullback."

"Top marks," said the psychiatrist. "Your reactions are quite normal. You would be surprised at some of the stupid answers I get."

*　　*　　*

IT was the jungle's soccer classic of the year, the annual grudge match between the animals and the insects, and by half time the elephants, zebras and cheetahs had proved too much for the grasshoppers, beetles and ants with a convincing score of 58 goals to nil.

However, when the match resumed the animals noted a substitute player run onto the field with the insects. It was a shiny black centipede.

From then on the centipede became the star of the game peppering the goals from all angles. Indeed, the animals failed to score another goal and the insects ran out winners, 59 goals to 58.

At the bar after the game the animals' captain, a tough looking elephant, said to the insects' skipper, a wily grasshopper, "Great game, but you were damned lucky that centipede arrived at half time."

"You're wrong," said the grasshopper. "He was here for the start of the game, but it took him until half time to put his boots on!"

*　　*　　*

THE champ from the bush was not all he was cracked up to be so the runner was sent out with a message.

"The coach says he will pull you off at half time."

"Great," said the country lad, "we only get oranges at Snake Gully."

## FOOTBALL FANS
See FOOTBALL

FOOTBALL fans are quite a different species from the rest of the human race. The average footy fan buys his final series tickets three months in advance, and waits until December 24 to do the Christmas shopping.

*　　*　　*

"I HEAR you had a difficult time explaining the grand final to your wife."

"Yes. She found out I didn't go."

AT the turnstiles it was being explained to McTavish that there were seats at $20, $15 and $10 and that programs were 50 cents.

"Okay," said McTavish, "I'll sit on a program."

*　　*　　*

CLASSIFIED Ad: "Young football supporter of good appearance and sound health offers hand in marriage to any young lady with two tickets to the grand final next Saturday. Please send photograph of the tickets."

*　　*　　*

THE two mates were down at the front fence for the rugby league match when the beer cans started to fly. One was so concerned about being hit he kept looking over his shoulder and couldn't concentrate on the game.

"Don't worry," said his mate, "as they say in the war, if there's one with your name on it ..."

"That's just it. My name is Foster!"

*　　*　　*

ON a crowded train going to the football game the fan resplendent in black and white colours had a large duck tucked under his arm.

Sitting directly opposite, at face level with the duck, was an old codger flaunting a scarf in the opposing team's colours. "They won't let you take a pig into the ground ya know," he said loudly.

"It's not a pig, it's a duck ya burk," said the fan in the black and white scarf.

"I wasn't talking to you," said the old codger.

*　　*　　*

"I BELIEVE you are a member of the school's football team," said the proud grandfather to his 13-year-old grandson. "What position do you play?"

"I'm not sure Gramps," said the lad, "but I heard the sports teacher say that I was the team's main drawback."

ONE-eyed supporter arrived at the ground. "How much to get in," he said.

"Sixteen dollars," said the ticket-seller.

"Well here's eight," said the fan, "I only watch one side."

\* \* \*

IT was the day of the grand final when the officials took a call from the gatekeeper. "There are two life-members here. They are close friends of the umpire and they have lost their tickets."

"Throw them out," said the executive. "They are liars. Whoever heard of an umpire having two friends!"

\* \* \*

WE all know that soccer is taken seriously in the United Kingdom, so when Ireland and Scotland clashed at Wembly a fan wearing the colours of neither side and cheering the goals of both teams was a thorn in the side of a Scot and an Irishman standing either side of him.

"Are ye from Scotland?" enquired the Scot.

"Or are ya from Ireland?" joined the Irishman.

"I'm neither. I'm English really," came the answer.

"Well then," said the Scot and Irishman together as they thumped him, "mind your own flaming business."

\* \* \*

IT was a mid-winter Saturday. The two footy fans were huddled together in the wind and rain. Their team was being thrashed, their feet were soaked and they were both beginning to shiver. Fred turned to his mate and said: "Harry, tell me how much fun we are having here today. I keep forgetting."

\* \* \*

A BLOKE took his black and white fox terrier in to the pub and was enjoying a few drinks until the footy scores appeared on telly. When it was announced that his team had lost the dog went mad, knocking over tables and snapping at customers.

"What's got into your dog?" asked the barman.

"He just can't take it when our team is beaten," explained the owner.

"Heck. What does he do when they win?"

"Don't know. I've only had him two years!"

* * *

A BLOKE went into the pub with his dog. Both were supporters of the local team and they watched the match on TV with great interest. Every time their team kicked a goal the dog yelped with delight.

The barman was impressed. "What does he do when the other side scores?" he asked.

"Somersaults" said the owner.

"How many?" asked the barman.

"Depends on how hard I kick him!"

## FUNERALS
See DEATH

IF you don't go to your friends' funerals... they won't come to yours.

* * *

THE difference between an Australian wedding and an Australian funeral is one less drunk.

* * *

AN Irish funeral is merrier than an English holiday.

* * *

A LARGE crowd had gathered at a funeral. A passer-by asked who had died.

"Dunno," he replied. "I'm only here for the beer."

* * *

IT was an overcast and threatening sky the day Fred buried his mother-in-law. In fact, just as the funeral party left the cemetery there was a loud clap of thunder and flash of lightning.

"Crikey," said Fred. "She's there already."

AFTER the funeral she took her husband's suits to the Op Shop. The manager noted the thin material and the holes in the trousers. "My goodness," she said, "your old man died just in time."

* * *

BRIDGET took one look at her late husband, lying in his coffin with a smile on his face.

"Look at him now," she said.

"He's smiling because he died in his sleep and he doesn't know he's dead yet. He is dreaming he is still alive, so when he wakes up and finds that he is dead, begorrah, the shock will kill him."

* * *

HE had died a very rich man, and at the funeral service Paddy was beating his breast and wailing louder than any of the other mourners.

One of the relatives comforted him. "We didn't know you knew him."

"That's the trouble. I didn't," wailed Paddy.

* * *

LOUIE had been a big time gambler and all his race-track friends had assembled in the small church for his funeral.

With heads bowed they heard the priest solemnly intone: "Our friend Louie is not dead. He merely sleeps," when a voice from the back of the church said, "I've got a hundred to say he won't wake up."

* * *

AFTER three weeks during which her husband had been slowly dying in bed the doctor came downstairs and told Mrs Murphy he had good news. He said her husband had made a remarkable recovery.

Mrs Murphy burst out crying. "What am I going to do now? I've sold all his clothes to pay for the funeral."

165

A LAWYER was merely fulfilling a duty by being present at the funeral service of a millionaire when a colleague arrived, a little late, and stood in the pew beside him.

"How far has he got?" said the newcomer referring to the vicar's eulogy.

"He's just opened the defence," replied the lawyer.

*   *   *

DID you know there is a law which prohibits anybody living south of the river being buried in the cemetery? It's on account of them being not dead yet.

*   *   *

HARRY had been a workaholic journo all his life and his friends at the office took up a collection for a head-stone, which read: "Erected in memory of Harry Bloggs, drowned in the river, by his relatives and friends."

The headstone had been installed hastily before the ground over the grave had settled. On inspecting the work next day the cemetery attendant found that it was tilting sideways. As a temporary measure he looped a wire around it and tied it to a nearby tree.

Harry's mates took the opportunity that afternoon to visit the grave for the first time. "Gawd, that's our Harry," said one, noting the wire. "He's still working. Now he's got the phone on!"

*   *   *

AT the funeral service the vicar and the undertaker had never seen a husband so grieved. Fred was sobbing his heart out and beating his breast. He was so distraught that the vicar took him aside in a bid to comfort him.

"It's tough, I know," said the vicar, "but believe me you will eventually get over it. And dare I say it," he paused, "in three or six months you might well meet another woman and ..."

"Yeah!" wailed Fred, "but what am I gonna do tonight?"

# G

## GAMBLERS

"DO you play cards for money?"

"No. But the blokes I play with do."

*     *     *

WHEN the little old lady fronted up to the bookie for yet another payout he was perplexed.

"You must study the form," he said.

"Oh, no," she said, "I just stick a pin in the paper."

"But how have you managed to pick four winners in one afternoon?"

"Oh, today I used a fork," she explained.

*     *     *

SLICK Sam was always winning at cards, and always losing at the races. "Why is that?" asked his mate Pete.

"Simple. They won't let me shuffle the horses."

*     *     *

DID you hear how Slick Sam lost $100 on the Melbourne Cup, and another $100 on the replay?

*     *     *

"WHAT'S the meaning of the three balls over the pawnshop?"

"It's two-to-one you won't get it back."

*     *     *

AFTER the last race a bloke who stuttered slightly approached a bookmaker who had a winning day.

167

"Excuse me, I b-b-backed a five-tt..."

The bookie was sharp. "There was no five-to-one winners, mate, nick off."

The bloke persisted. "I b-b-backed a five-tt."

"Look," said the bookie, "I've had a good day. Here's a fifty-note. Now nick off."

The punter shrugged his shoulders with resignation, accepted the note, walked over to his mate and said. "That bookie's a nice bloke. I tried to tell him I backed a five-ton truck into his Rolls Royce, and he gave me fifty dollars."

\* \* \*

THE lads had arranged to go fishing on Sunday morning. All turned up on time except Fred. He finally arrived ten minutes late. "What kept you?" they asked.

"It was a toss-up if I went to church or joined you blokes fishing."

"Well, that shouldn't have taken you long."

"I had to toss up 23 times."

\* \* \*

WHEN he got to the tote window a little voice in his ear said: "Put it all on number six."

He did, and it came in at 100 to one.

When he fronted the window for the second race a little voice in his ear said: "Put the lot on number 13."

He did and it romped home by a street.

When he pushed ten thousand over the counter at the tote window for the third race a little voice said: "Put it all on number nine."

He did and it ran stone motherless last, and the little voice in his ear said: "Oh well. Win some, lose some."

\* \* \*

THE gambler who had just won the $100,000 jackpot on the Melbourne Cup was asked by reporters how he would spend the money.

"Oh, I've got it all figured out," he said. "First I'll spend

$25,000 on whisky and beer, $25,000 on horses, dogs and cards, and $25,000 on women and wild living."

"Wow, and what of the other $25,000?"

"I will probably just squander that," he said.

\* \* \*

ONCE again he had to explain his bad luck to his wife. "As I walked into the racecourse a sudden gust of wind blew my hat off. It was a sure sign," he said. "So I put it all on a horse called Gone with the Wind."

"And it didn't win?"

"No. Some foreign horse called Mon Chapeau won by a mile."

\* \* \*

PETE the Punter was at the pub early and got a few under his belt before he noticed a large sign on the wall: Lunch 12 to 1.

"Bloody good odds," he said to himself. He called the barman over and said he wanted to put down a hundred for a win.

"No gambling here," said the barman, and ordered him out. Pete wandered down to the next pub where he saw another sign: Lunch 11 to 2.

"The odds are down already," he muttered. "It must be a good thing." He went straight in to the bar and said he wanted to place a bet.

He was immediately thrown out for a second time.

Pete wandered around the corner where a third pub displayed the sign: Lunch 1 to 2.

"That's blown it. It's odds on now." But he decided to go in and listen to the result. As he entered the pub the chef delivered a plate on the bar and called "Sausages one!"

Pete the Punter breathed a sigh of relief. "Just as well I didn't back that bloody Lunch!"

\* \* \*

WHEN the well-dressed gambler left the club he was

accosted by a down-and-outer who asked him for a few dollars for a meal.

The gambler took pity. "Come inside and I'll buy you a beer."

"No, I don't drink," said the man.

"Well, how about a cigar?"

"No, I don't smoke."

"Well, I know a certainty tomorrow. I'll put a $100 on it for you."

"No. Just a few dollars for food," insisted the man.

"Then come home with me for a meal. I want my wife to see what happens to a man who doesn't drink, smoke or gamble."

* * *

"HOW come you always come back from the races with a small fortune?"

"Cos I always go there with a bigger one."

* * *

AFTER six months at Gamblers Anonymous, Fred believed he was cured. "I'd like to thank you all for helping me kick the habit," he said.

"I'll never gamble again. I'll wager a fortune on it."

* * *

THEY had been gambling mates for years and finally it came to Fred's attention that his poker playing mate was having an affair with his wife.

"Let's settle this in a civilised way," said Fred. "We will play a hand of poker for her. And just to make it interesting how about a $50 wager on the side?"

* * *

TWO London gamblers were on holiday in Italy and visited the Vatican. They were the last to leave the Cistene Chapel and happened to see a white robed figure fall down some stairs. They recognised him as the Pope and he was stone dead.

The first Vatican authorities on the scene begged them

not to say anything for 24 hours. There were world-wide implications. The two gamblers agreed. After all, they were flying home that night.

On the plane one of them had a brilliant idea. "As soon as we land I am going straight to Ladbrokes and getting great odds on the life of the Pope."

"Sounds like a great idea," said Paddy, his mate.

It was two days before the Pope's death was announced and the first gambler made a clean up.

"And what about you, Paddy?" he asked.

"Nothing at all," admitted Paddy. "I took the Pope in a double with the Archbishop of Canterbury."

## GARDENERS

A GARDENER is a bloke who calls a spade a spade; until he falls over one.

\*     \*     \*

NOW is the time of the year when the bulbs you forgot to plant last autumn will fail to bloom.

\*     \*     \*

FRED'S specialty was growing vegetables and he eventually won the Nobel Peas Prize, for being outstanding in his field.

\*     \*     \*

WE know a bonsai tree grower who has been so successful he is now looking for a house with a smaller garden.

\*     \*     \*

SHE talked to the trees. That's why they took her away.

\*     \*     \*

"DO you really think talking to plants makes them grow?" confided one keen gardener to the other.

"Nah," said Fred. "My Missus hasn't stopped talking to me for the last 25 years, and I haven't grown one iota."

MY wife talks to the rhododendrons for hours on end. One day I asked them how the heck they could stand it.

"Who listens?" they replied.

*    *    *

"I CAN'T find anything to say to my plants," she said while laying newspaper on the garden beds, "so I'm giving them something to read instead."

*    *    *

IT was such a serious drought the government placed a ban on sprinkler hoses. Then suddenly the drought broke and the heavens opened up with a downpour that flooded everybody's garden. "If this rain keeps up," said Fred, "we will be able to use our hoses again."

*    *    *

PHIL, the philsophical gardener, was asked how he remained so tranquil in such a frustrating hobby. "I learned long ago," he said, "that when it wants to rain the best thing to do is just sit back and let it."

*    *    *

"WHAT causes rain?" asked the horticultural student.

"Weekends," was the unanimous answer.

*    *    *

"MY husband is an invertebrate gardener," she said.

"Don't you mean inveterate?"

"No. Invertebrate. He's got no backbone for it."

*    *    *

THE customer in the nursery was spending such a long time looking at two wheelbarrows an attendant eventually asked if he wanted assistance.

"Yes," he replied. "I can't decide between the red one or the green wheelbarrow. It is a present for my wife's birthday."

"Will it be a surprise?" asked the attendant.

"I predict it will. She is expecting a diamond ring."

*    *    *

THE nurseryman was running a special on ferns this

week and filled his shop with fronds of every species. But the customer insisted he wanted an anemone.

"With fronds like these who needs anemones?" said the nurseryman.

* * *

THE vicar was delighted to see Fred working up a sweat in his front garden. He leaned over the fence and gushed: "Your garden is looking lovely. Isn't it wonderful what man and God can do when they work in harmony?"

"Maybe," said Fred wiping his brow. "But you should have seen this yard when God had it on his own."

* * *

WOULD you believe it? Forty-three years ago, while sunbathing in her garden, Mrs Gladys Nurkle, of 7 Paradise St, Moonee Ponds, lost her gold wedding ring.

Yesterday, while digging the garden in the very same spot, her son Clarence ruptured himself.

* * *

GRANDPA was proud of his garden, and when it was admired by visitors he would say the key to his fine crop was "manure, manure, manure."

It embarrassed his daughter. "Can't you make Dad call it fertilizer?" she asked her mother.

"It took us years to make him say manure," she replied.

* * *

OLD Jake from the Outback said his pumpkins grew so fast he kept a pack of greyhounds to round them up. And when they did it only took five to make a dozen.

* * *

"WHEN are you going to prepare the garden beds?" she asked.

"I'm thinking about it."

"You mean you're turning it over in your mind?"

* * *

THE local handyman letter-boxed his neighbours with

173

a handbill which read: "Don't kill yourself in the garden this spring. I will do it for you!"

* * *

HARRY Henpecked had been ordered by his wife to buy only organic vegetables from the market garden.

"These vegetables are for my wife," he said. "Have they been sprayed with any poisonous chemicals?"

"No," said the gardener, "you will have to do that yourself."

## GOLF

FUNNY how man blames fate for all accidents, yet claims full responsibility for a hole in one.

* * *

QUESTION on golf etiquette: What do you do when your opponent claims to have found his ball in the rough, and you know he is a liar because you've got it in your pocket?

* * *

THEY called it golf because all the other four-letter words were already taken.

* * *

HER golf is improving. Yesterday she hit a ball in one.

* * *

NOW she has improved so much she misses the ball much closer than she used to.

* * *

A BELOW par golfer always takes two or three lumps with his tee.

* * *

"I GOT a set of clubs for my husband."

"Lucky you, what a swap!"

* * *

FRED seemed off his game. He was morose and sulky. By the fifth tee his partner said, "What the hell's the matter with you, Fred?"

"It's Madge, my wife. Ever since she has taken up golf she has cut my sex down to only twice a week."

"Think yourself bloomin' lucky," said his partner. "She's cut me out altogether!"

*     *     *

IN Africa native tribes beat the ground with clubs and utter blood-curdling screams. Anthropologisits call it the release of primitive expression. Here we call it golf.

*     *     *

FRED had swum through heavy seas to rescue a millionaire who fell from his yacht. The rich man was insisting that he accept some token of gratitude for saving his life. Fred said it wasn't necessary, but the millionaire persisted. "Okay," said Fred. "I'm a keen golfer. Maybe you might like to buy me a club?"

The millionaire, as good as his word, went out and bought two; Royal Melbourne and Huntingdale.

*     *     *

IT was a tight game in the Scottish Highlands.

"How many strokes was that?" said McTavish when they finished the fifth.

"Six," said McSporran.

"Well, I had five, so that makes it my hole."

When they finished the sixth McTavish said. "Well, how many strokes was that then?"

"Hang on," said McSporran. "It's my turn to ask."

*     *     *

A TOURING golf professional was having a drink at the club's bar when he was approached by a chap with a white cane and dark glasses who introduced himself as a golf champion.

"I am champion of the Blind Golfers' Association and as one champion to another, I would like to challenge you to a match which could be a fund-raiser for the blind." He said he didn't want any favors and told the pro he was keen to play for $50 a hole.

The embarrassed pro tried to avoid the challenge, but the blind man was so insistent he finally agreed.

"Okay, when will we play?" he asked.

"Any night. Any night at all."

* * *

THIS middle-aged couple had played golf together for most of their married life. One night over the evening meal she mused: "If I die before you, will you get married again?"

Although he was absorbed in the evening newspaper he muttered, "I guess so."

"Would you play golf with her?"

"I guess so," he mumbled.

"Would you take her to our club?"

"I guess so," he said.

"Surely you wouldn't let her use my clubs?"

"No, of course not. Anyway, she's left-handed!"

* * *

"I AM not playing my best game today,"

"Really, what other games do you play?"

* * *

ONE golfer was taking so much care before driving from the fifth tee that his partner asked: "Why the concentration?"

"I'm very anxious to make this shot a good one," said his partner. "My mother-in-law is down there in the clubhouse watching me."

"Impossible," said his mate. "You could never hit her from this distance!"

* * *

TWO businessmen took time from the office to play a round of golf during their lunch break but were hampered by two women playing ahead and slowing their game.

Finally one said, "Listen Jack, I'll go and ask if they mind if we play through."

He had only gone a hundred metres before he turned and hurried back. He was visibly shaken. "Jack, you won't believe this," he said, "but those two women... one is my wife and the other is my mistress."

Jack was a cool hand. "Listen Reg," he said. "Keep your head down while I approach them and we'll sneak past."

Jack had only gone a hundred metres when he turned back. "Listen Reg, you won't believe this ..." he began.

* * *

HIS drive from the third tee sliced to the left of the fairway and the ball ended in an impossible lie in front of the greenkeeper's tractor shed.

His wife summed up the situation. "No need to take a penalty shot darling," she said. "Just open the doors of the garage, push the tractor out, open the rear doors, and with a number three wood you could hit straight through the shed."

"Brilliant, darling," he said. He took a mighty whack but the ball hit the rear of the building, cannoned back and struck his wife, stone dead.

The following day he was playing the same hole and by sheer coincidence landed at the same place in front of the shed.

"No need to take a penalty shot," said the caddie, "we can push the tractor out and open both sets of doors. You can hit straight through the shed."

"No way," he said. "I tried that yesterday and ended up with a double bogey."

* * *

THERE were no caddies left when Fonsenby arrived at the clubhouse, but the manager said old George, sitting in the corner could do the job. "He has amazing vision. Has eyes like an eagle," said the manager.

Fonsenby had his misgivings but he gave the old bloke

the benefit of the doubt and hit his first drive a magnificent 500 metres down the fairway.

"Did you see where that went?" he asked.

"Of course I did," said the old bloke.

"Good," said Fonsenby, "Where is it?"

"I can't remember," said George.

*     *     *

THEY were leaning on the bar at the 19th when Fred produced a golf ball from his pocket and proudly set it on the bar. "Have a look at this," he said to his mate Charlie. "It's a digital golf ball."

Indeed, the ball was a bright irridescent orange. It had a small antennae. "It sends out beeps," explained Fred. Charlie was impressed. "Where did you buy it?"

"I didn't," said Fred. "I found it."

*     *     *

THEY were watching the golf classic on television when Fred entered the room and was immediately interested.

"Turn it up a bit," he called.

"Sshh. Not while Norman's putting!"

*     *     *

WHEN the club secretary explained to Fred that he couldn't play because the course was fully booked out, Fred was more than upset. He had been a member for 20 years too.

"Look," said Fred, "If the President of the United States lobbed here for a game today I bet you would make room for him."

The secretary admitted that he would have to.

"Well I just happen to know that he's in Washington today, so I'll take his place!"

*     *     *

FRED said during his last game of golf he stepped on a rake. "They were the best two balls I hit all day!"

*     *     *

ABE and Louie had made a pile in the rag trade and decided to take things easy and join a prestige golf club.

On the first day they went into the club bar for a pre-game drink.

"How much?" said Abe when the two whiskies were placed in front of them.

"First day at the club? New members? Well it's on the house," said the barman.

They went into the dining room and ordered lunch. "How much?" asked Louie.

"It's complimentary to new members, sir," said the waiter.

Then they wandered over to the pro shop and ordered half a dozen balls each. The pro obliged. "How much?" asked Abe.

"First day in the club?" asked the pro.

"Yes," chorused Abe and Lou.

"Well, that will be fifty-five dollars and seven cents each," said the pro.

When they finally got onto the green Abe muttered to Louie: "It sure aint by the throat that they've got you in this club."

\*　　\*　　\*

KEVIN had made his money as a car salesman and had done so well he thought it was time to move up in society and join the golf club.

On his first day he slashed and bashed his way around the course cutting divots from fairway and the greens alike. He left a trail of disaster.

He was in the club dining room half way through dinner when he was tapped on the shoulder.

"Excuse me," said the stern official. "I am chairman of the green committee ..."

"Just the bloke I want to see," said the new member. "These brussels sprouts are hardly fresh."

# GORILLAS

A GORILLA swaggered into a waterside pub, slapped a five dollar note on the bar and asked for a beer.

It quite took the barman by surprise for a moment, but ever ready to make a quid he capitalised on this unusual situation, pulling the beer, scooping up the fiver and giving the gorilla 60 cents in small change.

But as the primate sipped his beer, the phenomena of a talking gorilla aroused the barman's curiosity to the point where it could be contained no longer.

"Out for a walk, are you?" he ventured.

"Yeah," mumbled the gorilla.

"We don't get many gorillas in here," pressed the barman trying to make conversation.

"No wonder, at $4.40 a glass."

*     *     *

THE advertisement in "Showbiz" read: "Non-speaking part, but athletic agility a must." Paddy applied for the job and found himself being directed to Taronga Park Zoo. It was explained to him that one of the zoo's major attractions, the gorilla, had died and they needed a substitute until the real thing could be imported.

"All you have to do is don this suit for a few weeks and swing around the branches," said the zoo's director.

The few weeks turned into a month and although it was hot in the suit the pay was good. Paddy had even worked out quite a routine leaping and tumbling about.

Indeed, the crowd's applause drove him to greater heights and more daring feats until one day, while attempting a somersault he lost his grip and fell out of the tree on the wrong side of the adjacent lion's enclosure.

When he recovered his senses he saw the lion approaching and his first reaction was to let out a shriek for help.

"Shut up, you fool," said the lion.

"Do you want to get us both the sack?"

IT was a month after World War 3 had devasted the earth. Not a human being survived. Indeed a battered and dazed chimpanzee had wandered for weeks through what was left of the smouldering jungle without seeing another living thing.

One day the chimp saw something move behind the rubble. He was delighted to find it was another gorilla, and a female at that.

He rushed up and embraced her, but she pushed him away. "No. Don't let's start all that over again," she said.

# H

## HEALTH

WHEN you feel like you need more exercise, lie down until the feeling wears off.

\* \* \*

THERE are probably better cures for a cold than three whiskies, but who cares?

\* \* \*

FRED thought he had a club foot for forty-two years. When he died they discovered he had his boots on the wrong feet.

\* \* \*

HE used to be an all-round athlete. Now he's just all-round.

\* \* \*

FRED took up exercising. Now he has the energy of a man twice his age.

\* \* \*

THE Irish are great believers in health. They are always drinking to other people's.

\* \* \*

DOC: "Do you suffer from stress?"
  "No, but I think I'm a carrier."

\* \* \*

DON'T tell your friends
  About your indigestion

"How are You?" is a greeting
Not a bloody question.

\* \* \*

IT was the healthiest town in the region. They had to shoot a bloke to start a cemetery.

The only bloke to die over the last ten years was the undertaker. And he died of starvation.

\* \* \*

PEOPLE who say they are going on a diet are just wishful shrinkers.

# HISTORY

THE Magna Carta ensured that no free man could be hanged twice for the same offence.

\* \* \*

SIR Francis Drake circumcised the world.
And did it with a 100 foot clipper.

\* \* \*

HISTORY'S mysteries are those of the past
   Present intrigues seem worse, and are vast
   But before you condemn
   This generation, pro tem
Remember, you're also one of the cast.

\* \* \*

NAPOLEON came home tired and weary, wet and wounded, and went straight round to Josephine's flat. He was shocked to find a pair of large gumboots on her front doorstep.

"Josephine! Josephine!" he called out. "What are those rubber boots doing out here?"

"They're not rubber boots," said Josie. "They're Wellington's."

\* \* \*

HISTORY records how the first union and the first time-piece occured at the same time. It was when the soldiers in Alexander the Great's army got cheesed off swinging their swords against the foe from dawn to dusk. The troops appointed the first shop steward to parly with Alexander about shorter hours. The problem was the watch had yet to be invented.

By mutual agreement it was decided that the soldiers would tie a piece of rag around the wrist of their sword arm. When it got well and truly soaked with sweat, then it was time to call it a day. They called this timing device Alexander's rag time band.

\* \* \*

WHEN Noah was sailing his Ark there was a great accumulation of bulldust in the bull's pen and the crew wanted to know what to do with it.

"Push it over the side," said Noah.

Then in 1492 Christopher Columbus discovered it.

# HORSES

THERE is nothing like horse riding, to make you feel better off.

\* \* \*

WHAT has four legs and flies?

A dead horse!

\* \* \*

HE named his horse Radish because he got a kick out of introducing the beast when he took it out to social functions. "This is my horse, Radish," he would say.

\* \* \*

THE American tourist was leaning on the bar telling all and sundry about the size of things back in Texas.

"Why, I would hop on a horse and it would take three days to ride to the other side of the ranch."

"Yeah," yawned a local, "I've got a horse like that, too."

\* \* \*

MURPHY the horse trader sold a nag to a bloke and

it dropped dead on the way home. The bloke went back to complain.

"That's funny," said Murphy, "I've had that nag for years and it's never done that before."

*　　*　　*

TRAVELLER's car broke down ten kilometres from a remote town and had the driver puzzled as he tinkered under the bonnet looking for the trouble.

"I think it's the carburettor," came a voice from behind him. The startled driver looked around. There was nobody there but a horse in a nearby paddock. "Undo the petrol lead to the carby and clean it through," insisted the horse.

Almost panic-stricken the driver did as the horse insisted. Put the carburettor together again. Pressed the starter button and the engine burst into life.

He raced to town as fast as possible and stopped at the first service station. "You won't believe it," he gasped to the attendant, "I had carburettor trouble about ten kilometres out of town and a horse told me how to fix it."

"Was it a white horse?" asked the proprietor.

"Yes," answered the amazed driver.

"Well it must be your lucky day," he said. "There is usually a black horse in that paddock and he knows bugger-all about carburettors."

*　　*　　*

A WHITE horse leant against the bar and pondered the array of drinks on the top shelf. "I feel like something different tonight," he told the barman.

The barman said: "Why not have the whisky named after you."

"Really? Okay, I'll have a double Trevor."

*　　*　　*

THE travelling parson had decided to retire from his circuit in the bush and wanted to sell his horse. Old Jack was down from the high country and recognising a strong horse when he saw one soon struck a bargain with the parson.

But when Jack swung up in the saddle, the horse refused to move.

"Oh, I forgot to tell you he is a very religious horse," said the parson. "I have trained him reverently and he will only go when you say the words Jesus Christ, and he will only stop when you say Amen."

Old Jack thanked the parson, said "Jesus Christ" and the horse took off at a fast rate. They were travelling back to the high country when thunder clouds darkened the sky, and a bolt of lightning cracked to the ground.

The horse bolted in fright and a low branch struck Old Jack in the face momentarily blinding him. As the horse galloped madly through the bush he tried to think of the word to make it stop, finally yelling "Amen."

The horse skidded to a halt and when Old Jack opened his eyes he saw that his mount had stopped right on the edge of a frightening mountain precipice.

"Jesus Christ," he said.

&ast; &ast; &ast;

A CITY girl arrived at the bush riding school. She said she had never been on a horse, so naturally, she wanted a horse that had never been ridden before.


## HORSE RACING

DURING racing trials a trainer took the jockey aside just before the start. "I've got an option to buy this horse, but I don't know its form," he whispered. "Try him out for me, and hold it to about fourth place."

The jockey had a strong pair of arms and held him back to finish fourth as instructed.

"He's a good horse," summed up the jockey.

"Do you think he could have beaten the first three?" asked the trainer.

"Easy," said the jockey, "but I don't know about the other 12 who finished behind him."

\* \* \*

A LEADING trainer was given an eye test and presented with a pair of glasses. The optician said they would cost $300.

"Too much," cried the trainer.

"They're bi-focal," said the optician.

"I don't care if they're by Phar Lap. It's too much."

\* \* \*

THE secretary of the bush racing club was worried about falling attendances. On the morning of the Boxing Day Cup race meeting he got a phone call. "I'm bringing a coach-load of people," said the voice. "What time is the first race?"

"What time can you get here," replied the secretary.

\* \* \*

THE drover looked over the field at the Oodnadatta Races and reckoned his nag could beat anything in the mounting yard, so he entered him for the main race.

"But what's his pedigree?" asked the steward.

"What d'yer mean, his pedigree?"

"What is he by, and what is he out of?" insisted the steward.

"He's by that bloody gum tree and out in that bloody paddock."

\* \* \*

AN old hack jockey had been killed in a car crash and a leading trainer had been called to the morgue to identify him.

The trainer lifted the sheet off one body and shook his head. It wasn't his jockey. He lifted the second sheet and shook his head again. He lifted the third sheet and sadly announced: "Again, he hasn't run a place."

\* \* \*

THE trainer was giving last minute instructions to the

jockey and appeared to slip something in the horse's mouth just as a steward passed by.

"What was that?" inquired the steward.

"Oh, nothing," said the trainer, "just a Mintie. He offered one to the steward. "Here, have one. And I'll have one myself."

After the suspicious steward left the scene the trainer continued with his riding instructions. "Just keep the horse on the rails. You are on a certainty. The only thing that could possibly pass you down the straight is either the steward or me."

\* \* \*

IT was the Grand National Steeplechase and there was a terrible pile up at the third fence. Horses and jockies everywhere.

Despite two broken ribs one jockey managed to remount and with agonising pain and great applause from the crowd he was the only one to finish the course.

The trainer greeted him with a kick in the bum. "You re-mounted the wrong horse, you dopey drongo!"

\* \* \*

THREE horses were in the pub talking about their racing days; about the times they were pipped at the post.

"Just missed the Melbourne Cup by a nose," said one.

"Same thing happened to me at Randwick," said another.

A greyhound sipping whisky at the bar moved over to their table.

"I couldn't help overhearing," he said, "but the same thing happened to me at Sandown."

The horses looked at each other. "Crikey Moses," said one, "that's amazing... a talking dog!"

\* \* \*

A HORSE was looking over the fence watching a game of cricket.

"Any chance of a game?" he asked the captain.

At first the cricketer was taken aback by the talking

horse, but when it insisted it was keen to play the skipper thought it might be a bit of a lark if he sent the horse in as opening bat.

The horse shaped up to the first ball and slammed it over the boundary for a six. He did the same with the second and third, indeed every ball he hit for six until the over ended.

He had been partnered by the captain, and when the bowler ran in from the other end and the captain managed his first hit for a meagre single he called for the horse to run.

But the horse stood there. Frantic calls by the captain to run were ignored and in the confusion the skipper was stumped out.

"Why didn't you run?" roared the angry captain.

"Listen mate," said the horse, "if I could run I would be at the racetrack today, not messing around with this cricket game."

* * *

IT had started as an odds-on favourite, but by the home turn it had run out of puff and was going through the field backwards.

The irate trainer approached the jockey: "What the hell was going on?"

"The horse simply wasn't good enough," explained the jockey.

"Rubbish," roared the trainer. "You could have done much better."

"Maybe I could," said the jockey, "but you know as well as I do the rules state I must stay on the horse's back."

* * *

THE tipster said this horse would walk it in. It did, but all the others galloped.

* * *

IN the old days when tick-tackers were the stars of race

track relaying the prices and trends with hand signals one of the best, Paddy O'Reily, died.

"I can't believe Paddy's dead," said his mate at the funeral service, just as the priest blessed the coffin.

"He's dead alright," said Moloney, "He's just drifted out to 33s."

*　　*　　*

CATHOLIC priests are often at the races, but Pete the Punter was surprised to see the priest sprinkle holy water over one nag which duly went out and won by half a street.

Pete followed him closely and witnessed another holy water sprinkle and another win, at ten-to-one.

Next time he had the money ready and as soon as the priest annointed yet a third horse, albeit a skinny nag, Pete was off to the bookies.

After the horse had dropped dead on the home turn Pete tackled the priest for an explanation.

"If you were a Catholic," said the priest, "you would have known the difference between a blessing and the last rites."

*　　*　　*

PADDY the Punter cleaned out the bookies and his friends were soon pressing him to divulge his system.

"I'm superstitious, and I watch for omens," said Paddy. "On my way to the races I took a Number 5 tram. It made five stops on the way and it cost me $5 to get into the track.

"It was three fives telling me something. So I added them up, three fives are 16 so I backed Number 16 and it won by a street."

# HOSPITALS
See DOCTORS

A MINOR operation is one performed on somebody else.

A HOSPITAL is a place where people who are run down generally wind up.

* * *

A HOSPITAL is a place where they wake you at five o'clock in the morning to give you a sleeping pill.

* * *

FRED was in hospital. At the end of his bed was a chart with lots of complaints listed on it. All the nurses had written something.

* * *

FRED was in hospital for a complicated operation. In fact, while he was in there the surgeon took his wife out.

* * *

RECOVERING from an operation in a bush hospital Farmer Brown asked why the blinds were drawn.

"Well," explained the doc. "There's a bushfire outside, and I didn't want you to wake up and think the operation was a failure."

* * *

A GIRL from the country called at the hospital. "I'd like to see an out-turn, please," she said.

"You mean an intern," said the nurse.

"Whatever you call him, I want a contamination," she insisted.

"You mean an examination," said the nurse.

"Yes, I need to see the fraternity ward."

"You mean the maternity ward."

"Call it what you will," said the girl with annoyance, "but I certainly know I haven't demonstrated for two months and I think I'm stagnant."

* * *

THE indignant patient complained: "Why did you put me in a ward with this bloke?"

"Why, is he giving you trouble?"

"He's a lunatic," said the patient. "He keeps raving on about getting rid of the monkeys in this ward and look, the ruddy room is full of them."

MATRON at a large hospital answered a phone call in her office.

"Could you tell me how Paddy Murphy is getting on in ward three?" asked the caller.

"Paddy Murphy," repeated the matron consulting her list. "Oh yes. He had his operation last night. It was a complete success and he will probably go home in two days. Who is this speaking?"

"It's Paddy Murphy in ward three. They tell you nothing in here."

*   *   *

SURGEON to his assistant as he begins an operation: "How's that for openers?"

*   *   *

OLD Jock was sitting up in bed when the matron approached him. "I want you to pass a urine specimen in that bottle on the trolley at the foot of your bed."

"What, from here?" said Jock.

*   *   *

TWO Indian doctors were having an animated discussion. "I say it's spelt W-H-O-O-M," said one. "No, it is W-H-O-M-B," said the other. A nurse passing by said "Excuse me, you are both wrong. It is spelt W-O-M-B."

"Thanks nurse," said one, "but we prefer to settle this argument ourselves, besides, we don't think you are in a position to describe the sound of an elephant passing wind under water."

*   *   *

TWO nurses were climbing back into the dormitory window, trying to sneak in as quietly as possible when one said, "This makes me feel like a burglar."

"Me too," said the other, "but where would we find two burglars at this time of night?"

## HOTELS
See PUBS

"DO you want the porter to call you in the morning, sir?"

"No. I always wake promptly at seven."

"In that case, would you mind waking the porter?"

* * *

AN American business tycoon had just arrived at his Australian hotel. "I am a man of few words," he said to the porter. "If I beckon with my finger that means come."

"I'm a man of few words myself," said the porter. "If I shakes me head that means I aint coming."

* * *

THEY spent their honeymoon in two hotels. He didn't like the manager in the first place, and in the second place the first place was too expensive.

* * *

THE drunk in the lobby declared he could fight anybody in the entire hotel.

The elevator man took him up.

* * *

LIKE most travel writers he headed for the bar first before checking in at the hotel's reception desk. After his second drink he got the eye from a blonde drinking alone. Quick off the mark he bought her a drink and started to chat. By the third whisky he suggested going up to his room. "Look, I haven't booked in yet, so why don't I register us as man and wife?"

The blonde saw the logic in this and they had a wonderful night together.

Next morning when the writer was checking out he was presented with a bill for $1500. "Hey, I was only here one night," he protested.

"Yes," said the clerk, "but your wife has been here for a week!"

* * *

ON his first holiday to the Gold Coast the oldtimer from the bush settled at the bar and ordered a beer. The barman served him and asked for $5.

"Blimey, a fiver for one beer?"

The barman explained that the charge included the piped music, the lush drapes on the wall and the magnificent view... etc.

Next day the oldtimer fronted the bar for his usual beer and once again protested at the exorbitant price.

The barman began to repeat his routine about the carpets, the music, the view ...

"Hang on," said the oldtimer. "I paid for them yesterday."

*     *     *

WHEN Fred was given the bill for an overnight stay in a French hotel he thought the $500 charge was a tad excessive and raised it with the manager.

"If you remember Sir," said the manager, "you and your wife had a room with a bath."

"But we didn't take a bath," complained Fred.

"I can't help zat," said the manager. "Eet was there if you wanted it."

Fred thought about this for a moment then scribbled some words on a piece of paper and slapped it down on the counter with a $100 note.

"What eez this?" asked the manager.

Fred explained that the $100 was fair tarif for the room and that the piece of paper was an account for $400 to the manager for sleeping with Fred's wife.

"But I didn't sleep with your wife," protested the manager.

"I can't help that," said Fred, "She was there if you wanted her."

*     *     *

"DID you sleep well, sir?"

"No. There was a gorgeous blonde banging on my door for most of the night. I finally had to get up and let her out."

*     *     *

THE guest approached the hotel porter. "I know it is four in the morning, but could you let me have a glass of whisky?"

"What on earth would you be wanting with whisky at this hour?" said the porter.

"Soda?"

*    *    *

IN a very respectable hotel the old bloke in charge of the cloak room had been in the job for years and never bothered to give a ticket when coats were handed over to him.

A reporter got interested in him and asked the manager how the old geezer kept track of so many coats without dockets.

"Oh, don't worry about old Ted. He's been doing the job for years. Never had a complaint," said the manager.

The reporter decided to put him to the test on the next busy Saturday night. When leaving he asked for his coat and when he received one said, "How do you know if this is my coat?"

"I don't," replied Ted.

"Then why did you give it to me?" said the reporter with a hint of triumph.

"Because that's the coat you gave to me, sir," said Ted.

*    *    *

THE hotel manager told the elderly couple that the only room available was the bridal suite.

"But we've been married for forty years," grumbled the husband. "What the heck do I want with the bridal suite."

The manager smiled and answered, "Well, if I gave you the ballroom you wouldn't have to dance all night, would you?"

*    *    *

AT a party a man introduced himself, "Hello, my name is John Smith."

The other replied: "Please don't talk shop. I'm the night clerk at the motel."

*    *    *

THE manager of a large chain of hotels liked to travel incognito to check on the staff. After he booked in he seated himself in the dining room and when the waiter handed him the menu he tossed it aside. "Just bring me a good dinner," he ordered.

He did this at every meal during his stay and at the end of the week revealed his identity to the waiter and expressed himself highly satisfied with the food and service.

"That's alright mate," said the waiter. Then leaning over the table he added quietly, "When you or any of your mates who can't read come to town, tell 'em to stay here and ask for 'Arry."

\*       \*       \*

FRED booked into a small country hotel and the proprietor's pretty daughter showed him to his room. He asked what the rates were.

"Fifty dollars," she said.

"That's great. I'll pay fifty dollars with pleasure."

"With pleasure it will be another twenty-five," she said.

\*       \*       \*

"YOU won't find a single flea in this hotel, madam."

"That's what I'm afraid of," she replied. "Probably all married with children."

\*       \*       \*

OVER dinner one evening Fred turned to a fellow diner and said, "They call this the Palms Hotel. I've been here three days and haven't seen a palm within miles."

"Wait until you are leaving, when the staff line up at the door," said his new friend.

\*       \*       \*

THE rodeo at the Outback Hotel had put a strain on accommodation, but the American tourist was at least glad to know they had reserved his room.

"But we're short of staff," said the proprietor. "Do you mind making your own bed?"

"Not at all," said the Yank.

And he was given a hammer, a saw and some timber.

# HUSBANDS
See WIVES

WOMEN's faults are many
   Men have only two
   Everything they say
   And everything they do!

*       *       *

SOME husbands come in handy round the house. Others come in unexpectedly.

*       *       *

THE smart husband thinks twice before saying nothing.

*       *       *

EVERY married man knows that the most perfect husband in the world belongs to the woman next door.

*       *       *

"A HUSBAND like yours is hard to find."
   "He still is."

*       *       *

"IF you were my husband I would give you poison."
   "If I was your husband I'd take it."

*       *       *

THE first time Ethel saw her husband he was outside a junk shop picking his teeth. Then he went in and bought them.

*       *       *

HUSBANDS regard themselves as the head of the household, and pedestrians know they have right of way. Both are safe until they try to prove it.

*       *       *

FRED described the bump on his head as a glancing blow.
   "The wife caught me glancing at a blonde," he said.

*       *       *

IT was tough luck for Ernie. He missed two maintenance payments last month and his wife repossessed him.

THE couple were on their way to a cocktail party.

"Now listen," she said, "if it's a dull party, then leave it that way."

* * *

"I DON'T think I look 35, do you?" she asked her husband.

"No, I don't," he said, "but you used to."

* * *

FRED told his mate at the bar, "I can't stay long. My wife thinks I'm in the bath."

* * *

THE drinker turned to Fred and said: "You are a typical hen-pecked weak-spined husband."

Fred replied, "You wouldn't have the guts to say that if my missus was here."

* * *

MEN have two reasons for staying at the pub all night. Either they've got no wives to go home to; or they have.

* * *

"ARE you married, Albert?"

"No, I was hit by a car."

* * *

"I WILL say this for Madge," said the henpecked husband. "Spending money is her only extravagance."

* * *

THE two women met in the supermarket. "I thought I'd lost 560 kgms of ugly fat. Then Fred came home again."

* * *

"HOW long have you been wearing that corset, Fred?"

"Ever since the wife found it in the car," he replied.

* * *

FRED was hammering away at some woodwork in his back yard when his mate Charlie looked over the fence. "Aren't you coming to work today?" he asked.

Fred said no. He had to stay home and mind his wife who was sick with a sore throat and the flu.

Hearing a strange gurgling noise coming from the house Charlie asked: "Is that her coughing?"

"Don't be stupid," said Fred, "she'd never fit into this. She's 17 stone. This is a cage for the cocky!"

\* \* \*

TWO husbands leaning on the bar. "Did you give your wife a lecture on economy like I told you?"

"Yes, I certainly did."

"And what was the result?"

"I've got to give up smoking."

\* \* \*

THE henpecked husband reached the end of his tether. "Money, Money, Money. Those are the only three things you are interested in."

\* \* \*

ANOTHER henpecked husband decided to revolt. "I'm fed up. I'm leaving you and going to join the Foreign Legion."

"Well, don't come back traipsing sand through the house," she said.

\* \* \*

GIVE a husband enough rope, and he'll skip.

\* \* \*

FUNNY how a wife can spot a blonde hair on a chap's coat, yet miss the garage doors.

\* \* \*

"TODAY is the wife's birthday."

"What are your getting for her?"

"What are you offering?"

\* \* \*

HE said he hasn't spoken to his missus for a month. "I've been unable to interrupt her," he said.

\* \* \*

"MY Missus always has her own way. Why, she even writes her diary a month ahead."

HE had a problem about the future. He was getting married in a month and he still had not found her a job.

*     *     *

THEY were leaning on the bar. "I can't understand it," said one. "The wife asks for twenty dollars every Monday, says she needs another twenty by Tuesday. Has her hand out for another twenty on Wednesday. Every week it is the same."

"What does she do with all that money," said his mate.

"I don't know. I never give her any."

*     *     *

HE used to sit on the front door step and whistle at every young woman that went by. "Why do you let him get away with that?" asked the woman next door.

"It's no problem," said his wife. "I've seen dogs chase cars, but they can't drive."

*     *     *

ALBERT had a long session at the pub. He arrived home late and was ready for trouble.

"Is that you, Albert?" called his wife as he stumbled up the stairs.

"It had flamin' well better be," replied Albert.

*     *     *

A RATHER demanding wife returning home after a long trip abroad was met at the airport by her husband. Her first question was: "How's the cat?"

"Dead," replied the husband.

His wife erupted angrily. "What a way to break the news," she said. "Why couldn't you tell me something like, well, the cat was playing on the roof, say, and it slipped off and injured itself, and although you took it to the vet it eventually passed away quietly. Why not break the news that way and not be so brutal about it. Mother always said you were brutal. By the way, how is mother?"

"Well," said her husband slowly. "She was playing on the roof …"

# HYPOCHONDRIACS

THE hypochondriac had only four words on his tomb stone: "See, I told you!"

* * *

SHE visited the doctor for the fifth time that week: "It's awful," she said. "The pain comes every 20 minutes and lasts for an hour."

* * *

THEY were the perfect pair. She was a hypochondriac, and he was a pill.

* * *

MRS Kelly rang the doctor. "Will you come round please. My husband says he is ill."

But the doctor replies, "Mrs Kelly, I'm not coming round again. He only things he is ill."

Next day Mrs Kelly rings again. "What is it this time," says the doctor tersely. "Does your husband think he is ill again?"

"Worse," she said. "He thinks he's dead."

# I

## INDIANS

GENERAL Custer's last words: "I can't make these Indians out. Just a minute ago they were singing and dancing!"

*　　*　　*

THE Lone Ranger and Tonto had been inseparable. Suddenly their path was blocked by a Navajo war party. To the left was a hundred Apache. To the right an equal number of Souix. And behind them they heard the blood-curdling cry of the dreaded Blackfeet.

"Looks like we're done for, Tonto."

"What d'yer mean, 'we', paleface?"

*　　*　　*

AN Australian travel writer touring Canada was checking out of the Spokane Hilton and as he paid his bill said to the manager, "By the way, what's with the Indian chief sitting in the lobby. He has been there ever since I arrived?"

"Oh that's Big Chief Forget-me-Not," said the manager. "The hotel is built on an Indian reservation and part of the agreement is to allow the chief free use of the premises for the rest of his life. He is known as Big Chief Forget-me-Not because of his phenomenal memory. He is 92 and can remember the slightest detail of his life."

202

The travel writer took this in and as he was waiting for his cab decided to put the chief's memory to the test.

"What did you have for breakfast on your 21st birthday?" said the Aussie.

"Eggs," was the instant reply, and indeed the Aussie was impressed.

He went off on his travel writing itinerary, right across to the east coast and on his return to the Spokane Hilton six months later was surprised to see the Indian chief still sitting in the lobby whittling away on a stick.

"How", said the Aussie.

"Scrambled," said the chief.

*　　*　　*

A RED Indian wishing to convert to Judaism was told by the rabbi that he would have to be circumcised.

"How much?" he asked.

"$100," replied the rabbi.

"Too much," said the Indian and he began to shop around.

Another rabbi offered $90.

"Too much," said the Indian.

Finally the medicine man said he would do it for nothing and wielded his tomahawk with one swift stroke.

The Indian looked at the result. "Too much," he said.

## INFIDELITY
See WARDROBES

THERE was an almighty row when Fred discovered his best friend, Bert, had been having an affair with his wife.

"But you mustn't blame her," said Bert. "It is all my fault. I was the one who answered her advert in the Truth."

*　　*　　*

OF course high fidelity is a drunk who always goes home to his wife.

A LAWYER and his wife were out walking when a blonde on the other side of the street waved and blew him a kiss. The wife demanded to know who she was.

"Oh, I just met her recently. Professionally of course," he said.

"Whose profession, yours or hers?" said the wife.

\* \* \*

WITH good reason she was always suspicious of her husband's philanderings and each night there would be a row when she would discover a blonde or a brunette hair on his lapel.

One night she was really puzzled as she studied his coat for ten minutes.

"Okay, who's this bald-headed tart you are flirting with now," she said.

\* \* \*

THE parish priest made his way to the front door of the farmhouse through a swarm of fighting kids. He knocked on the door repeatedly but there was no answer. He moved along to the bedroom window, looked in and was shocked to see them in a passionate embrace on the bed.

The priest made a discreet retreat through the fighting kids and went to the next property where the farmer met him at the gate.

The priest said: "Your neighbour sure likes making babies."

"He sure does," said the farmer. "His wife is in hospital having her tenth, and my wife is over there helping him out."

\* \* \*

THE lovers were entwined in a passionate embrace on the loungeroom floor when suddenly a car was heard coming up the driveway. "Quick!" the woman shrieked. "That will be my husband. He's a policeman and he's twice as big as you."

Her companion hopped about frantically and said, "Where's the back door?"

"We haven't got one," she replied.

"Well, tell me quickly," he said, "where would you like one?"

* * *

A RATHER fat woman was puffing away in the aerobics class with a worried look on her face.

"What's up?" said the instructor.

"I work out here every night because my husband says he wants to make love to a woman with a trim figure," she said, "and I'm just beginning to figure out what he means."

* * *

SHE had her suspicions about her husband, Fred, so when they had an invitation to a fancy dress party at the Smithson's she conceived a plan to catch him.

When Fred was dressed in his gorilla suit ready to leave she feigned a headache, said she would stay home, but insisted Fred should go on without her.

Later she donned her own disguise and arrived at the party to see him flirting with every floosie at the party.

In her own masked outfit she approached him, whispered a seductive phrase in his ear and was surprised at the immediate response. He rushed her outside and made passionate love to her. She resisted declaring who she was in an effort to get all the evidence possible.

Just before the unmasking at midnight she left the party and drove home, and next morning was all set to confront Fred with his infidelity.

"How was it at the Smithson's?" she asked at breakfast.

"Dullsville. Boring without you, darling," he said. "When I arrived I saw Ben and the Murphy brothers without partners so we went upstairs and played poker. I lent my gorilla suit to Harry Forbes, and he said he had a wow of a time."

# INSECTS

THE fly walked almost to the top of the window pane, then had to go back. He left his specs behind.

*    *    *

THE last thing to go through a grasshopper's mind, as it slams into a sports car's radiator grill at 100-kmh, is its bum.

*    *    *

"NO! no!" cried the lady centipede, crossing her legs, "A thousand times no!"

*    *    *

LITTLE Johnny was watching two lanky-legged spiders.

"Hey, Dad," he said. "Is there such a thing as a Mummy Long-legs?"

"No, Son."

"I thought so," said the boy slamming his fist on the spiders. "Bloody queers."

*    *    *

A SINGLE gnat lays per day
  A hundred thousand eggs, they say
  It makes one gasp
  And wonder, too
  Just what a married one would do.


# INSURANCE

THIS policy guarantees absolute security in the event of any fatal accident.

*    *    *

WHEN Fred's house burned down he went off to the insurance company and demanded his compensation money. But he was soon to learn that the company didn't operate that way.

"It is our policy to replace your house and anything else you lost exactly in the same style and condition," said the manager.

"Hell," said Fred. "In that case I would like to cancel the policy I took out on my mother-in-law."

* * *

SITTING beside her old husband in his hospital bed she had to crane forward to listen to him.

"I am worried about the cost of this treatment," he wheezed. His voice was hardly a whisper: "How will we ever pay the bills for the specialists, the hospital, the operations," he wheezed.

"Don't worry about it," said his wife. "It's all taken care of. I have had a talk with the hospital and they say I can pay as soon as I've collected your insurance!"

* * *

THE pub was sending him bankrupt so Fred decided to burn it down and collect the insurance. But not without a master plan.

After he set it ablaze he called the police and told them a gorilla had done it.

"Would you be able to recognise him again?" asked the cop.

"It would be difficult," said Fred. "He was wearing a mask!"

* * *

THE insurance company noted with suspicion that Fred's premises were burnt down the very day he took out the insurance policy. Suspecting fraud the company sent him the following message: "Sir. You took out a policy with us at 11-am, and the fire didn't break out until five the same evening. Will you please explain the delay?"

* * *

ROZENBROCK and Solzberg met on a cruise ship, got to talking and found that they were both retired from the rag trade.

"Yes," said Rozenbrock, "when I got the settlement from the insurance company after the fire, me and Rachel decided to retire."

"Same here," said Solzberg. "The floods wiped us out, but the insurance company settled quickly."

Rozenbrock looked puzzled. "Tell me, Solzberg," he whispered, "how do you start a flood?"

* * *

HE left the court in his wheelchair, and a compensation payment for half a million dollars. But the insurance detectives followed him down the street. "You won't get away with this fraud," said one. "We will be watching you for the rest of your life," said another.

"No worries," he replied. "You can watch all you like. You can watch me go on my world trip and you can watch me go to Lourdes and you can watch, with your own eyes, one hell of a miracle."

# INVENTIONS

ONE of the greatest inventors was Pat Pending. He sure came up with a lot of gadgets, but the man who invented the convertible sofa should have been one of the richest men in the world. Millions have been made on it.

* * *

DID you know Alexander Graham Bell invented TWO telephones?

* * *

HE discovered a cure for amnesia, but forgot what it was.

* * *

AN Israeli chemist invented a new laxative and patented the brand name: 'Let My People Go.'

* * *

IT was the Irish who invented the helicopter ejection seat and the solar-powered torch while the Irish medical team developed the appendix transplant.

* * *

MY Old Dad was an inventor and among his accomplishments were:

Water-proof tea bags. Peddle wheelchairs. Parachutes which open on impact. L-shaped mobile homes.

The one-piece jigsaw puzzle.

An inflatable dartboard for campers.

An index for a dictionary.

Beer glasses with square bases that don't leave rings on the bar or tables.

\* \* \*

HE invented a marvellous appliance for speeding up production in factories. He called it a whip.

## IRISH

THE reason there are so many Irish jokes is because the Irish have a quaint way with words. Like the Irish patient who hobbled into the surgery's waiting room: "I hope to God the doctor finds something wrong with me because I'd hate to feel like this if I was well."

\* \* \*

ANOTHER example of Irish logic: "Hey Paddy, here's the five dollars I borrowed last week."

"Thanks, Mick, I had forgotten all about it."

"Then why the bloody hell didn't yer say so?"

\* \* \*

THE O'Flaherty family were small. They were all small. Even the smallest was no bigger than the rest, and what's more they never went anywhere alone unless they were together.

\* \* \*

MURPHY dropped dead the day he arrived back from a vacation in the tropics. He was laid out in the coffin for friends and neighbours to pay their last respects.

"He's got a great tan," mused Mrs Doolan from next door. "The holiday did him the world of good."

"And he looks so calm and serene," said Mrs McGinty.

"That's because he died in his sleep," explained Mrs

Murphy, "and he doesn't know he's dead yet. But when he wakes up and finds out, the shock will kill him."

* * *

THERE was a power failure in a Dublin department store. Thousands of shoppers were stranded on the escalators for hours.

* * *

"YOUR glass is empty O'Flaherty, will you be having another?"

"And why would I be wanting two empty glasses?" replied O'Flaherty.

* * *

THEY were two of the IRA's top men and the lay in ambush for the Chief Provost of the Ulster Brigade. "Okay," says Paddy, "let's go through the schedule once more.

"At 4.45 he leaves his office. At 4.50 his car leaves police headquarters with an escort through peak hour traffic. At 5 pm the first of his bodyguard turn this corner and we keep low and let them pass. At 5.10 the provost himself comes by in his disguised car and we let him have it. Is that all clear?"

"Clear as a bell," says Shaun looking at his watch. "But it is 5.15 now. I hope nothing terrible has happened to him."

* * *

MURPHY arrived home late from the pub, well oiled and ready for trouble. As he stumbled up the stairs his wife called out: "Is that you, Murphy?"

"Be Crikey it darned well better be!"

* * *

McTAVISH knew he was in an Irish pub, but nevertheless, when he had a few under his belt it always made him feel boisterous.

"Down with the Pope," he roared for his fifth toast. And Paddy O'Reilly stepped forward and flattened him.

When he came to his friends asked McTavish, "Didn't ya know O'Reilly was a Catholic?"

"Of course I did," he said. "But why didn't somebody tell me the Pope was?"

* * *

TWO tough union men were working on a building site when Murphy fell from the second floor scaffolding.

"Are ya dead?" cried Gallagher calling from above.

"To be sure I am," replied Murphy.

"You are such a liar Murphy that I don't know whether to believe you or not," called Gallagher.

"That proves I'm dead," said Murphy's voice from the rubble below, "because if I was alive you wouldn't be game to call me a liar!"

* * *

PADDY was coming through customs at the airport carrying a large bottle.

"What have you there?" asked the suspicious officer.

"'Tis Lourdes holy water. I am bringing it home with me," said Paddy.

The officer took the bottle and tried some. "Why, it's Irish whisky," he spluttered.

"Lord bless me," said Paddy. "Another bloomin' miracle."

* * *

PADDY had just become the proud father of twins and he was asked if they were identical.

"The boy is but the girl's not," he said.

* * *

YOUNG Teresa came home and related the awesome news to her parents. She was pregnant.

"How do you know it's yours?" asked her dad.

* * *

"TERESA has just had twins," roared Murphy angrily. "Wait till I get my hands on the other fellow."

* * *

PADDY: "Hey Shaun, what's Mick's surname?"

Shaun: "Mick who?"

ON his way home one night Paddy dropped in to the pub. The barman poured him a beer and asked if he wanted to be in a raffle.

"What's it for?" asked Paddy.

"It's for a poor widow with 13 kids," said the barman.

Paddy shook his head. "No good to me. I'd never be able to keep them."

\* \* \*

DUBLIN'S contestant in the international quiz was waiting for his first question.

"First, what's your name and occupation?" the compere asked.

"Pass," came the reply.

\* \* \*

PADDY had been stranded on the deserted island for two years. Then one afternoon a lifeboat drifted close enough for him to swim to it and drag it to the beach, where he knocked it to bits and made himself a raft.

\* \* \*

SHAMUS asked Paddy how he got his black eye.

"You'd never believe it," said Paddy, "but I got it in church."

He said he had been sitting behind a fat lady and when they all stood for a hymn he noticed her dress was creased into the cheeks of her bum.

"All I did was lean forward and pull it out and she turned round an hit me," said Paddy.

It was a week later and Shamus was surprised to see Paddy had another black eye. "I got it in church," he began to explain.

He said he found himself behind the same fat woman and when they stood for the hymn her dress was once again creased into the cheeks of her bum.

"My little nephew reached forward and pulled it out. But I knew she didn't like that, so I leaned over and tucked it back!"

PADDY and Shamus were hitch-hiking.

"It's best if we split up," said Paddy. "I will meet you in the next city under the town hall clock."

Later that night Shamus was waiting at the appointed place when Paddy drove up in a swank car.

"Where the hell did you get that?"

Paddy explained that he had just walked a little way when a beautiful woman picked him up. She drove to the wood, got out and took all her clothes off.

"She said I could have anything I wanted, so I took the car," said Paddy.

"Good choice too," said Shamus. "You'd look ridiculous in her clothes."

\*　　\*　　\*

PADDY: "If you can guess how many chooks I have in this bag you can have both of them."

"Three?" suggested Shaun.

\*　　\*　　\*

PADDY was intent on saving the man on the edge of the cliff. "Don't jump," he said. "Think of your wife and kids."

"I have no wife and I have no kids," replied the man.

"Then think of your family."

"I have no family."

"Then think of St Patrick."

"Who is St Patrick?" said the man.

"Jump ya bastard," said Paddy.


## INSULTS

"CAN I have this dance?"

"Sure, if you can find someone to dance with."

\*　　\*　　\*

IF there is ever a price on your head, take it.

HE told her he was a self-made man.

She said she would accept that as an apology.

\* \* \*

YOU are the kind of person Dr Spooner would have called a shining wit.

\* \* \*

"I WROTE that song myself," he announced.

"It's nice of you to take the blame," they replied.

\* \* \*

SHE said their neighbour must have taken offence at something as she hadn't been over for days.

"Be sure to find out what it was," he said, "and we'll try it on her again."

\* \* \*

THE barmaid complained that it was only an hour to closing time and two improper suggestions had been made to her. She was quite upset about it. Normally she has nine or ten.

\* \* \*

ONE night Fred took his mother-in-law to the pub and a stranger, a little the worse for wear, leaned over and offered her a double gin and tonic. Fred said she was affronted, but she managed to swallow the insult.

\* \* \*

"I WOULD like to buy my girlfriend a ring but I don't know what she'd like."

"Does she like you?"

"Of course."

"Then she'd like anything."

\* \* \*

"THAT'S a nice suit you are wearing. I wonder if the style will ever come back?"

\* \* \*

"I WENT by your place yesterday."

"Thanks!"

AN Englishman boarded a train with a large shaggy dog and sat opposite an Irishman. Paddy looked at the dog awhile then said, "And what type of dog would that be?"

The surly Englishman replied: "It's a cross between an ape and an Irishman."

Paddy was quick with his reply: "You mean its related to both of us!"

*     *     *

BERT had just been fired and told his boss: "You are nothing but a miserable rogue and blackguard, and I've got a darned mind to tell you so."

*     *     *

IT was in the outer at the cricket match when Fred returned with two beers only to find his mate, Bert, laying flat on his back. Worse, he was dismayed to find Bert's face swollen with bruises, a cut lip and a black eye.

"Which rotten so-and-so did it?" asked Fred, all fired up. "Can you describe him?"

"That's exactly what I was doing when the whacker hit me," said Bert.

*     *     *

HE: "I've got an idea"

She: "Beginner's luck."

He: "Are you trying to make a monkey out of me?"

She: "No. Why should I take the credit?"

He: "So this is a battle of wits between us?"

She: "No. I never pick on a man that's unarmed."

He: "I manage to keep my head above water."

She: "That's because wood floats."

He: "I won't stand these insults. I've gots lots of backbone."

She: "Yes, but the bone is all at the top."

He: "Intelligence reigns supreme in our family."

She: "Well, you must have been born during a dry spell."

He: "I'm nobody's fool."
She: "Perhaps you can get someone to adopt you."
He: "My mother thinks I'm a great wit."
She: "She's half right."
He: "You are going to drive me out of my mind."
She: "That's not a drive, it's a putt."

# J

## JAIL

THE prisoner was banging on the bars making a heck of the racket. "What do yer want?" said the warder.

"I want to know the time," said the prisoner.

"It's 1992," said the warder.

* * *

JOE was in for the term of his natural. He was given the job of organising the social events, because he was usually the lifer of the party.

* * *

IN prisoner of war camps it is tougher. One day the commandant marshalled all the inmates together and announced he had good news.

"For the first time in five years we are changing the sheets," he said. "Those in Hut A will change them with those in Hut B."

* * *

AFTER years in a high security jail Pat devised a way of communicating with his mate Mick. It was an ingenious ploy using a secret code to tap out messages on pipes.

However the scheme was eventually thwarted when they were transferred to separate cells.

# JEEVES

JEEVES said as a hostess, Lady Entwhistle was hopeless. She couldn't even entertain a doubt.

*     *     *

THE lady of the manor was becoming increasingly alarmed at Jeeves' practice of walking in to her bedroom without knocking. Finally she took him to task.

"It could be very embarrassing if I was in a state of undress," she admonished.

"No need to worry about that, m'lady," said Jeeves. "I always take a peek through the keyhole first!"

*     *     *

SHE called Jeeves into her bedroom. "Jeeves, please unzip my dress." With a great deal of embarrassment he did so.

"Now Jeeves," she said. "Take off my stockings." Jeeves was now in a sweat.

"And now take off my underwear … and if I ever catch you wearing them again you will be instantly dismissed."

*     *     *

JEEVES was interviewing a prospective maid for the household and asked the girl for her references.

She began rumaging around in her handbag. "I am afraid I've lost my reference from the Dorchester," she said, "but I've got these two spoons with the Dorchester crest to prove I worked there."

*     *     *

WHEN the squire announced that he was to get married Jeeves was alarmed about his future at the manor. And although the squire assured him that his position was safe, Jeeves still worried while they were away on their honeymoon.

"Jeeves, how many times do I have to tell you it's business as usual," said the squire on his return.

Sure enough, next morning, the squire was up at dawn for his breakfast, promptly at 6-30 his horse was ready, and at seven Jeeves went into the bedroom slapped the bride on the bottom and said: "Okay, back to the village my lass!"

\* \* \*

JEEVES was called by Lord Ponsonby. "Jeeves, could you ride down to the village and fetch a bottle of whisky, a box of cigars and a few ounces of snuff. That free-loading bishop will be calling in this afternoon."

Jeeves mounted his trusty bicycle and was off on his errand. It was not until the return trip and he had pedalled up the long hill to the manor gates that he realised he had forgotten the snuff.

What to do? It was too hot and too far to ride back down to the village. By chance the problem was solved, right there on the nature strip was a barker's nest with three of those white eggs dogs leave in neat little clumps. When dried in the sun and ground back to powder it looks for all the world like snuff.

Did he dare take the chance?

Jeeves quickly bent down, snatched up three portions and put them in his pocket.

"Did you get the whisky, Jeeves?"

"Yes, M'lord."

"And the cigars, and the snuff?"

"Yes M'lord," said Jeeves as he prepared to leave the room.

"I say, Jeeves," said Lord Ponsonby sniffing the air. "You didn't by any chance stand in something down in the village?"

"No M'lord."

The bishop arrived soon after and headed for the Scotch. "You don't mind if I have a drink, Ponsonby old boy?"

"Not at all, Bishop, go for your life," but Ponsonby was pre-occupied with the pervading odour.

"I say bishop, can you smell dog's doings in here?"

"Can't say as I can dear boy," said the bishop. "I happen to have a heavy head cold."

"In that case, take a pinch of snuff," said Ponsonby.

The bishop responded by taking two pinches and sniffing it up both nostrils.

"Gracious me," he said. "You always get the best snuff. That's cleared my head completely and I can smell that dog's stuff now!"

*　　*　　*

THE lady of the manor decided to dismiss the parlour maid and dressed her down with some sarcastic remarks about her unsatisfactory service as a cook and general housekeeper.

But the fiery parlour maid took the opportunity for a parting shot. "Your husband happens to think I am a better cook and a better housekeeper than you are," she retorted. "And what's more I am a damn sight better in bed than you are."

"Oh, and my husband told you that too?"

"No, Jeeves told me that!"

*　　*　　*

LADY Fontigue-Smythe took more than the usual care of her staff. So when her butler was hurt in an accident she was quick to attend the hospital.

"Sorry," said the nurse. "No visitors except family. Are you his wife?"

"Indeed not," said her ladyship. "I'm his mistress."

*　　*　　*

HIGH society couple were making love.

She: "Darling, do poor people do this?"

He: "I believe so, my sweet."

She: "It's much too good for them, don't you think?"

*　　*　　*

THE squire of the manor awoke with a raging erection one morning and immediately called his valet.

220

"Congratulations sir," said Jeeves. "Shall I awaken madam?"

"No, Jeeves. Get me my baggy shorts and we'll smuggle this one down to the village."

# JEWISH

PREP school son was studying his arithmetic and asked for help from his dad. "What's two and two, Dad?"

"Depends, son. Are we buying or selling?"

★　　★　　★

"PAPPA," said the lad. "What's Yiddish for a hundred per cent?"

"Izzy, my son, a hundred per cent is Yiddish."

★　　★　　★

OLD Abraham Cohen is knocked down by a tram and is laid gently on the median strip. A lady gets a pillow from her car and places it under his head.

"Are you comfortable?" she asks.

"Ah well," he says, "I make a living."

★　　★　　★

A JEWISH mother gave her son two ties for his birthday, a striped one and a spotted one. Next day she saw him wearing the striped one.

"So what's the matter with the spotted one? You don't like it?"

★　　★　　★

THE reporter was interviewing the socialite who had organised the charity ball and couldn't take his eyes off a massive diamond on her left hand.

"Oh, that," she said. "It's the famous Guggenheimer diamond."

The reporter was dazzled by it.

"Unfortunately it has a curse attached to it," said the socialite.

"A curse?" gasped the reporter. "What curse?"

"Mr Guggenheimer," she said.

* * *

ABRAHAM wandered into Sam's pawnshop and placed a leather coat on the counter. "How much will you give me for this jacket?"

Sam checked it over. "$20, and that's the best."

"But that jacket is worth $100."

Sam was adamant. "$20 or nothing."

"Are you sure that's all it's worth?" pressed Abe.

"Positive."

"Okay," said Abe. "Here's your $20. The jacket was hanging in your doorway and I was wondering how much it was worth."

* * *

IN a small school in Dublin the teacher told the class she would give 50 pence to whoever could name the holiest man in history.

Only one hand went up, that of little Izzy O'Cohen. "That would be St Patrick, Miss," he said.

Teacher handed over the money and said to Izzy, "How come the only boy to know the answer was Jewish?"

To which Izzy replied: "In my heart of hearts I know it was Moses, but business is business."

* * *

THE aircraft was flying into Honolulu when the man in the window seat spoke to his fellow passenger for the first time.

"How do you pronounce it, Hawaii or HaVaii?"

"HaVaii." said the passenger.

"Thanks."

"You're Velcome."

* * *

MRS Goldberg was heartbroken when young Moishe told her he was getting married to Rosie McEvoy.

"Oh, why are you not marrying a lovely Jewish girl? Why are you marrying a shikseh?"

"Jewish girls are terrible, Momma," said Moishe, "they grow fat and get varicose veins."

"So do all the shiksehs," cried his mother.

"Yes, but who cares about shiksehs?" said Moishe.

* * *

MRS Plotkin was waiting for an appointment with Dr Goldstein and the only other person in the waiting room was a young businessman reading the Financial Review.

"Excuse me young man," she said. "Are you Jewish?"

"No I'm not," he replied.

A little later she repeated the question: "Are you sure you are not Jewish?"

"Definitely not," he said without looking up from his newspaper.

But she kept her eyes on him, and a little later: "Are you really certain you are not Jewish?"

The young man threw his paper aside. "Okay," he said in utter exasperation, "I am Jewish."

Another five minutes went by. "That's funny," she said. "You don't look Jewish."

* * *

A JEWISH man went into Izzy's corner shop and asked for some ice-cream.

"We don't sell ice-cream to Jews," said Izzy.

"But you are Jewish yourself. This is disgraceful."

"Have you tasted our ice-cream?" said Izzy.

* * *

IZZY entered the room all agitated.

"There is a new Nazi party and their manifesto states they intend to kill a million Jews and five postmen."

"Why five postmen?" somebody asked.

"That's typical," cried Izzy in despair. "Nobody ever cares about the Jews."

* * *

IZZY and Rachel went to Switzerland for a holiday and

223

while in the mountains Izzy decided to try his hand at skiing. Down the slope he went and disappeared with a scream over a crevasse. When he didn't return that night a Red Cross rescue team was despatched to the area.

They searched all night and most of the next day until they discovered some tracks.

"Mr Guggenheim, Mr Guggenheim," they kept shouting. "It's the Red Cross."

And finally a feeble voice was heard in reply. "I've given already."

\*　　\*　　\*

IT was interval at the opera when Mrs Sternberg rose from her seat and called: "Is there a doctor in the house. Is there a doctor in the house?"

A man in a tuxedo pushed his way towards her. "I'm a doctor," he said.

"Oh doctor," she said, "Have I got just the loveliest daughter for you!"

\*　　\*　　\*

THE rabbi was hit by a bus and first on the spot was his old friend the Catholic priest who thought it was an excellent opportunity for conversion.

"Do you believe in the Father, Son and the Holy Ghost?" whispered the priest.

The rabbi opened his eyes. "I'm dying and he asks me riddles!"

\*　　\*　　\*

MOISHE was on his death bed and raised his head gently. "Moira, are you there?"

"Yes, Moishe, I am here."

A moment later Moishe said, "Izzi, are you there?"

His son, Izzi assured him he was by his side.

"Joshua," said the ailing Moishe, "Are you there?"

"I'm here poppa," said Joshua taking his hand.

Moishe raised himself on his elbow, "Then who the hell is minding the shop?"

GOLDSTEIN and Plotkin had spent a lifetime in competition climbing the social ladder, but Izzi Goldstein's barmitzvah was to be the calendar event of the year. It began at the London Ritz where guests were delivered in white Rolls Royces. The cabaret featured Liza Minelli and Barbara Striezand accompanied by the London Philharmonic Orchestra. The food was flown in from Vienna. Then the 100 guests were flown first class to Kenya where they set out on safari riding a team of elephants.

Two hours out from the village there was an elephant jam and the safari came to a halt.

"What's the hold-up?" demanded Mr Goldstein of the lead elephant boy.

A runner came back with the message: "There appears to be another barmizvah up ahead, by the name of Plotkin," he said.

\* \* \*

IT was with much wringing of the hands that Rachael discovered her husband, Hymie, had a mistress. Rachael, however, was not the sort to kill the goose that lays golden eggs, rather, she decided to find out what the mistress had that she didn't.

After long interrogation Hymie finally relented. "Well to tell you the truth, Rachael, you are too cold. When we make love you don't do anything. You just lay there, whereas she moans and groans with feeling."

"Is that all," thought Rachael. "Is that all there is to it?"

That night she dressed in her most alluring lingerie, slipped Hymie a shot of his favourite cognac and got him into bed.

Half way through the business she decided to give her most passionate moans and groans.

"Oh Hymie, darling," she began. "I've had the most terrible day. Our shares have dropped two points. The washing machine broke down. You don't give me enough housekeeping money..."

A TOURIST asked a Jewish gent where Plotkin's jewellery store was located.

The Jew was loaded with parcels and began handing them over until the tourist was holding them all.

When his arms were completely free he shrugged his shoulders: "How should I know?" he said.

\* \* \*

MOISHE is on his death-bed and and finally realises that he is about to cash in his worldly chips.

He calls for his wife, Beckie and says, "I want to leave the business to Izzi."

"No, not Izzi, he's too much of a gambler. Leave it to Abie," said his wife.

"Okay, the Rolls I will leave to Michael."

"Na, not Michael. He has smashed up three cars this year," said Beckie.

"Okay," said Moishe, "Then the summer house I will leave to Rachael and her husband."

"Na, don't let that schmuck get his hands on that property, leave it to Rachael herself."

Moishe raised himself on his elbow. "Listen Beckie. Tell me who's dying here?"

\* \* \*

MR GOLDBERG ran a clothing factory and had the reputation of wringing a full day's work from his employees. Abe had worked there for 30 years and had never been late... until today.

He limped in an hour late on crutches with his head bandaged. Mr Goldberg pointed to the clock and asked him to explain.

Abe said he was on his way to work when he stepped on his son's skate and crashed down seven flights of stairs. He tumbled out into a laneway only to be hit by a truck.

Goldberg listened to the story and then said: "And this takes an hour?"

THE eldest son took his father aside and said he had a problem. "I have had a bit of a fling Dad and unless I come up with a thousand dollars she will sue me."

Dad reluctantly wrote a cheque to save the family name.

A week later his second son approached him. "Father I have had a bit of a fling and unless I pay a thousand dollars she will sue me."

Dad coughed up another cheque to save the family name.

A week later his daughter approached him. "Father, I am ashamed to say that I have had a bit of a fling and…

Her father interrupted, and rubbing his hands said, "At last. We make a collection this time."

*   *   *

A JEWISH man boarded an overnight train and found himself sharing a sleeping compartment. As they were preparing for bed the Jew said: "Excuse me, I wonder if I could borrow a towel." The man lent him a towel.

"Excuse me," said the Jew again, "I appear to have left my pyjamas at home." The man lent him a tracksuit.

"Excuse me," said the Jew yet again, "Will you lend me your tooth brush?"

This time the man refused.

When he was met by his son at Central Station he was asked if he enjoyed the journey.

"No, I had to share with an anti-semite," he replied.

*   *   *

WHILE Abe Rosenberg waited at the Pearly Gates, St Peter thumbed through his lengthy personal file with an ever darkening frown. Finally, he said, "I am afraid you can't come in Mr Rosenberg."

"Look at this file," said St Peter, "it's nothing but good deeds, practically every day. The problem is Abe, we've got popes, archbishops and rabbis up here and if we let you in with this impecable record it would cause great embarrassment to the social order, not to mention putting a few pontifical noses out of joint. We can't have a mere tailor coming up here with a clean slate."

Old Rosenberg didn't protest. He was that type of bloke.

"Tell you what," said St Peter leaning forward on the counter in a confiding manner. "I'll zap you back to earth for the afternoon. You've got six hours to blot your copy book with a little sin. Do you think you could commit just one minor infringement? Then we could let you in without disturbing the heirarchy up here."

Rosenberg said he would do his best, and in a flash he found himself sitting in his lounge chair by the fireplace in his flat.

The mantelpiece clock chimed 12 noon and he began thinking. "What sin could I commit?"

He didn't smoke. He didn't like strong drink and no way would he risk a dollar on a horse.

He spent the first three hours racking his brain before he remembered the middle-aged spinster in the flat above, Miss Leonski. Yes, it was definitely a sin to make love to a woman to whom you were not married. And hadn't Miss Leonski gone out of her way at the last Body Corporate social function by deliberately sitting beside him and offering him tea and biscuits?

"That's what I'll do," he thought, and putting on his hat and coat he made his way up to her flat and knocked on the door.

"Oh, Mr Rosenberg," she said, "This is a surprise. Last thing I am hearing of you is that you are very sick, maybe dying. Will you come in for a glass of tea?"

Rosenberg sat there sipping tea, checking his watch and mentally noting that his life was fast ticking away while he was wasting time with small talk. By five o'clock he was beginning to panic as he realised there was no tactful way to dive into sin.

So suddenly he jumped up, grabbed Miss Leonski,

pushed her into the bedroom, ripped off her clothes and threw her onto the bed.

Then he sinned.

And while he was at it, he thought that if this was to be the only sin in his life he might as well give it all he had.

About five-to-six he began to feel life slipping away and he got out of bed to reach for his clothes. He turned to smile down at Miss Leonski and said: "Miss Leonski, I want to thank you. This afternoon you have shown me the way to heaven."

Miss Leonski looked up with a tired little smile. "Mr Rosenberg," she said. "You shouldn't mention it. Only me and the good Lord will know what a good deed you have done for me today!"

## JOBS

MOST young blokes stop looking for work the moment they get a job.

\* \* \*

MY father works as a blacksmith in a butcher shop. He shoos flies.

\* \* \*

MY uncle works as an espionage agent at the Mint.
  He's a Mint Spy.

\* \* \*

I ONCE worked at factory that made fire hydrants, but there was nowhere to park.

\* \* \*

"ARE you looking for work, my man?"
  "No. But I wouldn't mind a job."

\* \* \*

BOSS: "How many times have I reprimanded you about being late?"
  "I don't know. I thought you were keeping score."

BOSS: "You should have been here at nine o'clock."

"Why, what happened?"

\* \* \*

BOSS: "It distinctly says on the notice out front that we have no vacancies."

"Yes, I saw that. But take a chance. The bit of work I do would make no difference."

\* \* \*

THE boss told the applicant there was a vacancy for a responsible worker. "Are you responsible?"

"I'm the right bloke alright," said Fred. "Every job I've had, when anything happened, everybody said I was responsible!"

\* \* \*

HE started as an office boy on January 1. By February he was a salesman. Two months later he was regional manager. By mid year he was assistant general manager, and by November he was general manager.

On the first anniversary of his start with the firm he took over as chairman of the board. As he met the outgoing chairman at the office door he shook his hand and said, "Thanks Dad."

\* \* \*

THE teenager was complaining that his job was menial and boring. His father reminded him that digging holes was the only job you can get where you start at the top.

\* \* \*

HE saw the sign "Handyman Wanted" outside the convent and immediately applied. Mother Superior gave him a quick approval and asked if he could mend the fuse.

"Oh, I'm no good at electical matters," he said.

"Well, the front fence needs painting," said the nun.

"Oh, I'm no good at painting," he said.

"Well, we need a new door on the kitchen," she said.

"Oh, I'm no good at carpentry, sister," he said.

"Well tell me," she said. "What makes you think you are a handyman?"

"Oh, I just live around the next corner," he said.

\* \* \*

HIS new job is touting for a doctor. He goes around making people sick.

\* \* \*

FRED said if the foreman didn't take back what he said that morning he was leaving the job.

"What did he say?"

"He gave me a week's notice," said Fred.

\* \* \*

"WHAT are you working at now?"

"Nothing, but it's steady."

\* \* \*

THE young man was having a very loud argument with his girlfriend. "That's it. I am going to end it all," he cried and climbed on the the parapet of the bridge.

"I'm going to jump and I don't want anybody to save me," he said as he leapt into the water.

A young bloke who had witnessed this dived in after him.

"I told you I don't want to be saved," cried the young man.

"That's okay," said the other bloke, "I don't want to save you. Just tell me where you work."

\* \* \*

THE manager was giving the applicant the job.

"I think you will be very happy with us," he said. "We have a bonus scheme, a non-contributory pension scheme, special medical and hospital insurance schemes, free training and recreational facilities and a profit-sharing plan."

"Sounds wonderful," said the applicant, "and what are the wages?"

"Wages?" said the manager. "Hell, with all that we can't afford wages!"

THE man at the employment centre said there was indeed a job.

"What does it involve?" asked Fred.

"It is a photographer's assistant. Seems he wants a bikini-line shaver to ensure there are no pubic hairs showing when he photographs models in the latest swim gear."

"I'll take it," said Fred.

"Then you will have to go to Bachus Marsh."

"Why Bachus Marsh?"

"Because that's the end of the queue!"

\* \* \*

THEY were arguing about which was the oldest profession.

The surgeon rose to his feet and said: "When God created Eve he took a rib from Adam in the first surgical operation."

The architect made his claim: "In order to restore order from chaos, God must have needed the services of an architect."

The civil servant came in with the clincher: "Ah, but who created the chaos?"

## JOGGERS

FRED joined Joggers Anonymous. Whenever he feels like a run they send someone round with a dozen bottles to talk him out of it.

\* \* \*

FATHER: "Why don't you go for a run around the block?"

Son: "Why? I'm already here."

\* \* \*

FRED was told that he should exercise and that jogging would add years to his life.

"How do you feel?" asked his wife when he staggered once around the block.

"They're right. I feel ten years older," he said.

WHEN the husband came home unexpectedly, Larry the lover had to leap from the bedroom window. Spotting some joggers running by he quickly joined them.

"Do you usually jog in the nude?" asked one of the runners after a while.

"Oh yes," said Larry. "It's very stimulating."

"And do you usually jog with a condom on?"

Larry kept his cool. "Well, to tell you the truth, it was raining when I set out."

*　　*　　*

HAVING trouble with his sex life, Fred was advised by the doctor to take up jogging.

"Take it easy to start with, just two miles a day," said the Doctor, "and give me a call this time next week."

Fred did so. "And how is your sex life now?" asked the Doc.

"Worse," said Fred. "I'm 14 miles from home."

*　　*　　*

AFTER a very heavy night he left the nightclub at dawn and being in no condition to drive he stopped the car in the first recreation reserve and tried to sleep it off.

He had just settled down when a jogger tapped on the window and asked for the time.

"It's 5.30," he grumbled.

He snuggled down again, but only a few minutes passed before another jogger rapped on the window and asked the time. "It's 5.35," he roared.

In desperation he scribbled a note in large letters and stuck it against the window. It read: "I haven't a watch and I don't know the time."

Five minutes later a jogger stopped to rap on the window and told him it was 5.40.

# JOKES

THE only catch in telling a good story, is that it usually reminds the other bloke of a bad one.

* * *

"I'VE got a million jokes," he said.

"Then why did you tell us that one," they said.

* * *

HE always wanted to be a comedian, but he was afraid people might laugh at him.

* * *

A MAN who says his wife can't take a joke forgets himself.

* * *

HE who laughs last doesn't get the joke.

* * *

"DID you hear my last joke?"

"I hope so."

* * *

THE comedian's first professional engagement was at the Oodnadatta Social Club and his first performance was greeted with stony silence.

He was sitting in his dressing room drowning his sorrows while the bingo session was in full swing and he heard the MC trying to call the crowd to order.

"Now then," said the MC. "If you don't shut the noise while we're running the bingo I'll get that comedian on again!"

* * *

THE travelling salesman's car broke down and he wandered across the paddock to the farmhouse and asked if he could sleep the night.

"You're most welcome," said the farmer, "but I must warn you that I don't have daughters, I am a bachelor and you will have to share the only bed with me."

"Oh hell," said the salesman, "I'm in the wrong bloomin' joke."

THE Taxation Department is putting jokes and cartoons on the back of the income tax form now, so that taxpayers can see the funny side.

*　　*　　*

FRED was often the butt of office jokes. "Have you heard the story of the dirty window, Fred?" they said.

When he said no, they said: "It's no use telling you. You wouldn't see through it."

Fred could hardly wait until he got home. "Darling," he said. "Have you heard the story of the window you couldn't see through?"

"No," she said.

"Well I can't tell you. It's too dirty."

*　　*　　*

"THE trouble with you, Mabel, is that you have no sense of humour," he said.

She thought about it for a moment. "Well, I don't think that's funny."

*　　*　　*

WHEN the little man came home, his rather formidable wife gave him such a wallop on the head with a rolling pin that his knees buckled and he fell to the floor.

Shaking his head groggily he said: "Was that a joke, or did you mean it?"

"I bloody-well meant it," she said.

"That's okay then. Because I don't appreciate jokes like that."

*　　*　　*

DON'T worry if your life's a joke
And your successes are but few
Remember that the mighty oak
Was once a nut like you.

*　　*　　*

WE editors may dig and toil
Till our fingertips are sore

But still a few are bound to say
"I've heard that joke before."

      \*     \*     \*

EVERYBODY'S idea of a joke is different. Like the fellow who hit his mate on the head with a dead chicken.

    "Hey," said the victim, "are you having a go at me, or was that a joke?"

    "I'm having a go at you," was the reply.

    "Well that's okay then. 'Cos I don't like that kind of joke."

      \*     \*     \*

A WISE man never laughs at his wife's old clothes.

      \*     \*     \*

HE is convinced women don't have a sense of humour. He asked one to his room and she said: "Don't make me laugh."

      \*     \*     \*

HE who laughs last usually has a tooth missing.

      \*     \*     \*

HISTORY records that when Churchill met Stalin at the famous Yalta conference they discussed their hobbies.

    Churchill said he collected jokes people told about him.

    Stalin said he collected people who told jokes about him.

# K

## KIDS

CHILDREN, what a comfort in old age. And how soon they bring it on.

*       *       *

PRIDE is something you feel when your kids run a garage sale and raise a few hundred dollars.

Panic is when you go to get your car, and find it gone.

*       *       *

YOUNG Billy brought a note home from school. His Dad read it and announced to his wife: "They want a written excuse for his presence."

*       *       *

THE little boy in the crowded showgrounds was obviously distressed. "I've lost my Dad," he sobbed when the policeman approached him.

"What's your Dad like?" said the cop.

"Beer, women and the odd bet," said the lad.

*       *       *

LITTLE Mary stuck her head around the kitchen door, "Hey Mum. Can an eight-year-old girl get pregnant?"

"Of course not," said her mother.

Mary turned round. "It's okay fellas, we can keep playing the game."

THE RSPCA inspector stopped three kids in a billy-cart. It was being pulled by a big mongrel dog they had harnessed to the cart. He accused the kids of cruelty.

"Rubbish," chorused the kids. "Bonzo loves it, he has been doing it for years. He doesn't look unhappy does he?"

The officer had to admit that the big dog seemed to be enjoying himself.

"Okay," he conceded, "but that piece of string hanging from his testicles will have to come off. That could hurt him."

"Arr hell," said one of the kids. "There goes our brakes!"

\* \* \*

"ARE you a gardening expert?" asked the small girl when the visiting neighbour was seated in the lounge.

"No Mary I'm not. What makes you think that?"

"Mum says if there is any dirt about you'll dig it up!"

\* \* \*

LITTLE Johnny was having a lot of trouble with his arithmetic and when teacher asked him what two plus two was he counted on his fingers and said, "four."

"And how much is three and three?"

Again Johnny counted on his fingers and came up with "six."

"Johnny," stormed the teacher, "it is cheating to use your fingers. Now put your hands in your pockets and tell me what is five and five."

There was a fumble and a pause before the answer came up. "Eleven," he said.

\* \* \*

WHEN young Billie returned from his first time at church they asked him how he liked it. He said the music and singing was good, but he didn't think much of the news.

\* \* \*

HIS dad asked what he had learned in Sunday school that morning.

"I learned about a cross-eyed bear whose name was Gladly," replied the youngster.

Dad was puzzled and had to press the point further to finally discover it was a hymn: "Gladly, the Cross I'd Bear."

\* \* \*

A COP saw a little boy standing in the pub smoking a cigarette and drinking a pot of beer.

"Why aren't you in school?" he asked.

"Because I'm only four years old," replied the kid.

\* \* \*

"MUM," said the little boy, "where did I come from?"

"The stork brought you, dear," was the reply.

"And where did you come from, Mum?"

"The stork brought me too."

"And what about grandma?"

"The stork brought her too."

"Gee," said the little lad, "Doesn't it ever worry you to think that there have been no natural births in our family for three generations?"

\* \* \*

"HEY Mum, where do babies come from?"

"From the stork of course."

"But who gets the stork pregnant?"

\* \* \*

SMALL boy watching his Mum do the washing. "Mum, where did you work before you got this job here with us?"

\* \* \*

LITTLE Tommy, aged eight, marched into the living room with an important announcement for his father. "Dad," he said with great seriousness, "I'm gonna get married."

His Dad grinned indulgently, "Who to, son?"

"My girlfriend, Mary, next door."

Mary was also eight and his Dad decided to carry the joke along. "Found a place to live yet?" he asked.

"Well, she gets 50 cents pocket money and you give me a dollar. So if she moves in with me, we can manage," said Tommy seriously.

His Dad nodded. "Well, $1-50 a week is okay for now, but what will you do when the kids start to arrive?"

"Don't worry," said Tommy confidently. "We've been lucky so far."

\* \* \*

GRANDMA was spending a few days with the family, and on the fourth morning when everybody was seated around the breakfast table little Freddy said: "When are you going to do your trick, Dad?"

"What trick is that, son?"

"You know. You said if Grandma stayed more than three days you would climb the wall."

\* \* \*

YOUNG Basil had moved to town from the country and had settled in at the suburban primary school fairly well; except for his constant swearing. It was "bloody" this and "bloody" that until he was sent home with a note: "If this boy won't stop swearing he will not be allowed to school anymore."

His father gave him a bloody hiding and sent him back next day with a note to say he wouldn't bloody-well swear again.

The teacher was impressed and sent home another note. "Basil has been so good he can come to the school picnic on Saturday week."

When the big day came, little Basil set off for the picnic, with a caution and yet another note. "If he swears again, please send the little blighter straight home."

In less than an hour Basil was back, weeping his eyes out, and copped another hiding from his father for swearing.

"I didn't swear," he protested. "You sent me off on the wrong bloody Saturday. The bloody picnic is not until next bloody week!"

TWO young brothers were sent home from their country school with a note to say they had been suspended for the afternoon for swearing.

. Their father gave them a hiding, a lecture and sent them to bed without dinner.

Next morning as they sat down for breakfast their father, in a more conciliatory mood, asked what they would like for breakfast.

The first one said: "I'll have some of those bloody cornflakes." He received an immediate thrashing from his father and was sent back to bed for the day.

The father then asked the second boy what he would like for breakfast. "I don't know," he said. "But it won't be bloody cornflakes, that's for sure."

\* \* \*

BECAUSE he had been heard swearing, young Billie had been put across his father's knee and given a few good whacks. "Now son," said his Dad, "tell me why I punished you."

The kid threw up his hands in despair. "That does it. First you belt hell out of me and now you don't know why you bloody-well did it!"

\* \* \*

"DAD, all the kids at school hit me and call me Pansy."

"That's all right son," said his father. "Next time they do that, whack them over the head with your handbag."

\* \* \*

LITTLE Johnny had just met the new kid at playgroup.

"How old are you?"

"I don't know," said the new kid.

"Do women bother you?"

"No."

"Then you are five."

\* \* \*

A YOUNG boy was approached by the young housewife who had just moved into the flat next door. "Sonny, I

241

need some bread at the corner store. Do you think you could go for me?"

"No," said the lad, "but I've heard Dad say he could."

\* \* \*

DAD had just settled down with a book when young Johnny came home from school and asked the question he had dreaded to hear: "Where did I come from, Dad?"

Wiping the sweat from his collar Dad began the lengthy explanation beginning with the birds and the bees right through to sexual intercourse, and after an agonising half hour summed it all up with, "Now, do you understand, son?"

"Not really, Dad," said the lad. "Luigi says he comes from Italy and Ng VanDong says he comes from Vietnam. Where do I come from?"

\* \* \*

WHEN his wife said she was going to change the baby, he said: "Well get a quieter one!"

\* \* \*

SHE married a sailor because she wanted to have children and rear admirals.

\* \* \*

"I HEAR you have finally cured little Tommy of biting his nails?"

"Yeah, we pulled his teeth out!"

\* \* \*

LITTLE Agatha was crying bitterly because her father drowned the three new kittens. He had promised her she could do it.

\* \* \*

"MUMMY, you know the vase you were always worried I would break?"

"Yes."

"Well, your worries are over."

242

# KIWIS

A BLOKE went into the fish shop and asked for some "Fush 'n chups."

"Ar! You're a Kiwi, eh?" said the proprietor.

The Enzedder got sick and tired of this so he spent the next three months at an elocution class.

He finally returned to the shop and asked, in perfect English for some "Fish and Chips."

"Ar, you're a Kiwi, eh?"

"How the hell did you know that?"

"Because this has been a hardware shop for the last two weeks."

\*　　\*　　\*

THE potato farmer had recently arrived from Rotorua and had taken up a farm in Gembrook. "You look worried," said his mates in the pub, "what's bothering you?"

"Sex!" he replied.

They gathered around for more information.

"Well," explained the Kiwi, "as you know this is my first harvest here. I've got a wonderful crop of spuds, but not enough sex to put them in."

\*　　\*　　\*

THREE couples went into a restaurant in Auckland and asked for a table for sex.

"And three pillows," they added.

# L

## LAW
See POLICE

IT'S illegal to make liquor privately, and to make water publicly.

* * *

THE lag in the dock said: "As God is my judge I am not guilty."

The magistrate replied: "He's not. I am. You are. Three years."

* * *

THE judge called the court to order to make a serious announcement. He said he had been bribed $2000 by the defendant and $3000 by the plaintiff.

"This is a serious matter and I have given it earnest consideration," he said. "I've decided to return $1000 to the plaintiff, and judge the case on its merits!"

* * *

THE judge, he populates
   The city jails
   By grave decisions
   Heads or tails

* * *

DAN Murphy was a popular bloke in the one-horse town, but he was charged with stealing cattle. After the bush

244

jury of his peers heard the evidence the foreman stood up and said: "Not guilty. So long as he returns the cattle."

The circuit magistrate was infuriated with the finding and demanded they go back and reconsider their verdict.

After a short wrangle among themselves the foreman stood once more. "Okay, not guilty, and he can keep the bloomin' cattle."

\* \* \*

"YOU seem to have more than an average share of intelligence for a man of your background," sneered the lawyer at the witness stand.

"Thank you," said the witness. "If I wasn't under oath I'd return the compliment."

\* \* \*

FRED knew that a former partner owed him $500 but he was unable to legally prove it. He asked his solicitor what to do about it.

"Easy," replied the legal eagle. "We will send him a letter demanding payment of the $1000 within seven days and ...

"But it is only $500," said Fred.

"And that's exactly what he will reply in his letter, and then we have the proof."

\* \* \*

THE clerk turned to the little bloke in the dock. "Prisoner at the bar," he said, "do you wish to challenge the jury?"

Fred eyed the jury. "Not all of them at once," he said, "but I think I could go a few rounds with the little fat geezer in the middle."

\* \* \*

A BLOKE due to appear in court was talking about the case in the bar and was advised by his drinking mate: "If you want to get off, just send the judge a case of whisky."

The defendant discussed this with his solicitor next morning. "On no account do anything like that," said the legal man. "We've got a thin argument already without complicating it with a bribe."

To the solicitor's astonishment our bloke won his case. "We would have lost if you sent that case of whisky."

"Oh, but I did," said our bloke, "but I put the other party's name on the card."

* * *

JUDGE: "Can't you settle this out of court?"

"That's what we were doing when the police interferred."

* * *

"THIS pen leaks," said the prisoner as the rain came through the roof.

* * *

THE Melbourne lawyer received a fax from his partner representing a client in Sydney. It read "Justice has prevailed."

The Melbourne man faxed back a message; "Appeal at once!"

* * *

McTAVISH was as shrewd as they come and when he sat down with the lawyer he said: "I'm not into throwing money about, but I will certainly pay if you can give me an undertaking that you can win my case."

The lawyer said that was fair enough and told McTavish to outline the story.

McTavish launched into a terrible tale of breach of contract, lying, cheating and fraudulent business practices.

"That's an open and shut case," said the lawyer. "I will cheerfully accept such a brief."

"Oh that's bad news," said McTavish.

"Why?" asked the lawyer.

"That was my opponent's side of the story."

* * *

THE defendant had just been convicted and fined and was asked by the judge if he could pay anything at all towards the penalty and costs.

"Not a brass razoo," he replied. "All the money I had has gone to my lawyer and five of the jurors."

*　　*　　*

CHARGED with stealing a barrel of beer from the back of the pub the old defendant was not familiar with legal jargon. So when the judge said he would have to dismiss the case due to insufficient evidence the old lag scratched his head and said "What d'yer mean?"

The clerk explained: "It means you are let off."

"And does it mean I can keep the grog?" he asked.

*　　*　　*

DAD is very popular in prison. He's the lifer of the party.

*　　*　　*

"YOUNG man, you are accused of stealing a petticoat."

"It was my first slip."

*　　*　　*

"HAVE you ever been cross-examined before?"

"Yes, your honour, I'm a married man."

*　　*　　*

"DO you plead guilty or not guilty?"

"What else have you got?"

*　　*　　*

"DO you plead guilty or not guilty?"

"How do I know. I haven't heard the evidence yet."

*　　*　　*

"HAVE you anything to offer before judgement is passed?"

"No, judge, my lawyer has left me skint."

*　　*　　*

"GUILTY. Ten days or two hundred dollars."

"I'll take the two hundred thanks, judge."

*　　*　　*

"ORDER, order in the court."

"Whisky, on the rocks for me thanks."

*　　*　　*

JUDGE: you are charged with habitual drunkeness, what is your excuse?"

"Habitual thirst, yer worship!"

247

BOSS to pretty secretary: "Just because I made love to you last night, who said you could come in late?"

Secretary: "My solicitor."

*     *     *

JUDGE, to jury: "What possible reason could you have for acquitting this man?"

"Insanity," said the foreman.

"What, all of you?"

*     *     *

FRED consulted his lawyer. "I've been receiving threatening letters," he said.

"That's terrible," said the legal eagle. "We'll put a stop to that. Who are they from?"

"The Taxation Department," said Fred.

*     *     *

TWO tramps were hauled before the court and charged with vagrancy.

"And where do you live?" asked the judge.

"Nowhere," said the first tramp.

"And where do you live," he asked the second tramp.

Indicating his mate he replied, "Next door to him!"

*     *     *

SHE was seeking maintenance for her baby.

"Do you know who the father is?" asked the solicitor.

"Yes," she sobbed. "It was Tommy."

"But we can't sue Tommy. Don't you know his surname?"

"No. You see I didn't know him personally."

*     *     *

TWO magistrates were rolling home from a reunion, arms around each other, singing Sweet Adeline.

"Hey," said one. "I think we're drunk."

"You're right. And according to law I will have to charge you with being drunk and disorderly," said his mate.

"And you will have to appear before me at 10 tomorrow," said the first.

Next morning in court the first pleaded guilty to the charge and was fined $10. They then changed places.

"Drunk and disorderly, eh, fined $20."

"Hey," protested the first. "When I was in the chair I only fined you $10."

"Yes," said the second magistrate. "But the offence is getting too prevalent. You are the second drunk to appear before this court this morning!"

* * *

JUDGE to habitual defendant: "Is this the first time you have been up before me?"

"I dunno yer honour. What time do you get up?"

* * *

THE solicitor told Paddy that if he wanted to be defended in court tomorrow he would need money, but Paddy was broke.

"All I've got is an antique gold watch," he said.

Solicitor: "Well that's okay, you can raise cash on that. Now what are you accused of stealing?"

Paddy: "An antique gold watch!"

* * *

"HAVE you got anything to say for yourself?" said the judge sternly after hearing the case.

"Stuff all," muttered the defendant.

"What did he say?" asked the judge learning forward to the clerk.

The clerk stood up, turned, and whispered quietly to the judge: "He said 'stuff all' your worship."

"That's funny," said the judge, "I'm sure I saw his lips move."

* * *

WHEN the stranger entered the bar the publican said, "Good evening, Sir, would you like a drink?"

"Yes," he replied, "I will have a double Scotch."

It was plonked in front of him and the publican said, "That'll be five dollars, thanks."

"No," said the stranger, "It's your treat. I clearly heard you invite me to have a drink."

Another gent at the bar who heard the argument said to the publican. "He's right you know. I am a solicitor and I distinctly heard you invite him to have a drink."

The angry publican told the stranger to drink his whisky and leave and never come back.

Ten minutes later the stranger returned. "I thought I told you never to come back," roared the publican."

The stranger protested. "I've never been here before in my life."

The publican grudgingly conceded, "Well you must have a double."

"Thanks very much," said the stranger, "and one for my solicitor friend."

* * *

TWO workers entered the same pub, pulled their stools up to the bar and opened their cut lunches.

"Hey," said the barman, "You can't eat your own sandwiches here."

So they swapped.


## LAZINESS

HE was so lazy he married a pregnant woman.

* * *

HE was so lazy he had his window box concreted over.

* * *

HE was so lazy he used to ride the underground in peak hours just to press his clothes.

* * *

THE only thing he ever took up at school was space.

* * *

HE called her Baseball because she would never play without a diamond.

* * *

THE lazy German lived by the sweat of his frau.

# LETTERS

HE got a letter from his wife: "Fred, I missed you yesterday. Come home and let me have another shot. — Beatrice."

*     *     *

SMOOTH Sam was confiding to Fred over a beer that he had a problem. "I'm worried, Fred," he said. "This letter came the other day and it said if I didn't stop making love to this bloke's wife he was going to kill me."

"So what's the problem?" said Fred.

"It wasn't signed," said Sam.

*     *     *

FRED was always coming home from the pub in the early hours of the morning, and eventually found this note from his missus:

"The day before yesterday you came home yesterday morning. Yesterday you came home this morning. So if today you come home tomorrow morning you will find that I left you yesterday."

*     *     *

"DEAR Sir. Please find enclosed $10.50 for one of your razors as advertised. — Billy Bong. PS: I forgot to enclose the money, but no doubt a firm of your reputable standing will send the razor anyway.

Dear Mr Bong. Thank you for your order and we have pleasure enclosing the razor as requested.

PS: We forgot to enclose the razor, but no doubt a man with your cheek doesn't need one."

*     *     *

"DEAR John. I have been unable to sleep since I broke off our engagement. Won't you forget and forgive? Your absence is breaking my heart. I was a fool, nobody can take your place. I love you. I love you. — Marsha.

PS: Congratulations on winning the lottery."

*     *     *

THE university chancellor discovered that one of his

professors had been messing about with his wife. So he sent him a letter demanding his presence in the office on Tuesday morning.

The offending professor sent the following reply: "I received your circular letter. I regret that I cannot attend, but rest assured that I will accept the majority vote."

* * *

LETTER from a travel agent: "Dear Sir, in reference to your proposed trip to London, the flight you requested is completely full, but we will keep in contact and inform you immediately somebody falls out, as is often the case."

* * *

## LETTER FROM AN IRISH MOTHER

DEAR SON. Just a few lines to let you know I'm still alive. I'm writing this letter slowly because I know you can't read fast. You won't know the house when you get home because we have moved.

About your father. He has a lovely new job. He has 500 men under him; he cuts grass at the cemetery. There was a washing machine in the new house when we moved in but it hasn't been working too good. Last week I put Dad's shirt in, pulled the chain and haven't seen it since.

Your sister Mary had a baby this morning but I haven't found out if it is a boy or a girl yet, so I don't know if you are an auntie or an uncle.

Your Uncle Patrick drowned last week in a vat of whisky at the Dublin Brewery. Some of his workmates tried to save him but he fought them off bravely. They cremated him and it took five days to put out the fire.

I went to the doctor last Thursday and your father came with me. The doctor put a small glass tube in my mouth and told me not to talk for ten minutes. Your father offered to buy it off him.

It only rained twice this week, first for three days and then for four.

We had a letter from the undertaker. He said if the last payment on your grandfather's plot isn't paid within seven days, up he comes.

— Your loving mother.

PS: I was going to send you $10 but I had already sealed up the envelope.

*    *    *

## WHY I FIRED MY SECRETARY

TWO weeks ago it was my 45th birthday. I didn't feel too well that morning, but I knew that when I went to breakfast my wife would be pleasant and say "Happy Birthday". But she didn't even say "Good Morning".

I thought, that's wives for you. At least the children will remember. But the kids came in for breakfast and didn't say a word, so when I started for the office I was feeling pretty low and despondent.

As I walked into the office, Janet said "Good Morning, boss. Happy Birthday." I immediately felt better because somebody remembered.

About noon she knocked on my door and said that it was such a lovely day we should go out to lunch. It was the best news I had all day.

We went to lunch. We didn't go where we normally go. Janet said she knew a little private place out in the country. We had two martinis and enjoyed lunch tremendously.

On the way back to the office she said, "You know, it's such a beautiful day it would be a shame to go back to the office." When I agreed she said: "Let's go to my apartment and I will fix you another martini."

We did just that, in fact she fixed two martinis which put me in a very pleasant mood. Then she said, "Boss, if you don't mind, I think I will go into the bedroom and slip into something more comfortable." I assured her I didn't mind at all.

She went into the bedroom and in about six minutes

she came out carrying a big birthday cake followed by my wife and children, all singing Happy Birthday, and there I sat with nothing on except my socks!

*     *     *

AUSTRALIAN EXPORT
MEIN Tear Herren.

Der last two pecketches ve got from you off coffee vas mitt rattschidtten mixt. Ve did not see any rattschidtten in der samples vich you sent us. It takes much valuable time to pick de ratten durden from der coffee. Ve order der coffee clean but you schipt schidt mixt mit it.

Ve like you schip us der coffee in vun sek, und der rattenschidtten in an udder sek. Und zen ve can mix it to suit der customer. Write please if we should schip der schidt bek und keep der coffee, or should ve chip bek der coffee und keep der shidt, or should ve schip bek der whole schidtten vurks?

We remain at your conwenience...


# LIARS

THE lie is an abomination to the Lord; but damned helpful in getting out of trouble.

*     *     *

SHE said she can tell by looking at your husband's face if he is lying.

"Yes," she said. "If his lips are moving, he's lying."

*     *     *

DOES your husband lie awake at night?

Yes, and he lies in his sleep, too.

*     *     *

THEY say the first lie detector was made out of the rib of a man. And they have been unable to improve on that model ever since.

*     *     *

THE vicar from the pulpit announced that his sermon

that day would be on the sin of perjury. "How many of you have read the 25th chapter?"

All in the congregation raised their hands.

"That's good," said the vicar. "There is no 25th chapter so you are exactly the people I want to talk to."

*     *     *

THERE are two kinds of people who live in Sydney. Those who admit they have cockroaches and the others who lie about it.

*     *     *

THERE is only one thing that stops him from being a bare-faced liar.

What's that?

His moustache.

*     *     *

MADGE fixed her eye on her husband Fred and said: "So, where are you going today?"

"I'm going to the pub."

"Ha, when you tell me you are going to the pub I know that you think that I'll think you are going to the races, but this time I know you are really going to the pub, so why are you lying?"

*     *     *

HE described his wife as having a keen sense of rumour.

*     *     *

HE's not really a liar. He just arranges the truth in his favour.

## LIFE

THE best way to face life is with a stiff upper lip, a firm chin, your feet planted firmly on the ground your head high in the air, your nose to the grindstone, an ear to the ground and a shoulder to the wheel... and you'll find it's damned uncomfortable.

IF I had my life to live over again, I'd start making the same mistakes earlier.

* * *

NEVER let life get you down. Remember, when one door closes, another slams in your face.

* * *

ABOUT the time you are financial enough to eat, drink and be merry, the doctor limits you to a glass of milk.

* * *

THE only certain way to reduce the cost of living is to drop dead.

* * *

LIFE is to be enjoyed. We will never get out of it alive.

* * *

LIFE. The first half is ruined by your parents. The second half is ruined by your kids.

* * *

IF you want to remember, tie a short string around your finger.

If you want to forget, tie a long rope around your neck.

* * *

LIFE begins at 40, but you could miss a lot if you wait till then.

* * *

LIFE is like a shower. One wrong turn and you are in hot water.

* * *

WHAT is the reason women live longer than men?

Because they have no wives.

(And of course the reverse applies.)

* * *

HE was asked if he ever realised any of his childhood dreams.

"Yes. When I was young and my mother kept insisting on combing my hair I often wished I didn't have any."

LIFE can be hard, but some hearts can be harder as the tramp found out when he knocked on the back door of the inn looking for a hand-out.

The landlady fixed him with a steely glare. "Would you eat yesterday's stew?"

"Yes," he said eagerly.

"Well, come back tomorrow," she said.

## LITERATURE

SHE went to Stratford-on-Avon to see her first play, A Midsummer Night's Dream, and was so moved by it that on the final curtain she stood and called: "Author! Author!"

\* \* \*

A CRITIC, said Kenneth Tynan, is a man who knows the way but can't drive a car.

\* \* \*

A CRITIC is a legless man who teaches running.

\* \* \*

AND the critic's response. "I can't lay an egg either, but I am a better judge of an omelette than any hen."

\* \* \*

"WHAT do you think of Kipling?"

"Don't know. I've never tried it."

\* \* \*

THE English teacher looked dejected. "I have just given that class a lecture on Keats, and I doubt if any of them know what a keat is."

## LOCAL GOVERNMENT

A TEDDY Bear got a job on a council road gang. Monday went well, Tuesday likewise, but on Wednesday when he returned from his lunch break he discovered his pick had been stolen.

He complained to the foreman who was undismayed and had the obvious answer.

"It's Wednesday," he said. "That's the day the Teddy Bears have their picks nicked!"

*　　　*　　　*

SOCIETY matron was crowing over her husband's re-election on the municipal council. "Yes. My John got elected for his third time and got in unexposed!"

*　　　*　　　*

WHEN the municipal council decided to build a fountain outside the town hall they put the project to tender and got three quotes, from contractors in Brisbane, Sydney and Melbourne.

The town clerk interviewed the Brisbane builder and asked his price. "$3000," was the reply.

"And how do you break that down?" asked the clerk.

"That's $1000 for the material, $1000 for the workers and $1000 for me."

The town clerk called in the Sydney contractor who quoted a price of $6000. "And how do you break that down?" asked the clerk.

"That's $2000 for materials, $2000 for the workers and $2000 for me."

The clerk called in the Melbourne bloke, whose price was $9000.

"And how do you break that down?" asked the clerk.

The bloke from Melbourne said, "$3000 for you, $3000 for me, and we give the job to the bloke from Brisbane."

*　　　*　　　*

THEY had never had a woman on the town council before and newly elected Cr Flossie Firebrand intended to make her mark.

The first item on the engineer's agenda was the cost of constructing a urinal.

"What's a urinal?" she asked.

When it was fully explained to her she immediately demanded that the funds be doubled.

"If we are gonna have a urinal I insist that we have an arsenal too."

*　　*　　*

PAYING his parking fine at the town hall the commercial traveller complained to the clerk that the town didn't have enough parking spaces.

"We're a small country town with lots of expenses," said the clerk. "If we can't catch you blokes for speeding, then we rip a little bit off for standing still."

*　　*　　*

HE was mayor of the town, and a justice of the peace which meant he sat on the bench on court days. He glared over his glasses at the tramp charged with vagrancy.

"Have you ever earned a dollar in your life?" he sneered.

"Yes, yer honour," answered the defendant. "It was a tenner remember, for voting for you at the last election."

# LOGIC

TWO Catholic women were enjoying a cup of coffee opposite a house owned by a notorious call girl when they saw a protestant minister go in.

"Disgraceful," whispered one to the other.

Later they saw the local rabbi emerge from the same door and they shook their heads in despair.

"What's the world coming to?"

They were on their second cup of coffee when they saw Father O'Kelly knock on the door and enter.

"Dear, the poor woman must be awfully sick," they agreed.

*　　*　　*

TWO travellers, one with years of experience, found themselves in a strange town without lodgings. It was a warm night so they decided to sleep out in what appeared to be a quiet lane.

The older of the two elected to lay in the middle of the road. His younger companion, declaring his mate a fool, settled down on the side of the road.

As they were sleeping a truck came down the road and the driver, seeing the old bloke in his path, swerved to avoid him and ran over the young man on the pavement.

\* \* \*

SOCIETY Sally said to the good-looking stranger: "Gee you look like my fifth husband."

The stranger was taken aback. "How many times have you been married?" he asked.

"Four," she replied.

\* \* \*

THE club's fund-raiser approached the born loser.

"Will you buy a raffle ticket for a keg of beer?"

"I don't like beer," he said.

"Not to worry," she said. "There are too many in it already. You haven't a chance of winning."

"Good," he said. "I'll take two."

\* \* \*

AFTER catching a stranger in bed with his wife the irate husband reaches for his gun.

"Wait!" cries his wife. "Remember the world cruise we went on after I told you I won the lottery. Well, Lionel paid for it. Remember the strange circumstances which caused our mortgage to be paid off. Well, Lionel actually paid it. Remember the diamond ring I found. Well, again, Lionel paid for it..."

The husband lowers his gun.

"For goodness sake, woman. Cover him up he'll catch a chill."

# M

## MAGIC

AN old magician was working the Titanic on its last fateful voyage. He used to put a rabbit in his top hat and pull a hair out of his bum. (No, that's not the joke).

The old-timer had been down on his luck and couldn't afford one of those attractive leggy blonde assistants. On the Titanic he had to make do with a parrot, but to give it credit, the parrot had developed repartee and would squawk to the audience: "It's up his sleeve", or "It's under his cloak, folks."

They were half way through their act when the Titanic hit the iceberg and sank.

The magician swam all night while the parrot fluttered overhead. He swam all next day and the parrot still fluttered overhead. It was evening of the second day when the parrot finally alighted on the magician's head.

"Okay, I give up. What have you done with the bloomin' ship?"

\* \* \*

AFTER the leggy blonde had flagged him down on the country road he asked her what she did for a living.

"I'm a magician," she said.

"Get away, prove it then."

And with that she touched him on the knee and turned him into a motel.

THE party had been very entertaining and now it was Paddy's turn to do a magic trick. He stretches his arms forward, thumbs up, and says to the person opposite: "Pick a thumb, any thumb at all will do."

The volunteer makes his choice and Paddy quickly whips his arms behind himself and fumbles for a moment. Then, holding his clenched fists forward he says: "Okay, okay. Which hand is it in?"

## MARRIAGE
See WEDDINGS, NEWLY-WEDS

REMEMBER, Socrates died from an overdose of wedlock.

\* \* \*

MOST marriages are happy. It is trying to live together afterwards that causes the tension.

\* \* \*

MARRIAGES are made uneven.

\* \* \*

MARRIAGE is the price men pay for sex and sex is the price women pay for marriage.

\* \* \*

MARRIAGE has its good side. It teaches you loyalty, forebearance, self-restraint, and many other qualities you wouldn't need if you stayed single.

\* \* \*

MARRIAGE is not a word, it is a sentence.

\* \* \*

MARRIAGE is not a lottery. In a lottery you have a chance.

\* \* \*

MARRIAGE is like a three ring circus. First the engagement ring, second the wedding ring and third the suffer-ring.

\* \* \*

THERE'S a lot to be said about marriage. But try not to say it in front of the children.

262

STATISTICS prove that at least 50% of all people who get married at Easter are women.

* * *

IF a woman does household chores for $250 a week, that's domestic science. If she does it for nothing, that's marriage.

* * *

LAUGH, and the world laughs with you. Quarrel with your wife and you sleep alone.

## MARRIAGE COUNSELLING

COUNSELLOR: "Are your relations pleasant?"
  "Mine are, his are horrible."

* * *

THE marriage counsellor asked the wife: "Did you shrink from love-making?"
  "No," she replied, "I've always been tiny like this."

* * *

"OF course we are incompatible," she said, "but he's far more incompatible than I am."

## MARRIEDS

DARLING is the wife's maiden name.

* * *

THEY got off to a bad start at the altar.
  When he said "I do," she replied, "Oh no you don't," and they have been arguing ever since.

* * *

ONE month after the wedding Arthur began to wonder if he has made the right decision. Every evening meal had consisted of wedding cake and chips.

* * *

"I SHOULD never have got married, Fred."
  "Why not, Harry?"

"Because the wife hates me when I'm drunk and I can't stand the sight of her when I'm sober."

*      *      *

"MONEY, money, money, they are the only three words you know!"

*      *      *

HE said his wife doesn't understand him, but it is his own fault. He shouldn't have married a Chinese girl.

*      *      *

"I'VE been married five years, and believe me, when it comes to making money you've just got to hand it to Madge."

*      *      *

"TELL me dear, before we were married did you say you were oversexed, or over sex?"

*      *      *

"DOES your wife pick your clothes?"
  "No, only the pockets."

*      *      *

"I HAVE a clever wife."
  "Mine always finds out, too."

*      *      *

"TELL me Charles," she said. "If I died before you, would you still go to our golf club on week-ends?"
  "Oh, I suppose so, dear."
  "I guess, after a time, you would take up with another partner?"
  "Oh, I suppose so, dear."
  "Tell me Charles, would you let her use my clubs?"
  "No dear, she's left-handed."

*      *      *

SHE nudged her husband awake when she thought she heard a burglar, but he refused to get out and investigate.
  "What's happened?" she whispered. "You were brave when you married me."
  "Yes, that's what all my mates said," he replied.

SHE arrived at the breakfast table in an old chenille dressing gown and her hair in rollers.

"Why can't you look like you did when I married you?" he grumbled.

"Because I'm not pregnant now," she said.

\* \* \*

IT was another domestic that had reached the stage where they were not talking to each other. Notes were in vogue.

She found a note pinned to her pillow: "I have to be at the office early. Wake me at seven."

When he woke at 9-30, there was a note pinned to his pillow which said: "It's seven o'clock, wake up!"

\* \* \*

THE old couple sat on the porch, as they had for many years. "I was just thinking," said the old lady, "we've had such a grand life together, but sooner or later one of us will pass on."

"Yes, but don't worry about that now," he said.

"Well I was just thinking," she said, "when it does happen, I'd like to go and live in Queensland."

\* \* \*

REMEMBER that your wife is a romantic and still enjoys chocolates and flowers. So show her that you too remember, by speaking of them occasionally.

\* \* \*

"WHAT'S your husband's average income?"

"About midnight."

\* \* \*

THEY say he married her because her aunt left her a fortune.

He hotly denies it, and says he would have married her whoever left her the fortune.

\* \* \*

MR and Mrs Offenbloo had been married for 20 years and they were still in love. She with the doctor and he with his secretary.

BLOKE came home to find his wife in bed with the next door neighbour.

"What the hell do you think you're doing?" demanded the husband.

The wife said to her bedmate: "There you are, I told you he was stupid."

* * *

THE wife was nervous as she got behind the wheel of their new car for the first time. "I hardly know what to do," she said.

"Just imagine I'm driving," he said.

* * *

"THERE must be something, even one thing," he said in a heated argument "that my family scores over your family."

She pondered for a while. "Yes. Your in-laws are better than my in-laws."

* * *

WIFE: "Before we were married you told me you were well off."

"Yes, but I didn't know it at the time."

* * *

THEY had been married for ten years. She looked up from her sewing and said: "Darling, why don't we go out tonight?"

He put his book aside and said, "What a splendid idea. And if I get home before you I will leave the light on."

## MECHANICS

WHEN her date, a young mechanic, arrived to take her out she was surprised to see a set of jumper leads around his neck with the clips holding up his trousers. "My braces broke," he explained.

She gave the jumper leads a dubious look and said: "Well okay, I will come out with you. But don't start anything."

266

THE mechanic itemised the bill for the woman driver: "$100 repairs to fender, $150 repairs to the tail-light fixture, $50 for not telling your husband and $50 for running over Pete, the petrol pump attendant."

*     *     *

THE car mechanic went to the psychiatrist and laid down under the couch.

# MISTRESSES

FRED has got so many mistresses that when he takes his wife for a drive she has to hide under the dash when they pass a woman in the street.

*     *     *

IZZY's wife became piqued when a woman passing their table gave Izzy the eye.

"Who's that?" she wanted to know.

"Actually, it's my mistress," explained Izzy. "She is vital for business. Got essential connections in the trade. You know how it is."

This didn't exactly calm Mrs Izzy but at that moment Mr Rozenbloom walked past with a rather brassy tart on his arm.

"Who's that woman?" demanded Mrs Izzy.

"That's Rozenbloom's mistress," explained her husband.

She pondered for a moment and then said, "Izzy, I think our mistress is much better than Rozenbloom's."

# MOTHERS-IN-LAW
See FATHERS-IN-LAW

MY mother-in-law thinks I'm effeminate. But compared to her I probably am.

*     *     *

ONE mother-in-law to another: "I have never made a

fool of my son-in-law. I always allow him the opportunity to develop his natural capacities."

* * *

I NEVER forget a face. But in my mother-in-law's case, I am willing to make an exception.

* * *

THE local Peeping Tom knocked on the door the other night and asked if the mother-in-law would mind closing her bedroom curtains.

* * *

WONDERFUL woman my mother-in-law, 75 years old and never uses glasses. Drinks straight from the bottle.

* * *

FOR 20 years my mother-in-law and me were happy.
  Then we met.

* * *

MY mother-in-law is musical and does a bit of singing. Yesterday she was practising and three factories knocked off for lunch.

* * *

MY mother-in-law has a speech impediment. Now and then she has to pause for breath.

* * *

FRED rented a little cottage by the sea and wired his wife that the holiday was arranged and to come and join him. But he got a shock to see both wife and mother arrive with luggage.

  First chance he got he took his wife aside and whispered: "Didn't you get the telegram not to bring your mother?"

  "Yes," she replied, "that's what she wants to talk to you about."

* * *

MARRIAGE Anonymous is a club for bachelors. If any member is tempted to get married they send over a mother-in-law in a dressing gown and hair curlers.

FRED was explaining to his mate at the bar that he had yet another fight with his mother-in-law.

"But at least she came crawling to me on her hands and knees this time," he said.

His mate was impressed: "Why, what did she say?"

"Come out from under the bed you pathetic, snivelling little coward and I'll clobber you again!"

\* \* \*

BLOKE on a caravan holiday in Far North Queensland with his wife and mother-in-law was wakened one morning. His wife said her mother hadn't returned from her morning walk and she was alarmed. They searched along the river bank for a while before the wife let out a scream when she saw her mother paddling in the shallows and a large crocodile stalking her from behind.

"Oh my Gawd," screamed the wife, "Do something, quick!"

The man considered the situation for a moment and said: "The croc got himself into this trouble, let him get himself out of it."

\* \* \*

THE same mother-in-law was kidnapped when they returned from their holiday. After three days they got a note from the kidnappers saying that if they didn't send the ransom money immediately, they would send her back.

\* \* \*

HE complained to the doctor that he was worried about his mother-in-law. "She keeps blowing smoke rings through her nose when she talks to me."

"Nothing unusual about that," said the Doc. "Lots of people blow rings when they are smoking."

"Yeah, but my mother-in-law doesn't smoke," he said.

## MOTORING

THE freeway is where drivers under 25 do over 90, and drivers over 90 do 25.

269

THE motorist on tour stopped his car at Oodnadatta and asked a local how to get to Tennant Creek.

"Well, I certainly wouldn't start from here," he said.

\* \* \*

THE garage mechanic lifted the bonnet. "If I was you, sir, I'd keep the oil and change the car."

\* \* \*

THE best thing to say for the advent of motoring, is that it has certainly stamped out horse-stealing.

\* \* \*

CITY couple were driving in the country and stopped in a one-horse town to ask a local how to get back on the highway.

He scratched his head and said. "I don't think you can get there from here."

"It's no use asking him," said the woman to her husband. "He's stupid."

"Me? Stupid?" exclaimed the local. "I'm not the one that's lost. You two are."

\* \* \*

COP stopped a motorist one night. "How long have you been driving without a tail light?" he asked.

The driver jumped out and went to the rear of the car and began to moan and groan. "Oh hell," he lamented.

His distress was so genuine the cop was sympathetic. "Oh c'mon Sir, it is not that serious an offence."

"Isn't it?" moaned the driver. "What about the wife and kids and the whole bloomin' caravan?"

\* \* \*

IRISH cop stopped a motorist. "Would you be having a driver's licence?" he asked.

"Indeed I have," said the driver.

"Well that's good. Because if you didn't I'd have to see it."

\* \* \*

SHE took her car to the service station. "What's wrong with it?" said the mechanic.

270

"It's got an indifferent horn," she said.

"What d'yer mean?"

"It doesn't give a hoot."

*　　*　　*

THE police stopped him because he looked as if he was a bit under the weather. He was approached with the breathalyser bag.

"What's that?" he asked.

"It tells you if you have had too much to drink," said the cop.

"Amazing. I'm married to one of them."

*　　*　　*

FRED drove his car back to the second-hand dealer.

"You remember you sold me this car last week and said its sole previous owner was a little old woman, quiet and reserved and only used the car to go to church on Sundays?"

"Yes," said the salesman a little cautiously.

"Well can you give me her name," said Fred. "I have cleaned out the boot and the glove box and I want to return her cigar butts, two empty gin bottles, a pair of silk garters with spangles on them and a pair of red knickers."

*　　*　　*

HE was parking his battered old jalopy in the main street when a policeman stopped beside him and asked if he had reported the accident.

*　　*　　*

SHE was explaining the damage to the side of their new car to her husband.

"An old man in a Ford ran into me," she said.

"Yeah, but how many times?"

*　　*　　*

"I GOT rid of that rear noise in the car."

"How?"

"I made her sit in the front with me."

271

MIDDLE-AGED couple were driving along when the traffic cop pulled them over. "You were travelling at 90," said the cop.

"Rubbish," said the husband, "It was only 60."

The cop insisted on 90 and the driver was getting angry, at which point his wife leaned over. "Don't argue with him officer. He's always pig-headed when he's had a few drinks."

\*　　\*　　\*

TRAFFIC Cop: "Hey, you are blocking traffic, can't you go any faster?"

"Yes, but I don't want to leave the car."

\*　　\*　　\*

TRAFFIC Cop: "Do you know you were doing over 100 kilometres an hour?"

"Impossible," she said. "I only left home twenty minutes ago."

\*　　\*　　\*

HIS wife was waiting for him when he got home. "Darling," she sobbed. "I'm afraid I dented the front bumper of your new car today."

"Oh that's okay darling," he said. "Where is it?"

"In the back seat."

\*　　\*　　\*

FRED was driving his van slowly and with great caution, but what attracted the traffic cop was the frequent stops when Fred would dash to the rear of the van and kick the back doors.

The cop stopped him and asked for an explanation.

"Well officer," he began, "I have three tonnes of budgerigars on board and if they all land at once the van's springs will collapse."

\*　　\*　　\*

IT was Saturday and the traffic cop signalled the bloke driving the horse float to pull over.

"What's your hurry?" he said.

The trainer looked at his watch. "I have to be at the track for the first race at 1.30," he said.

The cop did a slow circumnavigation of the vehicles, looked in the float, and finally re-appeared at the driver's window.

"You've got no horses on board," he said.

"I know, I know," said the trainer. "I'm taking the non-starters aren't I?"

*    *    *

FOR some learner drivers, L-plates are more like destination boards.

*    *    *

THE distinguished old gent driving the Rolls had finally spotted a parking space and was sedately reversing into the kerb when a flash little sports car zipped in, skidded to a halt and stole the space from under his nose.

The cheeky driver hopped out and said, "You've got to be young and nippy to do that, Pops."

The old gent ignored him and the Rolls continued reversing until there was the sound of breaking glass and crunching metal and the sports car was reduced to a crumpled heap.

When he got out the old gent said: "You've got to be old and rich to do that, Sport!"

*    *    *

HIS car was veering from one side of the road to the other. He nearly ran off the road, when the cop pulled him up.

"You are drunk," said the cop.

"Thank goodnesh for that offisher. I thought my steering had gone."

*    *    *

PADDY was leaning on the bar enjoying a "point" when somebody yelled, "Hey Paddy, there's a bloke stealing your car!"

Paddy dashed from the pub but came back five minutes later all puffed out.

"Did you get him?" pressed his mates.

"No, I got close," puffed Paddy. "But it's okay, I took the number."

* * *

TWO Aussie tourists were motoring in England along one of those tight country lanes when the squire, in his Rolls, approached from the opposite direction. As the cars drew close the squire wound down the window, looked the Aussies in the eye and shouted, "Pigs!"

Our lads were taken aback and were still getting over the shock when, right around the next bend, they ran into a herd of pigs.

## MOVIES

HE said he saw a good film last night. It was called Moby Dick.

"I don't like sex films," she replied.

He said it wasn't about sex. "It was about whales."

"I don't like the Welsh either," she said.

* * *

WHEN the matron's eyes got accustomed to the dark she realised a young lad was sitting beside her.

"Why aren't you at school?" she said.

"Because I've got chicken pox," he replied.

* * *

A WOMAN rushed from the front stalls to tell the manager she had been molested. He tried to calm her down but when two more complained about the same thing he thought he had better investigate. In the second row he found a man on his hands and knees.

"I've lost my toupé," said the luckless patron. "I had my hand on it three times but it got away."

* * *

A MOVIE star is a person who strives for years to be well-known, then goes down side streets with dark glasses to avoid being recognised.

A HOLLYWOOD marriage is a great way to spend a weekend.

* * *

HE was only six years old, but he decided to take his girlfriend to the movies.

"How much is it?" he asked at the box office.

"Well, sonny, for grown ups in long pants it is eight dollars, but as you are only wearing short pants it is four dollars."

"Well in that case," piped up his girlfriend, "I should get in for nothing!"

* * *

THEY snuggled down in the stalls at the movies, but the woman in front was wearing a large hat which obstructed their view. He tapped her on the shoulder. She turned round and it was his wife.

## MULTI-NATIONAL

THE author just happens to be multi-national. He's part Irish and part Italian. That's Irish from his mother's side, and Italian by a friend of his father's.

* * *

BEFORE this country became multi-cultural a traditional Australian seven-course meal consisted of a six-pack and a pie.

* * *

AN Englishman, an Australian and a Scotsman were invited to a party. The Englishman took six bottles of Guiness, the Aussie took six cans of beer, and the Scotsman took six of his friends.

* * *

THREE soldiers met in the pub. The Australian stood a round, the Englishman stood a round and the Scotsman stood six feet tall.

"I'M Murphy, Irish, and proud of it."

"I'm McTavish, Scotch, and fond of it!"

* * *

IF a paddock full of Irishmen is a Paddy Field, then a paddock full of Ockers must be a vacant lot.

* * *

WHEN Paddy emigrated from Ireland to Australia, it lifted the IQ of both countries.

* * *

YOU can tell a Pommie, but you can't tell him much.

* * *

A LAZY German lives by the sweat of his frau.

* * *

BRITONS have an infinite capacity for churning themselves up into a terrific calmness.

* * *

A SCOTSMAN had been playing the pools and eventually won £500,000.

"We've made it at last," he told his wife.

"What are you going to do about the begging letters?" she asked.

"Keep sending them I suppose," he replied.

* * *

AN Irishman went for a job and was told he would have to pass an IQ test. When he asked what an IQ was the employer explained that anyone with an IQ of 150 would be admitted to university, but a bloke with an IQ of 50 would have trouble tying his shoe laces.

"Oh," said the Irishman, "So that's why so many Australians wear thongs."

* * *

IT was the bad old days and an Englishman, an Irishman and a Jew were sentenced to 50 lashes. The commandant said the rules allowed for oil or ointment on their backs.

"Then I will have olive oil, please," said the Englishman.

The Irishman was defiant. "I despise the English. I'll have nothing on my back, because I'm tough."

Then the Jew was asked what he wanted on his back. "The Irishman," he said.

\* \* \*

THREE different nationalities were discussing the meaning of 'savoir faire'.

The American said, "It means that if you came home and found your wife in bed with another man and you refrained from killing the son of a bitch, that's 'savoir faire'."

The Englishman said: "Hardly chaps. If you found your wife in bed with another man and excused yourself for interrupting and invited them to carry on, well that's 'savoir faire'."

The Frenchman had a different view: "If you came home and found your wife in bed with another man and you said 'Please continue, monsieur' and he was able to, then HE'S got 'savoir faire'."

\* \* \*

IT was Luigi's first day on the job, high on the scaffolding of the 51st level of a sky scraper when the hook of a crane knocked him off balance.

He fell into the rubbish shoot, and for the next five minutes he crashed, banged and walloped his way to the ground until he was discharged in a cloud of dust on the footpath.

"Where the hell did you come from?" asked the surprised foreman.

"Italy," said Luigi.

\* \* \*

PADDY got into a fight at the pub and was knocked down five times.

"Well, have you had enough?" said his much bigger opponent.

"Don't know," said Paddy. "This is my first fight."

THE Scottish publican picked up the phone to hear a voice say that there was a bomb planted under the pub and it would go off in ten minutes.

He put the phone down and called: "Last orders, gents!"

\* \* \*

AND what's the difference between a Scotsman and a coconut?

You can get a drink out of a coconut.

\* \* \*

TWO Scots met in Collins Street. They hadn't seen each other since they migrated from Edinburgh together 25 years ago. They hugged and slapped each other on the shoulder.

"Let's have a drink, like we did in the old times," said Jock.

"Aye, and don't forget, it's your shout," said the other.

\* \* \*

THE Greek businessman went to his favorite taverna and was surprised to be served by a Vietnamese waiter who spoke perfect Greek.

When paying his bill to Con the proprietor he raised the point. "How come the waiter speaks perfect Greek?" he asked Con.

"Ssh! Don't mention it. He thinks it's English."

\* \* \*

NEW Zealanders get the mickey taken out of them because of their funny accents when ordering "fush and chups." But we know of a chap in Auckland, when out with his girlfriend and two other couples, who went into a restaurant and ordered "a table for sex," and then added, "and three pillows."

\* \* \*

THE Chinese take-away and the Greek fruit shop were side by side, and each Friday morning the two owners would sweep the pavement.

Con the Greek would take the opportunity to have his little joke: "What day is it today, Charlie?"

"It's Fliday," the Chinaman would reply, and Con would roll about laughing.

Each week it was the same and Con would even get some friends to come along and listen to Charlie say "Fliday."

It got on Charlie's wick. So he went along for elocution lessons and concentrated on "Friday, Friday, Friday."

Next morning he was waiting for the big showdown, sweeping a clean pavement for ten minutes before Con appeared. "What day is it today, Charlie," grinned Con.

"It's Friday ... you Gleek plick!"

\*   \*   \*

RED Adair's fame in quelling oil rig fires stretches around the globe, so when a well in the middle of the Sahara Desert spewed smoke and flame the alert went out: "Get Red Adair."

But Red had his hands full with a fire crisis on the other side of the world, and nobody can be in two places at the same time. The Exon magnates were frantic. Without the famous Red Adair they were in heaps of trouble.

"Why not try Green Adair?" suggested a lackey.

"Who?" But as the flames roared higher in the sky, why not try Green Adair indeed.

Green Adair was contacted in the Limerick Arms in Belfast and offered one million pounds to do the job.

Within a few hours the oil engineers were amazed to see an air transport land in the desert. They gasped as the nose of the aircraft opened and a truck, bearing Green Adair and his crew sped towards the fire. They watched in amazement as the truck approached the wall of flames and disappeared into the very heart of the fire. They could see Green Adair and his men leaping about, jumping and stamping out the flames.

Finally, all charred, singed and blackened they emerged from the smoke to the cheers of their incredulous admirers.

"What will you do with the million pounds?" asked the first reporter on the scene.

"The first thing I do," said Green Adair, "will be to get some brakes for that bloomin' truck!"

*     *     *

IN a pub Harry the car dealer was trying to flog a heap of junk parked outside to a Chinese student.

"It's a reliable car," said Harry. "It is yours for five hundred dollars, but if you have the cash I will take off 20%."

The student was too shrewd to admit he didn't understand the discount and said he would think it over.

When he got the chance he asked the barmaid quietly, "If I give you five hundred dollars, how much you take off?"

"Everything except my earrings, honey. No worries."

*     *     *

THREE men answered an advertisement to join a mining survey expedition into the Outback. They were a Scotsman, a German, and a Chinaman. The boss said the Scotsman would be in charge of the engineers, the German would be in charge of the mechanics, and the Chinaman, well, they are all good cooks, so he said the Chinaman could be in charge of supplies. "But we leave promptly at eight tomorrow," he said.

Next morning, the Scot and the German showed up, but there was no sign of the Chinaman. They waited for half an hour before the boss gave a curse and ordered that they set off without him.

The party had travelled only a few hundred metres up the road when the Chinaman jumped out from, behind a tree and shouted: "Supplies, supplies!"

AN Englishman, American and an Irishman were arrested in South America for smuggling. "We'll give you gringos a fair trial and shoot you tomorrow," said the "capitan" of the guard.

The three spent a restless night. "But not to worry, chaps," said the Englishman. "I shall invoke the natural disaster plan. These South Americans are terrified of natural disaster. Just watch me."

So at dawn the Englishman said he would face the firing squad first and the other two watched from their cell as the capitan said "Ready ... Aim ..."

"Earthquake! Earthquake!" roared the Englishman at the top of his voice. The South Americans panicked and in the confusion the Pommie escaped.

Later the American was led to the stake and the capitan said: "Ready ... Aim..."

"Flood! Flood!" roared the Yank and in the confusion he escaped too.

The Irishman had picked up the drift of the plot. It was all a matter of timing, so he listened as the capitan ordered, "Ready... Aim..."

"Fire!" yelled the Irishman.

\* \* \*

JILL, she was a pretty girl,
and Jack, an ardent male
He praised her shapely beauty
In English, French,
And Braille.

## MUSIC ✓

THE serious music lover is the bloke who, hearing a soprano in the bathroom, puts his ear to the keyhole.

\* \* \*

AN earnest young man with a violin case under his arm asked a London Bobby: "How do I get to the Albert Hall?"

The bobby replied: "Practice, practice, practice."

THE old lady asked the busker: "Do you always play by ear?"

"No, Ma'am, sometimes I play over there."

* * *

"WHY do you play the same piece all the time?"

"It haunts me."

"So it should. You've murdered it often enough."

* * *

"I AM always breaking into song."

"Well, if you found the right key you wouldn't have to break in."

* * *

"CAN you sing opera?"

"Yes."

"Can you sing Faust?"

"Faust or slow, any way you like."

* * *

PADDY Murphy thought the Guinness Book of Records was an LP of Irish drinking songs.

* * *

AFTER the concert she said, "My word, that soprano had a wonderful repertoire."

"Yes," he said, "and that tight dress showed it off well."

* * *

THE Scotsman said his singing voice was a natural gift.

We all agreed, it would have to be.

* * *

HE was a short-sighted musician, and one day he fell over a clef.

* * *

SHE went out with a musician once, and has never been composed since.

* * *

I CAN'T sing. So I am looking for a ravishing blonde accompanist who can't play the piano.

INTRIGUED by the complications in trying to fold road maps while seated in a Mini Minor, Arthur persevered until he became a celebrated accordian player.

*　　*　　*

HE had just landed on English shores from Dublin and went straight to a pub and bought a round of beers.

"Will an Irish tenner be alright?" he asked the barman.

When the barman replied, "no problem" he broke out in the chorus of "Oh Danny Boy..."

*　　*　　*

FRED played the trombone and eventually got a gig in Las Vegas. Tired from the long flight he booked into the swank hotel and turned in early but was awakened by a knock on the door about midnight.

"Hello there," said a ravishing brunette. "Are you Frank Sinatra?"

"No Miss, I'm Fred Nerd from Moonee Ponds, Melbourne," and he shut the door and climbed back into bed.

An hour later there was another knock. Fred wearily opened the door to see a lovely redhead. "Hi there, are you Frank Sinatra?"

"No," he said, "I'm Fred Nerd," and slammed the door and dived back into the blankets.

You've guessed it, there was yet another knock on the door. This time a ravishing blonde wearing a see-through negligee says: "Hello, are you Frank Sinatra?"

"Am I Frankie, baby?" And throwing his arms out wide Fred starts singing at the top of his voice, "Strangers in the night ... New York, New York ..."

*　　*　　*

THE old maestro had fallen on hard times, mainly due to tippling the whisky bottle. He had been a concert pianist of great renown in his time and his drinking pals at the Pig and Whistle decided they should be responsible for putting him back on the concert circuit.

They chipped in and bought an old tuxedo from the Opportunity Shop, not knowing that the trousers had a split in the crotch.

They booked him for the next benefit concert at the Mechanics' Hall and lined the front row on the opening night. When the maestro came on stage, bowed and sat on his chair at the piano there was a gasp of concern from the front row, and one of his friends was so bold as to leap onto the stage and whisper.

"Do you know your old flannel shirt is flapping through a hole in your tuxedo?"

"No," said the maestro thoughtfully, "But if you hum the tune I will soon pick up the melody!"

*    *    *

A SAILOR who had been six months at sea was hunting the waterfront looking for a bar where he could have a quiet drink. He inspected a few, but the one that took his fancy had a South Sea Island motif, a monkey swinging around the chandelier and a pianist tinkling out a tune in the corner.

He went in and ordered a martini. As the barman put the drink on the counter the monkey swung down from the rafters, spun around and dunked his feet in the glass.

Naturally, the sailor reacted with loud abuse at the barman.

"Did you see that!" he roared. "Get me another drink."

The barman dutifully delivered another martini and set it on the bar, but before the sailor could reach for the glass the monkey dropped from the roof again, spun round and once more dunked his feet in the drink.

The sailor was furious. He gripped the barman by the shirt-front and lifted him across the bar.

"It's not my monkey. Not my monkey," protested the barman. "It belongs to the pianist over there."

The sailor dropped the bartender on the floor and strode over to the pianist.

"Do you know your monkey is paddling his feet in my martini,?" he roared.

"No," replied the pianist thoughtfully, "But if you hum the tune I'll soon pick up the melody!"

* * *

THE guest had heard the strains of classical music but when he entered the drawing room he was amazed to see a large tomcat playing the piano.

"And there is no music," he noted with further astonishment.

"No," said the proud owner. "He writes his own music, and the piece he is playing now is one of my favourites."

"You should have it orchestrated," said the guest.

The cat leapt out of the window and has never been seen since.

* * *

THE busker was repeating the same old tune on the corner of the street until the lady shopkeeper came out and said: "Do you play the refrain?"

"Yes Ma'am," he said.

"Then would you please refrain from playing it here," she said.

* * *

THE vicar's sermon was again interrupted by the arrival of yet another late straggler. "There have been more late entries than an Irish orchestra," he said.

* * *

HE is an original player. He makes a lot of mistakes, but they are always different each time.

* * *

AN Indian psychiatrist from New Delhi visiting Salt Lake City called at the local asylum and heard the inmates singing. Investigating further he saw a large group of choristers holding an apple and tapping the apple with the other hand. "Are they inmates?" he asked.

"No, that's the Moron Tap-an-Apple Choir," he was told.

So he hot-footed it back to India and told Indira Ghandi that there was a lot of money to be made with choirs.

Hadn't the Vienna Boys Choir been successful?

So they got 500 young boys together and trained them for weeks until they were ready for their first audition before a visiting Italian maestro. He listened to their first rendition with eyes averted and then said "terrible, terrible. They are not castrata." Indira Ghandi was told they had to have that little operation that made all the difference. They did and they were ultimicimo, and began their world tour as the Indian Nackerless 500.

*    *    *

THE band had just finished its first bracket when the master of ceremonies came on stage. "Ladies and gentlemen. I have wonderful news. Our band leader's wife has just presented him with a fine bouncing baby boy. I would like the proud father to stand and take a bow.

As the leader stood and bowed, so did the entire band behind him.

*    *    *

IN the orchestra he plays piano. At home he plays second fiddle.

*    *    *

MY brother was known as the Van Gogh of the violin. He had no ear for it.

*    *    *

MY sister used to play the banjo until she married. Now she picks on her husband.

*    *    *

THE young musician with a violin case under his arm was boasting of his prowess.

"The director of the National Symphony Orchestra was trying to get me for months."

"Who were you playing with at the time?"

"His wife!"

IT was amateur night down at the local and Fred stood on the table and rendered "An Irish Lullaby."

He noticed one young lady reach for a handkerchief and wipe a tear from her eye. Thinking she was overcome with emotion he later approached her.

"Are you Irish then?"

"No," she said with a sob. "I'm a music teacher."

\*　　\*　　\*

THE professor had a theory that music would sooth the savage beast so he took his violin and trekked deep into the jungle of darkest Africa. All around were the roars and screams of ferocious animals.

When he came to a little clearing he opened the violin case and began playing classical music. One by one the animals came out to listen, and soon, sitting quietly in a circle, was an elephant, a gorilla, three buffalo, a few snakes and a pair of tigers.

They were listening enraptured, when with a loud roar a lion sprang into the clearing and bit off the professor's head.

"What did you do that for?" chorused the other animals. "First time we get to hear lovely music and you spoil it," they said.

The lion cupped a paw to his ear and said "Eh?"

\*　　\*　　\*

FRED has a musical nature
He can yodel, whistle and hum
He goes out fit as a fiddle
And comes home tight as a drum.

# N

## NAMES

RUTH is stranger than fiction.

*     *     *

I WAS born on the first of the month, so they called me Bill.

*     *     *

ARE you chewing gum?
　No, I'm Harry McGillicardy.

*     *     *

"I LOVE men who are frank."
　"Bad luck. My name's Algernon.

*     *     *

"WHAT are the names of your parents?"
　"Mum and Dad."

*     *     *

THE new vicar in town even entered the country pub in a bid to introduce himself and approached an old-timer at the bar with outstretched hand.
　"My name is Paul," he said.
　The old-timer studied him for a moment and then said: "Did those Thessalonians ever write back to you?"

*     *     *

THE track official approached the new athlete. "Are you a pole vaulter?"

288

"Yes," he replied, "I am from Gdansk. But how did you know my name vas Valter?"

* * *

AS the MC said when introducing the prime minister: "I am keen on genealogy. I've made a study of names and I can tell you that Keating means bright and intelligent.

Unfortunately, Paul means 'Not Very'."

(Change name to suit guest of honour).

## NEIGHBOURS

EVER since we put the "Neighbourhood Watch" sign on our gate every nosey neighbour comes in and wants to know the time.

* * *

IT'S been tough keeping up with the Jones. Especially since Tom moved next door.

* * *

DON'T keep trying to keep up with the Joneses. Drag them down to your level.

* * *

BERT stuck his head over the fence and asked Fred if he could borrow his mower.

"Sorry, Bert," said Fred. "The neighbour on the other side has had it for a week. I've just got it back and I've got to cut my own lawn. It will take me all day."

"In that case then," said Bert, "you won't mind if I borrow your golf clubs?"

* * *

THE easiest way to meet your new neighbours is to play the stereo full blast at 2 a.m.

* * *

A NEIGHBOUR is a person who listens to you attentively, through a wall.

A GOOD neighbour is the one who, when borrowing a corkscrew, says bring it over.

## NEWLY-WEDS

HERE today, gone home to-momma.

*　　*　　*

HE has a problem about the future. He's getting married in a month and he hasn't found a job for his wife.

*　　*　　*

A YOUNG bride was explaining her problem to her long-married friend. "How can I keep my husband in line?" she asked.

Her older and wiser friend didn't hesitate: "My dear," she said, "your husband shouldn't have to wait in line!"

*　　*　　*

THE newly-weds had been married for a month and some of the novelty appeared to be wearing off.

"Well I'm getting sick of the same meal morning noon and night," he complained. "Nothing but wedding cake and chips."

*　　*　　*

SHE had served him so many burnt offerings that on their first anniversary he bought her an altar cloth.

*　　*　　*

THE new husband sat down at the table after his young bride had just cooked her first chicken.

"What did you stuff it with?" he asked in hungry anticipation.

"I didn't stuff it," she said. "It wasn't hollow!"

*　　*　　*

BILL and Beryl had been married only a few weeks when Bill had to travel interstate on a job. While he was away, Beryl's sister Betty moved in to keep her company.

Bill finished the job sooner than expected and was

quickly on a plane home. When he arrived at the airport he dashed to a phone.

Betty answered the call.

"Is Beryl there?" he asked.

"No, she's having a bath," said Betty.

"Don't disturb her then. Just tell her to put a couple of stubbies in the fridge and I will be home about midnight. Tell her to put on her sheerest nightie and a dab of perfume and I will sneak in and wake her with a kiss."

"Okay, and who will I say called?" asked Betty.

*   *   *

HE had only been married six months when he confided to his mate: "I've just had a terrible shock. I have just discovered my wife is a liar."

"How do you know?" asked his mate.

"She said she was out with Betty last night. But I was out with Betty last night!"

*   *   *

THE newlyweds had just settled on their farm and she brought his lunch out to the home paddock. As he was finishing his last sandwich a little red hen dashed by being chased by a rooster. He threw the rooster a piece of crust and it stopped dead in its tracks and began to peck the bread.

"I hope you never get that hungry," mused the bride.

*   *   *

"HOUSEWORK, it's so boring," said the first-year bride. "You make the beds, clean the floors and do the dishes. Then three months later you have to do it all again."

*   *   *

(R) THE new bride was too embarrassed to talk about sex, so the groom explained it as delicately as he could.

"No need to talk about it," he said. "Whenever we are in bed and you want it, just pull it once. If you don't want it, just pull it about 350 times."

# NEWSPAPERS

NEWSPAPERS are still credible, provided you read between the lies.

*     *     *

YOU should never tell a journalist what you don't want to read in the papers.

*     *     *

LIKE a dead wombat, a good journalist always keeps his ear to the ground.

*     *     *

THE reporter was pressing the old gent on his 100th birthday as to why he had lived so long.

"Two reasons," said the old-timer, "The first is my life-long practice of having two whiskies a day."

"And second?" asked the reporter eagerly.

"Cancelling my voyage on the Titanic," said the old gent.

*     *     *

NEWS Flash! A helicopter crashed into the cemetery of an Irish village this afternoon. At last count, 705 bodies had been recovered.

*     *     *

THE Free Press: Where three men impose their prejudices on 15 million.

*     *     *

SHE was only the newsagent's daughter, but she loved her Daily Mail.

*     *     *

MY dad was an old newspaper man. He went broke. Nobody wanted old newspapers.

*     *     *

AS a reporter he was trained to ask Who? What? Where? When? and Why? Then his first assignment turned out to be a wedding.

"PAPER, paper, gigantic fraud!" roared the newsboy. "Fifty-six victims in gigantic fraud!"

Chap stopped to buy a paper and quickly scanned the front page.

"Just a minute," he said. "This is yesterday's and there's nothing about a fraud."

"Paper, paper! Fifty-seven victims in gigantic fraud," roared the paperboy.

\* \* \*

THE advertisement in the local newspaper read: "Editor urgently needs poof reader."

\* \* \*

LETTER to the advertising manager. "Last Friday I lost a gold watch which was a valuable heirloom. I advertised in the Lost and Found column of your Saturday edition with almost immediate results. Yesterday I found the watch in the pocket of another suit in my wardrobe. Congratulations."

\* \* \*

A FRONT page panel on the newspaper read: The Daily Bugle was the first to report the death of Cr Grabalot, and was the first to announce that this report was untrue. The Daily Bugle is always first with the news.

\* \* \*

CORRECTION: The China Seafood Restaurant advertisement in Saturday's edition was incorrect. It read #/ @%°°%#. It should have read !°°&/#@°&##. We regret any inconvenience this may have caused.

\* \* \*

THE businessman stopped by the newsboy. "Anything new in the paper today?" he asked.

"Naw," said the lad. "Just the same things happening to different people."

\* \* \*

THE country newspaper was prospering so well with advertising it couldn't cater for all the news. The pointer on the front page explained it all: "On account of lack of space this week, 15 births and three deaths have been held over until next issue."

* * *

IT was rare for the Archbishop of Canterbury to visit a small town so at the press conference the local reporter desperately wanted to scoop his metropolitan rivals. He managed to get the first question away: "Will you be visiting the nightclubs?"

The archbishop was a little surprised. "Are there nightclubs in this small town?" he said.

The newspaper had its headline. "ARCHBISHOP'S FIRST WORDS: ARE THERE ANY NIGHTCLUBS IN THIS TOWN?"

* * *

IT had been a slow day, so when a bloke got hit by a bus, reporters from both rival newspapers were on the scene. One was a seasoned journo, the other was a cadet.

Next day the cadet's editor called him in to show that the old scribe had gleaned a more interesting item from a routine event. It happened to be the victim's birthday.

"Ask more questions," roared the editor.

The lad was a quick learner and at his very next accident he crawled under an overturned bus to reach a moaning victim to ask, with notebook in hand: "Don't suppose it's your birthday today?"

* * *

HE was sent to cover the earthquake and began his first bulletin with "God has caused tremendous devastation ..."

He received an urgent message from his editor: "Forget the earthquake. Interview God."

* * *

AT the press conference the boring politician groaned along on his dreary speech, ad nauseum, until one reporter, a little the worse for drink, actually threw a bottle at him.

Unfortunately it missed the politician and hit another journalist a glancing blow on the head, to which his immediate response was: "Hit me again, I can still hear the bludger."

* * *

THE cadet had been assigned to do the annual story on Colonel Frobisher. "He has the reputation of being England's bravest soldier," said the editor. "The story has been done before, but if you can get a new angle, then you are well on the way m'lad."

The cadet went off to the Old Soldier's Home with the advice of his chief still ringing in his ears. "If only there was a time Frobisher had been scared ..."

He found the colonel sitting in his wheelchair and soon came to the point. "Surely, Sir, surely there was a time when you were frightened?"

The colonel looked thoughtful for a while. "Well there was the time I was with the fusiliers in India and this rogue tiger had eaten two or three of the native chaps," he began.

"I remember tracking the beast through the jungle, followed his tracks and got a glimpse of him hiding behind some tall grass.

"I cocked my gun and crept right up to the grassy patch and I was about to peep through when the monster leapt straight at me and roared 'Aaaarrgh!' My God, I shit myself."

The cadet whipped out his notebook. "When was that?" he asked eagerly, "when was that?"

"Just then when I went 'Aaaarrgh'," said the colonel.

* * *

A SUB-EDITOR had doubts about a cadet's story on a farmer who had lost 2025 pigs from a small farm in the outer suburbs. It seemed too many pigs, so the sub rang the farmer.

"Is it true that you owned two thousand and twenty-five pigs?"

"Yeth," lisped the pig farmer. "That wath the thituation."

The sub said thanks, hung up and corrected the copy to read: Two sows and 25 pigs.

*     *     *

THE businessman was testifying that advertising got results. "We advertised for a nightwatchman, and that very same night our safe was robbed," he said.

*     *     *

A SHARK alarm at Bondi sent everyone rushing from the surf, except three young boys who didn't hear the siren. Those on the beach were aghast to see the dorsel fin moving towards them.

A tall, blonde, bronzed young man took a deep breath and plunged into the surf, swam right past the shark and brought in two of the boys.

He took another deep breath and plunged through the surf again to snatch the third boy from the jaws of the monster.

When all three were safe on the beach he took yet another deep breath and with a knife between his teeth, swam out for a third time to tackle the shark in a struggle to its death.

When he finally staggered up the beach a reporter who had witnessed it all ran up to him. "That's the most heroic feat I have ever witnessed. What's yer name? This is bound to make the front page tomorrow. I can just see the headlines: AUSSIE HERO KILLS SHARK, SAVES THREE!"

The young man interrupted him. "Thanks, that's nice of you, but I must correct you on one point. I am not Australian. I am an Englishman out here on holidays."

The reporter looked a bit crestfallen but said, "No worries, it's still a great story."

The headlines next day read: "POMMIE BASTARD KILLS KIDS' PET!"

HEADLINES:

"DON'T PRINT STORY OF MY DIVORCE" sobs
Actress. See sensational exclusive, page 7.
WOMAN RECOVERING AFTER FATAL CRASH
POLICE MOVE IN BOOK CASE
BISHOP TURNS SOD

\* \* \*

AFTER a man escaped from an asylum, raping a washer-
woman as he fled, the headline that afternoon read: NUT
SCREWS WASHER AND BOLTS.

\* \* \*

THE sub was handling a sports report from the local
cricket club secretary who spelt bowling, b-o-e-l-i-n-g.
"That," said the sub, "is the worst spell of bowling I have
seen."

\* \* \*

AND full credit to American journalist William Safire
for this advice on, How to Write Good:

Avoid run-on sentences they are hard to read.

No sentence fragments.

It behoves us to avoid archaisms.

Also, avoid awkward or affected alliteration.

Don't use no double negatives.

If I've told you once, I've told you a thousand times:
resist hyperbole.

Avoid commas, that are not necessary.

Verbs has to agree with their subjects.

Avoid trendy locutions that sound flaky.

Writing carefully, dangling participles should not be
used.

Kill all exclamation marks!!!

Never use a long word when a diminutive one will
do.

Poofread carefully to see if you any words out.

Take the bull by the hand, and don't mix metaphors.

Don't verb nouns.

Never, ever use repetitive redundancies.
Last but not least, avoid cliches like the plague.

★　　★　　★

THERE was a young lady from Stawell
   Wore a newspaper dress to a ball
   But her garb caught on fire
   And burned her entire
   Front page, sports section and all.

# O

## OCKERS ABROAD

KEVIN and Bruce had overstayed their English holiday and were in desperate need of a job, so the advertisement they saw in the "Times" was most appropriate. It read: "Two butlers needed for Scottish country manor. References a must."

The references were an initial problem, but was solved with simple Aussie ingenuity. Keven wrote Bruce's reference and Bruce gave Kevin a splendid wrap.

When they were ushered before the lady of the manor they proffered their references but she waved them aside. "Later," she said, "First, I'd like to check your knees. Formal wear here means wearing kilts so if you would be so kind as to drop the tweeds ..." The lads thought it a little strange, but they did so.

"Not bad," she said. "Now you can show me your testimonials."

When they picked themselves up from the gravel driveway, Kevin said: "With a little more education we would have got that job."

&ast;  &ast;  &ast;

TWO Ockers from the same town met in London. "Fancy meeting you over here," said Bruce to Merv. "Listen mate, you've got to come over to my flat tomorrow night. We're having a small gathering."

Merv said he'd be in like Flynn.

"Get the tube to Earl's Court, straight down the High Street, second on the right, number 35 and you can ring the bell with your elbows."

"What's with the elbows bit?" said Merv.

"Well you're not coming without bottles are ya?"

*　　*　　*

AT the Ockers picnic they were selling coffee at 50 cents a mug. The queue of mugs stretched back around the corner.

*　　*　　*

THE pretty fraulein approached the Ocker at the Munich beer hall and invited him to her flat. She gave him a nice meal and he stayed the night.

In the morning after a hearty breakfast he was about to leave and made a little speech about the outstanding hospitality he had received.

"Ja, the words are nice," she said, "but what about marks?"

"Bloomin' oath, nine out of ten I reckon," he said.


## ODDS

I KNOW a woman who has got more brains in her head than I've got in my little finger.

*　　*　　*

"DO you know a bloke with one leg called Moloney?"

"No. What's the name of his other leg?"

*　　*　　*

"HEY Fred, what's Billie's other name?"

"Billie who?"

*　　*　　*

ETHYL says her husband is a man of few words, and every one of them unprintable.

*　　*　　*

"FRED'S taken up meditation."

"Well, that's better than sitting around doing nothing."

HE spent a fortune on deodorant before he realised that people didn't like him anyway.

\* \* \*

"WHAT'S that mark on your shoulder?"
   "A birthmark."
   "Had it long?"

\* \* \*

A SNAIL got rich and fulfilled a lifelong dream by buying a racing car and lodging an entry in the Grand Prix. He painted the letter "S" for snail on the side of his speedy machine and when he raced down the straight the crowd roared: "Look at that "S" car go."

\* \* \*

THE nun who always slept with her clothes on just couldn't get out of the habit.

## OFFICE

THE boss is the bloke in the office who is late when you are early, and early when you are late.

\* \* \*

HE nervously faced the boss: "My wife told me to ask you for a rise."
   "Okay. I will ask my wife if you can have one."

\* \* \*

TESTY boss: "Answer that phone."
   "It hasn't rung yet."
   "Well, why do you have to wait until the last minute?"
   And to the latecomer: "You should have been here at nine o"clock."
   "Why, what happened?"

\* \* \*

HE advertised for a secretary: "Wanted. Young lady assistant who can type. One who has no bad habits and is willing to learn."

THE boss's secretary had been hired for her legs and figure, but her sloppy arithmetic was getting too much to bear.

Finally, the boss said, "Next time you deliver the day's figures make sure you add up the column at least three times."

She went one better the very next day. "Mister Smithers, I have added these figures ten times," she said dropping the papers on his desk with a dazzling smile, "and here are my ten answers."

*　　*　　*

"WHAT do you think of our new boss?"

"He dresses smartly."

"And quickly too!"

*　　*　　*

THE salesman set the computer up on the executive's desk at W.F. Fotheringham & Son. "This is the latest technology, Mr Fotheringham," he said. "Ask it any question. Even personal questions."

The executive was sceptical. "Okay," he said, and typed in: "Where is my father?"

The answer came back instantly: "Your father is playing golf at Royal Melbourne."

"There you are," said the boss. "It's wrong. My father died five years ago."

The salesman was surprised, but not flustered. "He typed in: "Where, exactly, is Mr Fotheringham senior?"

The answer was just as prompt. "Mr Fotheringham senior died five years ago, but Bill Fotheringham's dad is still at the seventh green at Royal Melbourne!"

*　　*　　*

SOME couldn't spell, others couldn't type, few could do shorthand. The businessman who wanted a private secretary was about to despair when the employment agency phoned to say they were sending round a girl who had a number of things going for her.

302

She turned out to be a ravishing long-legged blonde, and the business executive was immediately entranced.

"I'll pay you $500 a week, with pleasure," he said.

"With pleasure, will be $1000 a week," she said.

* * *

NOTICE in the office: In an effort to spread the work more evenly would all staff take advantage of the stenographers earlier in the day!

* * *

GLOSSARY of Management terms:

Delegate: Pass the buck.
Pending: Haven't figured it out yet.
Delayed: Forgotten.
Urgency: Panic.
Extreme urgency: Blind panic.
Frank discussion: Bloody argument.
Analytical projection: Guess.
Forecast: Guess.
Long-range forecast: Wild guess.
Scheduled: Hoped for.
Deficiency analysis: Search for scapegoat.
Ambitious: Ruthless.
Strategy: Low cunning.
Shrewd: Devious.
Profit: Profit.
Profit before tax: Loss.
Deficit: Staggering loss.
Industrial by-product: Waste.
Environmental pollution: Other people's waste.
Pilfering: Theft by employee.
Fringe benefit: Theft by executive.
Terminal payment: Golden handshake.
Supplementary statistical information: Padding.

# OLD CODGERS

DO not complain about growing old. Many are denied the privilege.

* * *

FRED was determined to keep healthy in his old age, and when he turned 60 he decided to walk five kilometres every day. He has now reached Adelaide.

* * *

BY the time you reach 75 years of age you've learnt everything. All you have to do is to try and remember it.

* * *

A GERIATRIC is a German cricketer who captures three successive wickets.

* * *

EVEN the parish priest was a welcome visitor for short-sighted Mrs Flannigan. "But that wasn't the priest," said her daughter after the man had left, "that was the doctor."

"Oh was it?" she exclaimed with relief, "I thought Father O'Reilly was getting rather familiar."

* * *

MRS Flannigan described herself as a sprightly old girl. "Actually I see seven gentlemen a day," she said. "I get out of bed with Will Power, then I go to my John, next it's breakfast with Uncle Toby, followed by Billy T.

Then the rest of the day is spent with either Arthur Ritis or Al Zymer until I finally go to bed with Johnny Walker.

* * *

OLD Fred fronted up to the Sperm Bank and insisted on making a donation. The matron looked at him doubt-fully. He was 83. But Fred would not be denied and protested that he was as fit as a prize bull.

Finally she gave Fred a little jar, ushered him towards

a cubicle and closed the door. For the next few minutes all she could hear was much grunting and puffing and it went on for so long she got worried. She knocked on the door.

"Are you okay?" she called

"No. I need some help," said Fred. "I can't get the lid off this bloody jar."

\* \* \*

THE old gent was backing his Rolls into the last available parking space when a zippy red sports car whipped in behind him to take the spot. The young man jumped out and said: "Sorry Pops, but you've got to be young and smart to do that."

The old man ignored the remark and kept reversing until the Rolls had crunched the sportscar into a crumpled heap. "Sorry son, you've got to be old and rich to do that!"

\* \* \*

AN old bloke was sitting at the bar sobbing with the odd tear dropping in his beer. "I got married to a lovely young widow last week," he explained to the barman. "She is a great cook, keeps my clothes in great nick and is insatiable in bed," he said.

"Then why the hell are your crying?" said the barman.

"Because I can't remember where I live," sobbed the old codger.

\* \* \*

OLD Jake went for his annual medical check-up. "Your hearing is getting worse," said the Doc. "And you will have to cut out drinking, smoking and sex."

"What?" cried Jake in alarm, "Just so I can hear better?"

\* \* \*

A YOUNG social worker used to call on Old Jake to cut up his steak and help with his meals. She noticed a bowl of almonds beside his tray. "They were given to me as a present, but I don't want them," he explained. "You can have them."

She said thanks and began to nibble away on them. "Funny present to give a man with no teeth," she remarked when she had eaten most of them.

"Oh no," he said. "They had chocolate on them then."

* * *

THE doctor had examined Old Jake's heart and summed up his advice with "No smoking, no drinking and no sex."

After much protesting by Jake the doctor relented: "Okay, one cigarette only after meals, and no more than two glasses of light beer a day.

"What about sex?" pressed Jake.

"Very occasionally," said the doctor, "and only with your wife because it is important you avoid any excitement."

* * *

AN old chap in his seventies was concerned about the lack of his sex drive and consulted his doctor.

"Well, what would you expect at your age?" said the medic.

The old geezer was still worried, "But my nextdoor neighbour is over eighty and he says he gets it every night."

The doc thought for a moment. "Well, why don't you say it too?"

* * *

A COUPLE of old timers were discussing their sexual situation. "You know Jack," said one, "I understand that drinking stout will put lead in your pencil. Why don't we try a bottle?"

"I don't know about you," replied Jack, "but I don't have that many women to write to."

* * *

ON his morning round the doctor stopped beside the little old lady he had been treating for asthma. He checked her over, asked a few questions and listened to her croaky replies.

"What about the wheeze?" he said.

"Oh, fine," she replied. "I went three times last night!"

* * *

THREE old codgers had been playing cards for a few days when one noticed that they had run out of beer. They pooled their money, drew straws and Old Jake was sent for the beer.

An hour passed. Three hours passed and there was no sign of Jake's return. One said, "I think the old bugger has run off with the money."

Jake's voice was heard from near the door. "One more smart comment like that and I won't go at all."

* * *

THE old farmer had married a comely young wench of 18 years and after a month of wedded bliss he visited his doctor for some advice.

"It's so tiring, Doc," he said. "I am still working the farm, and when I am out in the field and get the urge I have to run back to the house, jump in to bed, and afterwards, I have to walk back to the job again. It's knocking me out."

"No wonder," said the doctor. "You are 82 and she is only 18. She should be running out to you," he said.

He solved the problem by suggesting that the farmer take a shot-gun out into the field, and every time he got the urge he could fire a shot to signal that his young wife should come running.

A month later the doctor bumped into the old man down the main street and out of curiosity asked him how the shot-gun scheme was working.

"Oh it worked well for the first two weeks, but then the duck season opened and I haven't seen her since!"

* * *

THE vicar called on the rich 80-year-old grazier who had recently married a 20-year-old bride to see how he was coping.

"Can't keep my hands off her," he said.

The vicar mumbled his approval and went on his way. He called back in a week. "How's the bride?" he enquired.

"Can't keep my hands off her," repeated the old farmer. "Worse, now she has run off with one of them."

* * *

THE old codger came to see the doctor for a check up. "I'm getting married next week," he said.

The doctor was surprised for he knew the old gent was 84.

"Why would you want to get married?" he asked.

"I don't want to, I have to," said the old codger.

* * *

OLD Jake came back from the doctor's anxious to show his missus his new $3000 silicon chip hearing aid.

"It looks fine," she said.

"Half past seven," he replied.

* * *

WHEN Old Jake returned to the doctor he was given a bottle of medicine. "This is potent stuff," said the doc, "don't take it every day." The doctor wanted to make sure Old Jake understood. "So take it on alternate days, do you know what I mean? Take it tomorrow, then skip a day, then take it the next day and skip another day, and so on."

A month later the doctor saw Jake's wife in the street and enquired after the old codger.

"Oh, he's dead," she said.

The doctor was aghast.

"No, the medicine wasn't that strong," she said. "It was all that skipping!"

* * *

"WHAT'S the matter little boy," said the old codger when he saw the lad sitting on the kerb crying.

"I'm crying because I can't do what the big boys do," he said.

The old man sat on the kerb and started crying too.

OLD Jake tottered into the clinic. "Doc," he said, "you've got to do something to lower my sex drive."

"C'mon Jake," said the doctor. "Your sex drive is all in your head."

"That's what I mean. You've got to do something to lower it!"

* * *

THE old codger came to the doctor with the exciting news that he was going to marry a 20-year-old bride. "Well, I think at your age you should take things easy. In fact I think you should take in a lodger," said the doctor.

A year later he bumped into the old codger and asked how was married life.

"The wife's pregnant, I am happy to say," said the old man, and with a wink and a nudge he added, "thanks for that advice about taking in a boarder. She's pregnant too."

* * *

OLD Jake was reminiscing. "I can remember the time I gave up both booze and sex at the same time. Crikey, in all of my life that was the worst half hour I've ever spent!"

* * *

THE exhausted bush-walker stumbled into a drover's hut high in the Southern Alps and was immediately welcomed by its lone inhabitant, a tough old mountain man.

The visitor was offered food and invited to sit by the log fire.

After the meal the old man pulled down an unlabelled bottle from a shelf and offered the visitor a drink. The bush-walker accepted, but when he pulled the cork and sniffed the evil home-brew he graciously declined and attempted to return the bottle.

"Drink it!" insisted the old-timer. When the lad declined again the old man reached for his rifle, cocked it and pointed it at the lad's head.

There was no other alternative but to take a swig of the vile firewater that had a kick like a mule. When the bush-walker gasped his way to recovery he handed the bottle back, and the old man handed him the rifle.

"Now you hold the gun on me while I have a drink," he said.

## OLD SOLDIERS

IT was a regimental dinner testimonial:

"Today we honour a man who doesn't know the meaning of fear; a man who doesn't know the meaning of defeat, quit or surrender.

"So we have all chipped in and bought him a dictionary."

\* \* \*

TWO old blokes in the Returned Servicemen's Club were talking. "Do you remember those pills they used to give us in the army to keep our minds off girls?" said one.

"Vaguely," said the other.

"Well," said the first, "I think they are beginning to work."

\* \* \*

WHEN old Fred went to join the Returned Servicemen's Club they asked him if he had a war record: "Bloody oath I have," he said, "I've got Vera Lynn singing the White Cliffs of Dover."

## ONE-LINERS
See PROFOUND STATEMENTS

A STRING of one-liners unashamedly woven into a yarn on a single topic can reduce listeners to tears. While they are short and punchy in themselves, they have far more effect queued up in the same story. Sure, it requires a good memory and a little practice for delivery, but with a prompt card in your hand ready for the occasional glance to find the key word, the story line should flow with each one-liner bolstering the next.

One of the easiest forms of monologue is your own "biography." We all find it easy to talk about ourselves, so it is comparatively simple to deliver your own preposterous life story around a dinner table of strangers or friends, or even from the rostrum.

Here's an example, but remember it is an overloaded version. It can be ready to be released at the drop of several trigger questions which are bound to crop up in such groups; like what do you do for a living, how long have you lived in these parts, or where do you come from?

Where do I come from? Actually, I am part Irish and part Italian. (If you have their attention with this line, follow with): I'm Irish by my mother's side, and Italian by a friend of my father!

The family was in iron and steel. My mother ironed and my father stole.

(Now ramble on)

I was born at an early age. Premature actually. I am a man before my time.

I am really only 25.

My birth was a surprise to my Mum

... and everyone else in the Tankerville Arms at the time.

It was during the Depression, and they were tough times.

I was abandoned on a doorstep.

I wasn't found there. No, the door opened out.

I was found two somersaults out on the roadway.

There was a note pinned to my shawl.

It read: "Keep your head down. The door opens out." It was signed, "Mum!"

Years later when Mum had enough coupons to get me out of the orphanage, I met my brothers.

That's when the tough times really started.

We were so poor the woman next door had my brother.

He was a Caesarian birth. It didn't effect him, but I noticed he always left the house through the front window.

We lived in a tough neighbourhood.

You could walk ten blocks without leaving the scene of the crime.

Any kid in our street with two ears was a sissy.

Any cat with a tail in our neighbourhood was a tourist.

We used to call the nuns the Little Sisters of the Rich.

Our school still retained capital punishment.

And when we went to school my Dad used to paint the house a different colour and change the number on the front gate.

When I was seven, my Dad took me aside. And left me there.

He was tough on us. He made us run two miles every night.

By the end of the week we were 14 miles from home.

His swimming training was tougher.

He threw us off the deep end of the pier.

Swimming to shore wasn't so bad. Getting out of the bag was the hard part.

Tough? We used to have bread and pullet most nights.

Except Saturdays. On Saturday night we always had Windmill Pie. (What's Windmill Pie?) You get a bit if it goes round!

Before our Mum and Dad ran away from home Dad gave me some serious advice about getting a job. I will never forget it. He had taken me aside one day and said, "Fred!" (he was hopeless with names).

He said: "Fred. There are three kinds of people in this world; those who can count and those who can't."

I knew he was in the latter category when he used to read us nursery rhymes: "One, two, three, buckle my shoe.

Three, four, five, open the door."

I got the message to dodge accountancy and took my first job which determined my destiny as a travel writer. I became a proof reader for a sky writing firm.

# P

## PARROTS

THE young woman got out of bed, slipped on a silk gown, drew back the curtains, switched on the coffee percolator and uncovered the parrot.

Then the phone rang and a man's voice announced he had just arrived on the morning flight and would be there in ten minutes.

The young woman switched off the coffee percolator, covered the parrot, drew the curtains, took off her silk gown and got back into bed.

And the parrot muttered: "Jeez, that must've been the shortest day of the year!"

\*       \*       \*

HE refused to buy her a pair of budgerigars. He said one could cheep as lively as two.

\*       \*       \*

WOMAN goes into a pet shop. "I'd like a parrot for my husband."

Proprietor: "Sorry, we don't do swaps!"

\*       \*       \*

OUTSIDE the petshop in the pouring rain was a galah in a raincoat.

"He's poly unsaturated," explained the proprietor.

AFTER buying a pair of talking parrots Miss Prim wanted to name them but found she couldn't tell Joey from Polly. She phoned the pet shop proprietor for advice. "Simple," he said. "Wait until you see them mating, then fasten something around the male's neck so that you can identify him."

Miss Prim watched and watched. One day she heard flutters and squawks and dashed in to tie a white ribbon around the male's neck.

A few day's later Miss Prim threw an afternoon tea party for the church. Joey spotted the vicar and said: "Ha, so she caught you at it too!"

* * *

(This is an action joke, best told with a loud squawk when imitating the parrot)

THE lady of the manor had called the plumber weeks ago, but the leeking pipe was far from her mind when she set off early one morning for a day's shopping.

No sooner had she left when the plumber arrived and knocked on the tradesmen's door.

"Squawk! Who is it?" came the raucous voice of the parrot on the enclosed rear porch.

"Tis plumber, come to fix pipes," said the man knocking again.

"Squawk! Who is it?" came the response.

"Tis plumber, come to fix pipes."

"Squawk! Who is it?"

"Tis plumber come to fix pipes."

To cut a long story short, this went on all day until late in the afternoon the frustrating repetition caused the plumber to have a seizure. He collapsed and died on the back steps.

The lady of the manor arrived home and was confronted with the shocking scene. She let out a squawk and cried: "Who is it?"

"Tis plumber come to fix pipes," replied the parrot.

CHAP said he wanted a canary that was a good singer. "Then listen to this one," said the proprietor and he produced a great little whistler that delighted the customer's ears.

"Yes, he's good alright," said the customer, "but I notice he only has one leg."

"Make up your mind," said the proprietor, "D'yer want a singer or a dancer?"

* * *

THE lady with the blue rinse entered the pet shop and said she wanted a parrot, provided it could talk.

"Got just the model for you, madam," gushed the proprietor leading her to a cage. "This little chap is in training," he said. The proprietor explained if madam pulled the string on the parrot's right leg it would say "Pretty Polly," and if she pulled the string on his left leg he would say "Polly wants a cracker," and he successfully demonstrated the exercise.

Madam was impressed. "What if I pull both strings together?" she asked.

"I'll fall off the bloomin' perch ya stupid old bag," said the parrot.

* * *

THE priest had two parrots and taught them religiously to say the rosary. He even had two sets of rosary beads made and after a year of rigorous training he was delighted to have them perform at fetes and country fairs.

The priest was so pleased he decided to teach another parrot the rosary and bought a new bird from the pet shop.

When he put it into the cage one of the originals said to the other. "Throw away your beads Fred, our prayers have been answered. It's a sheila!"

* * *

TALL bloke entered the pet shop and said he wanted a parrot. "It has to be a big red and green one, exactly like the one in Treasure Island," said the customer explaining that he was going to the Arts Fancy Dress Ball as Long John Silver.

The proprietor said he could get such a parrot if he called back on Wednesday.

"Oh, not Wednesday. That's the day I'm having my leg off!"

\* \* \*

HERBIE operated his SP bookie business in a pub and had a pet parrot called Percival who became a perceptive talker. Always looking for the chance to make some money on the side Herbie taught the parrot to sing Advance Australia Fair and when he was word perfect took him down the pub to clean up on a wager or two.

At the bar Herbie turned the conversation round to the fact that not too many Australians knew the words of the national anthem.

"It's a disgrace," said Herbie. "Why even my parrot knows it."

That brought in the suckers. They were queuing up to place their fivers, tenners and hundred dollar notes at 25-to-one against Percival singing the national anthem.

When Herbie had scraped in all the money on offer he gave the parrot the nod. But not a word.

He cajoled, begged, threatened and swore at the parrot, but not one squawk.

After a disastrous payout Herbie stormed off home and threw the cage into the corner.

"Hang on," said Percival. "Don't get upset. Think of the odds we will get tomorrow night!"

# PEARLY GATES

AN elderly spinster approached the pearly gates and knocked.

"Who is it?" asked St Peter.

"It is I," came the reply.

"Oh no," muttered St Peter. "Not another school teacher."

*     *     *

ST PETER: "How did you get up here?"

New arrival: "Flu."

*     *     *

TWO Rotarians died and arrived at the Pearly Gates. St Peter asked the first if he had ever been unfaithful to his wife. "Once," was the reply.

"That's not bad," said St Peter, and he gave him the keys of a Rolls Royce. "You can drive around Heaven in that," he said.

St Peter put it to the second Rotarian: "Have you ever been unfaithful to your spouse?"

"No more than a dozen times," he replied. "Okay," said St Peter. "That's your battered old Holden. Fix the tyres and you can drive around Heaven in that."

The very next day when the Holden was repaired he was chugging along Celestial Way when he saw the Rolls parked on the side of the road and his friend crying his eyes out.

"Why the grief?" he said. "You got the best deal. Look at the heap I've got to get around in."

"It's not that," said the Rolls owner, "I just saw my wife go past on a skate-board!"

*     *     *

TWO Kiwis in black singlets, shorts and thongs arrived at the Pearly Gates. St Peter took one look at them and said, "Nick off. You look like wharfies. We know all about you thieving Kiwis. Pinch anything that wasn't nailed down. Nick off."

St Peter informed God he had just got rid of two Kiwis. God went berserk. "You can't do that. Everyone is entitled to get to heaven. Go and get them back."

317

St Peter went off to do his bidding but soon returned. "They've gone," he said.

"Who? The Kiwis?"

"No, the bloomin' Pearly Gates," said St Peter.

\* \* \*

THERE was an orderly queue outside the Pearly Gates as people waited patiently to get into Heaven. But suddenly there was commotion along the line as a man, muttering and grumbling, began pushing people aside and barging his way up to the gates. He went straight in, past St Peter.

"What a cheek," said some.

"Who was that?" enquired others.

St Peter replied. "Oh, that was God. He sometimes likes to think he is a journalist!" (Or a lawyer, an accountant, a doctor, a politician, the Member for Somewhere... whatever the audience)

\* \* \*

THERE were two signs outside the Pearly Gates. A long line of men were queued at the first sign which said: "Hen-Pecked Husbands Report Here."

At the other sign which read: "Liberated Men Report Here," there was only one small timid man.

St Peter said to him: "Why are you standing here?"

He said: "Because my wife told me to."

\* \* \*

THREE nuns died at the same time, arrived at the Pearly Gates simultaneously and intended to go straight in, but St Peter barred their way.

"Just because you are nuns," he said, "doesn't mean you barge straight in without the religious test."

"You," he said to the first one. "What was the name of the first man?"

"Er, Adam?" she answered, and the bells clanged and the trumpets blew and in she went.

"You," said St Peter addressing the second, "What was the name of the first woman?"

"Er, Eve?" she ventured, and the bells clanged and the trumpets blew and in she went.

"You," he said to the quaking third nun, "What were the first words Eve said to Adam?"

"Oh, gee. That's a hard one." And the bells clanged and the trumpets blew and in she went.

\*     \*     \*

NOTICE came to St Peter at the Pearly Gates that the Devil and his mob had challenged Heaven in a football match.

St Peter was quickly on the phone to accept. "By the way," he told Satan, "you haven't much of a chance, all the best footballers are up here."

"Maybe," said Satan, "but we've got all the umpires down here."

\*     \*     \*

ST PETER was interviewing a new arrival:

"While on earth, did you ever drink?"

"Good gracious no."

"Ever go with women?"

"Indeed I did not, no sir."

"Gamble then?"

"No, no, never."

Said St Peter, "Well, what took you so long?"

\*     \*     \*

AN old farmer died at the age of 90 and arrived at the Pearly Gates. "Now I will have my reward, thanks," he said to St Peter.

"What reward is that?" asked the saintly gate-keeper.

"When I was a lad," said the farmer, "my old Dad took me out of school and put me on the ploughs. When I constantly complained that I wanted an education he said I would get my reward in heaven. Now I am here and I want my reward. I want an education."

St Peter said he was a fair-minded bloke but told the farmer he would have to mark time for a while and sent him off on a heavenly tour for a hundred years.

When he returned a century later the old farmer once more demanded his education.

"Sorry, not ready yet," said St Peter, and put him on yet another 100-year heavenly tour.

When he returned from the second trip the old man was adamant. "No more procrastination. (which is a big word for an uneducated farmer) I want my education," he insisted.

"Okay," said St Peter. "I'm sorry Pops, I will have to level with you. As soon as a teacher arrives up here you will get your education as promised. In the meantime, take another trip."

\*　　\*　　\*

ST PETER was in a sour disposition when the young and handsome negro rapped on the Pearly Gates.

"I am not letting anybody in today unless you have done something really extraordinary."

"Well I can meet that criteria," said the young negro. "I once made love to a ravishing white woman against the wall of a hall where the Ku Klux Klan was meeting."

"Well, I am impressed," said St Peter. "When was that?"

"About three minutes ago," said the negro.

## PETS
See DOGS, CATS

PETS come in all shapes and forms.

A bloke was walking up High St with a crocodile on a lead when a concerned policeman said: "Where are you going with that beast?"

"I am taking him to the zoo," replied the bloke, which satisfied the cop.

Next day the same cop saw the same bloke with the same crocodile on the same lead.

"I thought you were taking that thing to the zoo?"

"Aye, I did, and he had a great time. Today I'm taking him to the pictures."

* * *

THE same bloke went into the pub and said: "Do you serve Catholics?"

The barman said he did.

"Well, I'll be having a pot of stout, and two Catholics for my crocodile!"

* * *

FRED had two monkeys as pets, but when they both died on the same day he was heart-broken. He took them to a taxidermist in the hope that they could be restored as near to life as possible.

The taxidermist said Fred would hardly know the difference and asked if he wanted them mounted.

"No, just shaking hands will do," said Fred.

## PHARMACISTS

CHAP went into the chemist and bought some phensic. He was three doors from the shop when the chemist came running after him. "Stop. Stop," he cried, and when he drew level said, "There's been a dreadful mistake. Instead of phensic I have given you arsenic."

The customer said, "is there any difference?"

"Of course," said the chemist in alarm, "it's another fifteen cents."

* * *

CHAP went into the chemist shop and asked for a packet of condoms.

"That will be $3.50 with tax," said the chemist.

"Forget the tax, I'll tie them on."

* * *

"DO you sell condoms, Miss?"

"Yes."

"Well wash your hands, I want a bag of jellybeans."

THE young couple had been cuddling in the back seat of his car and he was eager to go on with it. "Not here," she said. "Come around tomorrow. It's Sunday and my parents go to Evensong. We can have the house to ourselves. Oh, and don't forget the condom."

Next evening the lad arrived at the front door just as her father announced that they were off to church.

"I'll come with you," said the lad smartly.

At the first opportunity the young girl whispered, "Why the change of plan and how long have you been religious?"

To which the lad whispered in reply: "How long has your father been a chemist?"

*　　*　　*

YOUNG socialite was advised that her miniature show dog would never win a prize because its hair was too long. It was supposed to be a smooth hair breed.

So she went to the chemist for some hair remover.

The chemist handed her the latest product. "When you slap this on, it is best to keep your arms up for at least three minutes," he said.

"Oh, you misunderstand," she said, rather embarrassed. "It is not for my underarms, it is for my chihuahua."

"Well, in that case," said the chemist, "don't ride a bike for half an hour."

*　　*　　*

THE irate young man entered the pharmacy.

"That ointment you sold me to increase the size of my penis doesn't work. I want my money back."

He assured the chemist he applied it according to the instructions on the packet which said 'Rub it in'.

"Ah, but you didn't read the small print," said the chemist. "By a woman between 16 and 25."

# PHILOSOPHY

AN optimist says the bottle is half full. The pessimist says it is half empty.

THEY were watching a television soap opera and he became irritated by the way his wife was taking it so seriously.

"How can you sit there and cry about made-up troubles of people you have never met?" he demanded.

"The same way you can jump and scream when some bloke you have never met kicks a goal," she replied.

*　　*　　*

IF you are looking for a helping hand, there's one on the end of your arm.

*　　*　　*

FRED had been contemplating the world's population. "It's amazing, Ethel," he said. "Every time I breathe in and out, someone dies."

"Have you tried mouthwash?" said Ethel.

*　　*　　*

"THE trouble with the human race," thundered the pub's philosopher, "is that the world is full of ignorant and apathetic people." And nudging the drinker beside him said: "Don't you agree?"

"I don't know and I don't care" was the reply.

## PHONES

OF course it should always be remembered that Alexander Graham Bell invented TWO phones.

*　　*　　*

"PARDON me Miss. I am writing a phone book, may I have your number?"

*　　*　　*

CAN you telephone from a submarine?

Of course, anybody can tell a phone from a submarine.

*　　*　　*

I RANG Madge and told her I was at St Alban's.

She wanted to know what I was doing at his place.

WHEN the vicar heard that the mayor's pretty wife had been ill he told the mayor he would call round and see her next morning.

When he was shown into her room the vicar said: "I prayed for you last night."

"Silly man," she replied. "You know I'm on the phone."

*　　*　　*

THE father of a teenage girl answered the phone.

"Is that Dreamboat?" enquired a voice.

"No," replied the father, "it's Supply Ship."

*　　*　　*

HE phoned his wife from the pub to say he had been delayed at the office, but before he got a word in he heard her voice at the other end: "A damned likely story. Never heard such rubbish. Get out of that pub this minute and come straight home. This is a recorded announcement."

*　　*　　*

BARMAN on the phone: "You will have to give me a better description than that lady, this pub is full of hopeless layabouts who should be home."

*　　*　　*

FRED finally sobered up from his lost week-end and, terror-stricken, realised he had to explain it to his wife. He reached for the phone: "Hilda darling. I have escaped. Whatever you do, don't pay the ransom money!"

*　　*　　*

FRED rang the wrong number at two o'clock in the morning.

When he realised his mistake he said, "Oh I am sorry to wake you in the middle of the night."

"Oh, that's alright," said the other party, "I had to get up and answer the phone anyway."

*　　*　　*

THE second time Fred made the mistake the other party wasn't so happy.

"Well, if you are telling me it is the wrong number," said Fred, "why the hell did you answer it?"

THE voice said: "Young Tommy won't be at school today. He is very sick."

The school principal asked: "Who is speaking?"

"My father," said the caller.

*　　*　　*

HE rang his wife to tell her the good news that he had the rest of the day off, but a small boy's voice answered. "G'day son, where's Mum?"

"She's in bed, Dad," said the boy.

"Is she sick?"

"No Dad, she's in bed with the butcher and I can hear her giggling. She's not sick."

There was a poignant silence while he figured out the gravity of the situation. "Are you still there, son?"

"Yes, Dad."

"Go and get my shotgun from the garage. Load it like I told you and give them both barrels."

He listened for an interminable five minutes or more until he finally heard two loud blasts, then the boy's voice again: "I did it, Dad."

"Okay, son, now drag them out and drop them in that big hole I dug for the compost pit."

There was another long silence before the boy, still puffing, came back to the phone and said "I've done it Dad, but I've got a bit of blood on my arms."

"Then jump in the pool and swim around for a bit."

"What pool, Dad. We don't have a pool."

After a few seconds silence Dad said: "Is that 584-8400?"

*　　*　　*

"IS that the motor pool?" asked a posh voice.

"Yus."

"Tell me, my man, what vehicles are operational at the moment?"

"Five trucks, three utilities, two staff cars and the Bentley that pompous old colonel swans around in."

There was a few seconds silence.

"Do you know who this is?"

"No."

"It is the so-called pompous old colonel you so insubordinately referred to."

There was another short silence.

"Do you know who this is?"

"No."

"Well you can go and jump in the lake," and the phone was slammed down.

\*　　\*　　\*

THE little old spinster rang Telecom's complaint department.

"The cord on my phone is toolong. Could you pull it back a bit on your end?" she asked.

\*　　\*　　\*

PEDANTIC boss; "Answer that phone."

"But it isn't ringing."

"Why do you have to wait until the last minute!"

\*　　\*　　\*

IT was six in the morning when the phone rang at the reception desk of the hotel. The night porter picked it up to hear a slurred voice say: "Excoosh me, my fren, hic. What time dush the bar open?"

The porter replied, "It doesn't open until ten, but by the sound of your condition you won't be allowed in."

"Allowed in?" shouted the drunk. "I've been waiting all night to get out!"

\*　　\*　　\*

THE drunk phones the police station: "I've been driving along the (hic) highway and I think itsh my duty to tell you I have knocked down two signposts, and a (hic) telephone box."

"Indeed, sir," says the cop. "And where are you?"

"Wouldn't yoush like to know?"

SHE answered the phone to hear a very repentent voice.

"I'm sorry darling," he said. "I have thought it over and decided that you can have the Rolls as a wedding present and we will move to the Gold Coast immediately, and, okay, your mother can come with us. Will you marry me?"

"Of course I will," she said, "who's speaking?"

*　　*　　*

HE answered the phone only to hear heavy breathing and the occasional obscene suggestion.

"It's for you dear," he said.

*　　*　　*

THE phone rings and Joe answers to hear a voice enquire: "Could I speak to Bobby Bonkbrake, please?"

"I don't know anybody by that name," said Joe, "but hang on a moment and I'll ask." Do we have Bonkbrake here?" shouts Joe.

"No, it's all we can do to get a coffee break," was the answer.

*　　*　　*

A MATHEMATICIAN named Paul
Has a hexahedronical ball
And the cube of its weight
Times his pecker, plus eight
Is his phone number,
Give him a call.

## PILOTS

AIR Traffic Control to Aer Lingus: "Identify yourself, and what is your height and position?"

"I'm Captain Paddy Murphy, I'm five-feet-two, and I'd be sitting up the front."

*　　*　　*

THE passengers were shocked to see a nude man dash up the aisle of the aircraft and into the flight deck, but then it was fully explained with the announcement: "This is your captain streaking."

* * *

THE airline pilot was having his regular medical check.

"When did you last have sex?" asked the doctor as a routine question.

"Nineteen fifty-eight," said the pilot.

"Hell, that was along time ago."

The pilot looked at his watch. "It's only twenty-two fifteen now," he said.

* * *

THE captain made an announcement.

"Does anybody on this aircraft know how to pray?"

The clergyman put his hand up.

"Good," said the captain. "You start praying. The rest of us will don our parachutes. We are one short."

* * *

THE aircraft was on its final approach and the intercom was still switched on when passengers heard the captain's comment to his co-pilot.

"First thing after we land I'll have a couple of beers, then I intend to make love to that blonde stewardess."

The stewardess turned red with embarrassment and dashed down the aisle intending to alert the pilots that the intercom was still on. But she tripped over a case.

A little old lady passenger helped her to her feet.

"It's alright miss," she said. "Plenty of time. He said he was going to have a beer first."

* * *

THE co-pilot had an unfortunate name, and he was late. When he finally stepped aboard the captain called: "Hi, Jack!" and most of the passengers tried to jump out.

* * *

IT looked like an Irish hijack. Paddy used one of those airline sleeping masks with no eye holes. He jumped up, with the gun pointing the wrong way and roared: "Hands down this is a stuff up."

"One move out of you and you'll be geography," he said.

"Er, don't you mean history?" ventured a passenger.

"Don't change the subject," roared Paddy.

## POEMS

SAID the young man to his new fiancee: "Have you told your folks that I am a poet?"

"Not yet," she said, "I've mentioned your police record, and that you smoked, drank, were presently bankrupt because of your gambling habit, but I thought we'd wait until we were married first."

*    *    *

A MAGAZINE ran a poetry contest setting out three rules for submissions: The poem had to rhyme, be brief and appeal to most people.

The winner is printed below:
Pay Day.

*    *    *

BEWARE of strong drink, my dear
And only have two, at the most.
Three, and you're under the table,
Four and you're under the host.

*    *    *

"DON'T drink nought but water,"
Was Mum's word to her daughter,
"Say no to men,
"Be home by ten,
"And behave just like you oughta!"

*    *    *

ROSES are reddish
Violets are bluish
If it wasn't for Jesus
We'd all be Jewish.

GOD is good,
Yet all his peoples
Put lightening rods
On top of steeples.

* * *

"AND what'll have?"
Said the waiter, idly picking his nose.
"I'll have two boiled eggs, ya drongo.
Ya can't stick yer fingers in those."

* * *

THE difference between prose and poetry is clearly illus-
trated by this sample of prose:
The young maiden entered the water
   First time away from her mum
   All her clothing was strewed
   So she stood there quite nude
   While the tide lapped up round her knees.
Now, had she gone in a little deeper it would be poetry.

* * *

WITH the police still hot on his trail
He was tempted by fanny for sale
So the crook went to bed
With a price on his head
With a girl with a price on her tail

* * *

THIS is the story of Signwriter Joe
While painting a sign he fell through the 'O'
No need to cry "shame"
What end could be better
He went as he came, through a hole in a letter.

* * *

MOST poets will tell you that rhyme doesn't pay.

* * *

SAY it with flowers
Or say it with sweets,
Boxes of chocolates

Or plush theatre seats,
Say it with diamonds,
Or say it with mink
But whatever you do
Don't say it in ink.

\* \* \*

THE limerick packs laughs anatomical
Into space that is quite economical
But the good ones I've seen
So seldom are clean
And the clean ones are so seldom comical

## POLICE
See LAW

"OFFICER," said the Sweet Young Thing coming into the police station, "where do I apologise for shooting my husband?"

\* \* \*

ROBBERS broke into a Dublin bank and stole half a million pounds and a quantity of gold bullion. Baffled police are trying to figure out a motive for the crime.

\* \* \*

POLICE are looking for a three-fingered pick-pocket who specialises in stealing bowling balls.

\* \* \*

THE detective wanted to know what the dead body was doing in the living room.

\* \* \*

MADGE always wanted to be a policewoman. Now she's on the beat. "It's not much of a job, but it's better than walking the streets," she said.

\* \* \*

A FRIENDLY cop found two young women crying their eyes out at the Railway Station and was unable to console them until he took them to a nearby cafe and ordered a pot of tea and a plate of cakes. They dried their tears and smiled.

Then he plonked the teapot in the middle of the table and said: "Now who's going to be mother?"

And they both burst into tears again.

*     *     *

A POLICE sergeant in the bush doubled as the local vet and late one night his wife answered the phone. "Is your husband there?" queried the voice.

"Do you need the services of the police or the vet?" she enquired.

"Both," said the caller, "we can't get our dog's jaws open and there's a burglar in them."

*     *     *

TRAFFIC cop stopped a very fast car and approached the driver with note-book in hand.

"You were doing 100 kilometres an hour in a 60 zone. What's your name?"

Driver: "Mickhaelovic Dubroevscnzkics."

Cop, flipping his note book shut: "Okay, don't do it again."

## POLITICS

POLITICIANS are ubiquitous. Everybody knows one, which makes them legitimate targets for lampooning in speeches or yarns. Jokes on politicians are perennial, only the names have to be changed to make them current, or switched to suit your own political bias.

*     *     *

NO matter who you vote for, a darned politician always wins. And the only thing wrong with political jokes is, they get elected.

*     *     *

MAKE your MP work — Don't re-elect him.

POLITICIANS are people who have to mind their appease and accuse.

* * *

WHAT's the difference between a flattened politician and a flattened kangaroo on the road to Canberra?

There are skid marks to the kangaroo.

* * *

NEVER believe anything about a politician, until he has made an official denial.

* * *

BOB Hawke died and went to heaven. As he approached the celestial chair God said: "Who are you?"

"I'm Bob Hawke and that's my chair you are sitting in."

* * *

"MR MINISTER!" boomed the back-bencher, "What are you going to do about the Abortion Bill?"

"Shhh, not so loud," said the Minister, "I'm paying it tomorrow."

* * *

PAUL Keating was asked if he had heard the latest political jokes.

"Heard them?" he said. "I work with the bludgers."

* * *

CABINET decided to adjourn business for a dinner break and they trouped into the parliamentary restaurant.

The prime minister ordered a mixed grill.

"And what about your vegetables?" asked the waiter.

"Oh they can order what they like," he replied.

* * *

WHILE on safari in cannibal country a traveller came across a cafe in a clearing in the jungle. The sign out front advertised: Fried Missionary $5, Boiled Hunter $4.50, Grilled Safari Guide $5, Stuffed Politician $15.

When the traveller asked why so much for the politician the chef replied, "Have you ever tried to clean one?"

\* \* \*

THE election campaign had become fairly bitter and when the two opponents met at a social gathering it was a chance to make a pact to stop insulting each other.

"Let's make a clean fight of it," said Smith. "I promise to stop telling lies about you."

"That's fair," said Brown, "and I will stop telling the truth about you."

\* \* \*

HE had listened to the politician's speech for a solid hour before going outside for a breath of fresh air.

"Is he still talking?" asked his mate outside.

"Yeah."

"What's he talking about?"

"He didn't say."

\* \* \*

THE commercial traveller was leaning on the bar in a country pub chatting to the locals when the subject turned to politics. "I can't stand Bob Hawke. He's got a face like a sheep's head," he said.

He was immediately thrown through the swinging doors into the dust of the main street.

"What was that for?" he asked in a daze. "I didn't think anyone would feel so strongly for Bob Hawke in the bush. Is this Hawke territory or what?"

"No," said a farmer. "This is sheep territory."

\* \* \*

HE walked into the general store of a country town and bought all the rotten fruit, tomatoes and eggs available. The greengrocer beamed: "I bet you are going to hear the visiting MP at the Mechanics' Hall tonight."

"No," he replied. "I AM the visiting MP!"

HOW come there is only one Monopolies Commission?

*     *     *

ON the headstone of a grave in the Cemetery is the most unusual epitaph: "Here lies the body of a great politician, an honest man and the Member for Wills."

It is unusual because it is not often they bury three men in one grave.

*     *     *

ONE thing about our local MP. He's an honest politician. When he's bought he stays bought.

*     *     *

THE Leader of the Opposition was walking along the banks of a river when he slipped and fell in and was soon in difficulties. The Prime Minister dived in, swam to his aid and hauled him ashore.

The Opposition Leader thanked him and said. "Can you do me one favour. Don't tell my party that I can't swim?"

"That's okay," said the Prime Minister, "provided you don't tell my mob I can't walk on water."

*     *     *

LATE at night the Prime Minister was walking by the lake and preoccupied by affairs of State, slipped and fell in.

A youth heard his cries for help and at great risk to himself dived in and saved him.

When he recovered the great man said to the lad: "Boy, you saved my life. Anything you can name you can have."

"I don't want anything," said the lad. "Just don't tell my Dad."

*     *     *

THE Prime Minister had gathered caucus about him to outline the strategy of the next campaign. "I am going to describe the tactics in the simplest possible terms, so if there are any idiots in the room will they stand up now."

After a pause one politician got to his feet. "So you are an idiot are you?" said the P.M.

"Not exactly, P.M., I just didn't like to see you standing alone!"

\* \* \*

THE proposition to put a king-sized statue of the Prime Minister in central park has been well supported. It will give shelter when its raining, shade in the summer, and the pigeons a chance to speak for us all.

\* \* \*

"AND as for the problem of the pigeons around the town hall," said the mayor, "it's no use trying to dodge the issue."

\* \* \*

GOD called the world's three greatest leaders up to heaven for a special caucus meeting. George Bush, Mikhail Gorbachev and Bob Hawke were told that the world would end in three days and to go back and prepare their communities.

George Bush went on television: "My fellow Americans, I have good news and bad news. The good news is that God exists, as we all believed. The bad news is that the world will end in three days."

Mikhail Gorbachev told the Soviet Union: "Bad news and worse news. God exists and the world will end in three days."

Bob Hawke went nationwide: "Good news and better news. God exists, I am no longer an agnostic. And in three days, no Australian child shall live in poverty!"

\* \* \*

OUR local Member of Parliament says at the forthcoming election he will stand on his record.

That's the only way he can stop people examining it.

\* \* \*

DON'T Vote. It only encourages the bastards.

336

DURING the pilots' strike a charter flight was carrying four passengers. One was a businessman, one was a priest, one was a back-packing tourist and the fourth was none other than the Prime Minister.

Somewhere over the alps the pilot made the shocking announcement that the aircraft would shortly run out of fuel. He said there were only four parachutes on board and apologising for being a coward he threw three into the cabin and jumped out with his own.

The priest said he was an important man with a large diocese to look after so he grabbed one of the three parachutes and jumped out.

The Prime Minister said he was the most important leader in history and must have a parachute, and so saying he made a grab and jumped out.

The businessman said to the hiker, "That leaves one parachute between us."

"Not so," said the back-packer. "We have a parachute each. The most important leader in history has leapt out with my haversack."

*   *   *

POLITICAL definitions:

Capitalism: You possess two cows. You sell one and buy a bull.

Socialism: You possess two cows. You give one of them to your neighbour.

Communism: You possess two cows. The government confiscates them and provides you with milk.

Nazism: You possess two cows. The government confiscates them and shoots you.

European Common Market: You possess two cows. The government confiscates them, shoots one, milks the other and pours it down the drain.

337

# PRAYER

AN MP, noticing his colleague on his knees asked if he was praying for the House.

"No," was the reply. "I've looked at the House. I was praying for the country."

\*　　\*　　\*

THE gambler was praying for a win.

"Oh God. Let me win the pools."

And God answered his prayer with a thundering reply: "Meet me halfway, and fill in the coupon."

\*　　\*　　\*

A JEWISH mother was standing with her toddler son in the shallows at the beach when a freak wave crashed ashore, knocked the little boy off his feet and dragged him into the surf and out to sea.

The distraught mother fell on her knees and prayed that God would take her life instead, so that her son should live.

In answer to her prayer the very next wave washed the boy ashore.

Again she fell to her knees. "Lord, thank you, thank you, this is truly a miracle. How can I ever repay you?"

Then taking a second look at her child she added: "Excuse me Lord, before you go, there's just one thing. He did have a hat!"

\*　　\*　　\*

TWO mates who had been out fishing all day couldn't get the motor started. Night had fallen and a strong off-shore wind was carrying the frail boat further out to an increasingly stormy ocean.

Jack fell to his knees in prayer. "Oh Lord, get us out of this and I promise to change my life. I promise to pay my debts, I promise to be faithful to my wife. I promise to give up the booze. I promise..."

He was interrupted by his mate. "Hang on Jack. Don't go too far. I think I can see a light coming towards us."

# PREGNANCY

A YOUNG woman looking as if she was in photo finish with the stork staggered into the maternity ward and grabbed a nursing sister. She said she needed immediate attention.

"Ah," said the sister, "due are you?"

"No, Church of England."

* * *

OLD Mrs Gerrarty staggered into the doctor's surgery and complained of stomach pains.

After an examination the doctor declared, "You're pregnant."

"But I can't be," she said in shock. "I'm 83."

The doctor said he was positive and when he calmed her down said, "You had better ring your husband."

"Brace yourself Fred," she said on the phone. "I'm pregnant."

"Crikey Moses," said Fred. "And who is speaking?"

* * *

THE unwed Irish girl settles down in the confessional and begins: "It's a shameful thing I have to confess. I am pregnant."

"Are you sure it's yours?" says the priest.

* * *

ON a crowded bus the young woman asked the gent: "Do you mind if I sit down, I'm pregnant?"

He stood up and gave her his seat, but then took a second look.

"You don't look pregnant. How long have you been pregnant?" he asked.

"Oh, about 15 minutes," she said, "but doesn't it make you tired!"

* * *

THE young woman looked at the beer gut on the Ocker with disgust. "If that stomach was on a woman, she would be pregnant," she said.

"It was and she is," replied the Ocker.

FRED was stunned by the news of his wife's pregnancy.
"It's impossible," he lamented. "I'm always so careful.
How could it possibly happen?"

"There, there," she consoled him. "Who says it was
your fault?"

*     *     *

SIGN in a maternity shop: We supply the accessories
after the fact.


## PROFOUND STATEMENTS
See ONE-LINERS

HERE is a most important segment of the book.

The Master of Ceremonies constantly has cause to
make an announcement or introduce somebody, and
claim attention over and above the clatter and buzz of
conversation.

Sometimes, one can say "Excuse me ladies and gentlemen, can I have your attention please?" And you can
repeat it ad nauseum while banging champagne glasses
together. Let's face it, "Ladies and gentlemen can I have
your attention?" is a pretty dull statement and grabs
nobody's attention.

On the other hand, step to the microphone and say:
"You can always tell a happy motorcyclist by the insects
on his teeth." Someone will hear it.

Follow with a number of the throw-aways listed below
and eventually there is dead silence while they strain
to catch these profound statements.

Some are so profound they should be dropped into
the middle of your address whether you have lost your
place or not, in case the audience has drifted away. Here
are a few which should recapture their attention.

*     *     *

TIMING is the essential factor in the success of any rain
dance.

SMOKING shortens your cigarettes.

LOCKJAW means never having to say you're sorry.

MONOGAMY leaves a lot to be desired.

NO woman has ever shot her husband while he was doing the dishes.

IF you feel strongly about graffiti, sign a partition.

THERE is no alcohol in Iran, but you can get stoned anytime.

AN optimist is one who thinks the future is uncertain.

ABSTINENCE is the thin edge of the pledge.

A CHRYSANTHEMUM by any other name would be easier to spell.

NEVER play leapfrog with a unicorn.

LET him among us to run the fastest cast the first stone.

CRIME doesn't pay, but the hours are optional.

ONE-legged girls are a push-over.

YOU can lead a horse to water but you can't lead a whore to culture.

A MAN is known by the company he floats.

ALL is fair in love and the war which follows.

ANY port in a storm is better than no rum.

ANYTHING for a quiet wife.

IF I'd known she'd take offence so easily I would have entered her in the Grand National.

PUNCTUALITY is something that, if you've got it, there is few to share it with.

THIN yaks leave light tracks.

NO leg is too short to reach the ground.

PORNOGRAPHY is in the groin of the beholder.

OBSCENITY is anything that gives the judge an erection.

WHEN God created man, She was only joking.

BEGGARS can't be boozers.

CONTRACEPTIVES should be used on all conceivable occasions.

CANNIBALS are not vegetarians. They are humanitarians.

W.C. FIELDS is alive and drunk in Alburqueque.

CIRCUMCISIONS alter cases.

STATISTICS prove that 50% of all people who get married at Easter are women.

DON'T put all your bags in one exit.

HALF a loaf is better than no tea-break at all.

HERE today, gone home to Momma.

IF you like home cooking, stay home.

GOING steady only means you've sobered up.

IF Labor is the answer, it must have been a bloody stupid question.

ONE good turn gets most of the bedclothes.

ONE door closes, another slams in your face.

PROCRASTINATION is the thief of time, especially if you can't spell it.

SEX is bad for one, but it is good for two.

RUTH is stranger than fiction.

THE opera's never over until the fat lady sings.

IF the epileptic fits, wear it.

HE who laughs last doesn't get the joke.

TWO can live as cheaply as one, but for half as long.

CONFUCIUS, he say too much.

A FRIEND in need is a pest indeed.

THERE is nothing like horse riding to make a person feel better off.

THERE are three kinds of women, the beautiful, the intelligent and the majority.

THERE are three kinds of men, the handsome, the caring and the majority.

THERE are three kinds of mathematicians, those who can count, and those who can't.

SOME girls are like flowers. They grow wild in the woods.

NOT to mention the monkeys.

THE man who goes into the bar optimistically, usually leaves misty optically.

HE may drink to forget, but he never forgets to drink.

YOU don't get a second chance to make a first impression.

TIME wounds all heels.

TIME is nature's way of stopping everything from happening at once.

DEATH is nature's way of telling you to slow down.

NEVER leave a turn unstoned.

NEVER put off till tomorrow what you can avoid altogether.

BETTER to be a coward for a minute than dead for the rest of your life.

SHE was only the horse trainers daughter, but all the horse manure.

THERE were more late entries than an Irish orchestra.

HE had an ego bigger than the outdoors.

DON'T come the raw prawn.

DON'T try to keep up with the Joneses. Drag them down to your level. It's cheaper.

A CULT is a group too small to be a minority.

IF you don't go to your friends' funerals, they certainly won't come to yours.

THE number of people at your funeral can depend on the weather.

I KEEP fit by wrestling, with my conscience.

MY wife keeps fit by jumping, to conclusions.

I LOVE women so much I think I'm a lesbian.

MY carma run over your dogma.

LIVE every day as if it is your last. One day you'll be right.

ALL babies are subject to change without notice.

ALL my life I have been doubtful. Now I'm not so sure.

A CLOSED mouth gathers no feet.

THEY were so progressive they tried to adopt a gay baby.

SHE had more chins than the Singapore phone book.

SHE was only a newsagent's daughter, but she loved her Daily Mail.

SHE was only a cab driver's daughter, but you sure auto meter.

SHE used to be married to a trapeze artist, but she caught him in the act.

HE'S very broad minded. He thinks of little else.

THEY were thicker than mourners at a brewer's wake.

SHE was so mean she used to heat the knives so the family would use less butter.

HE'D steal the harness off a nightmare.

I AM so miserable, it is as if you hadn't left.

NEVER go round with another man's wife, unless you can go a round with her husband.

SILENCE isn't always golden... sometimes it's guilt.

DIPLOMACY is the art of saying "nice doggie" until you can find a rock.

## PROPOSALS

YOUNG Jock McTavish got down on his knees to propose to her when a 25-cent coin dropped from his pocket and rolled under the sofa. In the 20 minutes it took him to find it she had lost interest.

\*　　\*　　\*

BLOKE walked up to a lovely blonde on the corner. "I'm

sorry to bother you," he said, "but I am a stranger in town and I don't know my way around. Could you tell me where you live?"

# PSYCHIATRISTS

ANYBODY who goes to a psychiatrist needs their head read, but read on.

\* \* \*

PSYCHIATRY is the care of the id by the odd.

\* \* \*

NEUROTICS build castles in the air. Psychotics live in them, and psychiatrists collect the rent.

\* \* \*

YOU go to a psychiatrist when you feel slightly cracked and keep going until you're completely broke.

\* \* \*

"DOCTOR, doctor," said the patient as he burst into the psychiatrist's room, "I feel invisible."
    Doctor: "I'm sorry, I can't see you now."

\* \* \*

HE stopped going to his psychiatrist. He asked too many personal questions.

\* \* \*

"NOW that I have cured you of your gambling addiction," said the psychiatrist, "I can present you with your bill."
    "Thanks doc. Toss you double or nothing."

\* \* \*

PATIENT: "How do I know if you can help me?"
    Doc: "I can guarantee a sure cure, or your mania back."

\* \* \*

THE friendly psychiatrist is the one who lies on the couch with you.

\* \* \*

GOING to the psychiatrist didn't cure Fred's drinking problem. He kept falling off the couch.

DID you hear about the psychiatrist who kept his wife under the bed because he thought she was a little potty?

* * *

A FELLOW phoned his psychiatrist. "Doctor, my wife needs help. She thinks she's a horse."

The doctor heard a few more details and said, "Mmmm, it seems serious. It could be a long and costly treatment."

"Money is no object," came the reply. "She's won her last three starts!"

* * *

"MY doctor insisted that I come and see you," said the patient to the eminent psychiatrist. "Goodness knows why, because I'm happily married, I like my job, got lots of friends and no worries..."

"Hmmm..." said the psychiatrist reaching for his notebook, "How long have you been like this?"

* * *

I TOLD my girlfriend the truth, that I was seeing a psychiatrist.

She told me the truth, that she was seeing a psychiatrist, a plumber and two barmen.

* * *

PATIENT: "Why do you think so many people take an instant dislike to me?"

Psychiatrist: "Saves time."

* * *

PATIENT: "Everybody hates me."

Psychiatrist: "Don't be silly. Everyone hasn't met you yet."

* * *

"DOC, my wife is a kleptomaniac."

"Is she taking anything for it?"

* * *

"I THINK I am going mad, doctor. Every time I ask someone the time I get a different answer."

"I USED to suffer from a split personality, Doc, but now we're both okay!"

*　　*　　*

SHE took her husband to the psychiatrist. "He says he is suffering from hallucinations, but I'm sure he is only imagining it," she said.

*　　*　　*

"NOW tell me," said the psychiatrist, "have you had any more of those sexually erotic dreams?"

"No," said the patient.

"Tough luck, I've had some beauties."

*　　*　　*

HE asked her to explain her dreams.

"I haven't had any this week, doctor," she said.

"Well how the hell can I help you if you don't do your homework?"

*　　*　　*

THE shapely blonde entered the psychiatrist's office. She stood nervously by his desk as he told her to lie on the couch. She hesitated.

"Come, come, now," said the psychiatrist, "how can I help you unless you lie down on the couch?"

Finally, she walked over and stretched out on the couch.

"Now then," he said, "tell me how your troubles began."

She looked him straight in the eye, "Just like this," she said.

*　　*　　*

PSYCHIATRIST: "So, you think you are a dog, eh? That's no problem. Just hop up on the couch."

Patient. "I can't. I'm not allowed."

*　　*　　*

HE helped cure my phone phobia. I was always scared of answering it. Now I answer it all the time, whether it rings or not.

*　　*　　*

THE patient explained to the psychiatrist: "Every time

349

I go to sleep I dream of cricket. It's the most important match of the year and every time I get a duck. Doc. it's driving me mad."

Doctor: "Well, when you go to bed tonight try thinking of something else."

"What, and miss my turn to bat?"

* * *

HE briskly entered the psychiatrist's rooms and settled himself down on the couch with his brief case. "Let's talk business," he said. "I want to rent advertising space on your ceiling."

* * *

HOW many psychiatrists does it take to change a light bulb?

Only one. But the bulb must want to be changed.

* * *

A PSYCHIATRIST on holiday became fascinated by the antics of an apparent simpleton who had set up a sign on the beach which stated "Seagulls for sale."

"That's why we are needed," he said to his wife. "I think I will humour him."

"How much are the seagulls?" asked the psychiatrist.

"Only a fiver each," the jolly hawker replied.

"Okay," said the psychiatrist, "I'll buy one."

The man took the note, and pointing skywards said: "That's your one, up there."

* * *

THE psychiatrist treated Bazza for two hours and finally solved the problem. "You've got a split personality. You are really two different people struggling for supremacy of yourself."

The doc then handed him a bill for $100. Bazza produced $50. "There's my half. Why should I pay for the other bloke's troubles?"

* * *

THE psychiatrist had listened for ten minutes while his patient insisted he had turned into a bell.

"Take these pills. If they don't work, give me a ring!"

350

THE middle-aged woman settled herself on the couch. "It's about my son, doctor. He keeps making mud pies."

"I wouldn't worry about it," said the doctor, "It's quite normal really."

"Well I don't like it," she said, "and neither does his wife!"

*　　*　　*

ONE psychiatrist to another: "All day long I have to listen to stories of pain and suffering, raw deals, persecution complexes, husbands complaining about wives, wives complaining about husbands, family feuds, everybody's problems, the world's troubles. It's getting me down.

"But tell me Dr Entwhistle, how come you look so serene after listening to everybody's troubles?"

"So, who listens?"

*　　*　　*

THE psychiatrist told Fred he was going to drop some ink on a blotter and he wanted Fred to explain what the random designs meant to him.

"That's Marilyn Munro in the nude," said Fred deciphering the first blotch.

"That's Jayne Mansfield taking a bath," he described the second.

He said the third spattering of ink was the Luton Girls Choir all singing in the nude.

"The trouble with you Fred," said the doctor with some satisfaction, "you are obsessed with sex."

"What, me?" exclaimed Fred. "It's you who's drawing the filthy pictures."

*　　*　　*

TWO psychiatrists met in the hospital corridor. One said: "You're feeling good. How am I?"

*　　*　　*

A PSYCHIATRIST spent two hours listening to a young woman pour out the details of her anxieties and emotional problems.

Finally he said there was nothing wrong with her, she was coping well, and she was quite normal.

"Normal?" she repeated. "But what about these caterpillars crawling all over me. I can't stand it any longer."

The psychiatrist jumped up and backed away. "Well, don't flick the damn things over me."

## PSYCHOLOGY

THE psychologist put it to Fred: "If you had to give up wine or women, which would you choose?"

Fred thought for a moment. "That would rather depend on the vintage of each," he said.

\* \* \*

AN attractive woman was sitting alone in a bar when a young man approached her. "Excuse me," he said, "may I buy you a drink?"

"What, to a motel?" she screamed.

"No, no," protested the man, "You misunderstood. I just asked if I could buy you a drink."

"You are asking me to go to a motel?" she screamed, even louder.

Completely bewildered the young man retreated to a corner table while everybody glared at him indignantly.

After ten minutes the young woman came over to explain. "I'm, sorry to have created such a scene," she said. "I am a psychology student studying human behaviour in unexpected situations."

The young man looked at her and shouted, "What? A hundred dollars?"

\* \* \*

OLD Jacob lived in a small side street in Fitzroy and was being annoyed by a group of kids who would play cricket in this alley, using a tin can as a ball.

The noise would irritate him and sleep was hopeless, so he decided to put an old business principle to work.

He called the boys together and explained that he was an old pensioner, and that nothing gave more pleasure than to see young lads playing cricket with a tin can. He said if they would come there every night and play cricket he would pay them fifty cents each, per night.

The kids thought this was great and turned up the following evening to make their usual noise and were duly paid fifty cents each.

The second night old Jacob explained to the boys that he was an old-age pensioner and would they mind copping 40 cents because he was a little short. The lads accepted the money.

The third night he told the boys that he had suffered some unexpected expenses and would they mind taking just 30 cents.

The fourth night he explained that his pension cheque hadn't arrived and the best he could do was five cents each.

The news wasn't taken gladly. The boys looked at each other and finally one said. "To hell with this. I'm not wasting my time playing cricket with a tin can for a measley five cents. I'm off."

The rest followed, and he has never seen them again.

\* \* \*

HE had suffered from insomnia for years and at last the psychologist was giving him some sound advice.

"Next time you are in bed relax your body bit by bit, starting from the toes," said the psycho.

"Go to sleep toes," he said that night. "Go to sleep feet, go to sleep ankles, go to sleep knees, go to sleep thighs..."

Just then his wife walked in to the bedroom in a sheer negligee.

"Wake up everybody," he yelled.

\* \* \*

FRED had been out with the boys. And as the night

developed he found himself among the girls, and one of them, a buxom blonde, eventually took him home to her flat.

It was three a.m. when he was set to leave and he was overtaken by remorse. "What will I tell the missus?" he muttered.

"No worries," said the blonde, "Here's the plan and put this bit of chalk behind your ear."

At four a.m. he was tip-toeing across the bedroom when the light flashed on. "Where have you been?" demanded his wife.

"I've been in bed with a big buxom blonde who wouldn't let me come home until I satisfied her five times," he began.

"You bloody liar," said his wife. "You've been out playing pool. You've still got a bit of chalk behind your ear!"

## PUBLIC RELATIONS

HYMIE was the world's first public relations officer and worked with Moses on the flight of the Israelites. When they reached the shores of the Red Sea, hotly pursued by Pharaoh's army, Moses sent for his PR man.

"Where are the boats? You forgot the boats," Moses roared at Hymie.

"When were boats in the contract?" asks Hymie.

Moses was in a rage. "I must have boats. Do you want me to part the sea and walk across it?"

"Great thinking Moses," said Hymie. "If you do that I will get you two whole pages in the Old Testament!"

## PUBLIC SPEAKING

VETERAN guest speaker: "I don't mind them looking at the time when I'm talking. But when they take their watches off and shake them to see if they are still going, then I find it disconcerting."

HE was pacing up and down when the young lady approached and asked if he was the guest speaker. He replied that he was.

"Do you get nervous before you speak?" she enquired.

"No," he lied.

"Then what are you doing in the ladies' loo?"

* * *

HE lacked confidence as a public speaker. "I'm afraid I'm not good at it," he admitted. "Last time I even stuffed up the minute's silence."

* * *

AFTER he addressed the Chamber of Commerce, the guest speaker stayed on for a while but was looking despondent.

"What's bothering you?" asked the chairman.

"Well, one of your members, that chap there, just told me that it was the most boring speech he had ever heard."

"Oh, don't worry about Smithers," said the chairman. "He's the type of chap who just goes round repeating what everybody else says."

* * *

"HAVE you ever spoken before a large audience before?"

"Yes. And I said Not Guilty."

* * *

"I HEARD your wife was an after-dinner speaker."

"Don't be silly. She couldn't wait that long."

* * *

AN ideal response from the guest of honour: "I really don't deserve this award. But then, I've got arthritis and I didn't deserve that either."

* * *

OPENING remark for a public speaker:

"The prime minister would have been here tonight but for a conflict of interest. He didn't want to come."

# PUBS
See HOTELS

ON the chest of the barmaid in Sale
   Were tattooed the prices of ale,
   And on her behind,
   For the sake of the blind,
   Was the same information in Braille.

\*    \*    \*

THINGS are so tough at this pub that they employ a chucker-in! Patrons are frisked for weapons. If they don't have any they are given some.

\*    \*    \*

SOME of the pubs around Sydney are the toughest in Australia. The drinkers can fight at the drop of a hat, have muscles like knotted wire, covered in tatts and swear like troupers. The men are just as wild.

\*    \*    \*    .

"WHY do you throw your drinks down so fast, one after the other?"
   "Cos I once had one stolen."

\*    \*    \*

IT was in a pub where unattended beers were unsafe and Jake had a need to go to the loo. So he left a note beside his beer, reading: "I've spat in this."
   When he returned there was an addendum to his note: "So have I."

\*    \*    \*

YOU can always tell the stranger in our local pub.
   He's the one who puts his drink down on the bar.

\*    \*    \*

A VENTRILOQUIST asked the barmaid for a gottle of gear and then drank it without moving his lips.

\*    \*    \*

"DO you serve women in this bar?"
   "No, you have to bring your own."

356

THE barman gave me a nasty look. I didn't need it. I already had one.

* * *

HE wanted to go to a topless bar.

So they took him to a pub without a roof.

* * *

THE barman at the bush pub was one of the toughest he had ever seen; muscles, tatts, unshaven, sweaty and pulling beers in a black singlet.

The shearer couldn't take his eyes off him. "What the hell d'yer think yer staring at?" said the barman eventually.

"I just can't get over the likeness. It's a truly remarkable resemblance," said the shearer. "You are a dead-ringer for my wife. In fact if it wasn't for the moustache..."

"I haven't got a moustache," interrupted the barman.

"No, but my wife has!"

* * *

THE barmaid wondered where the voice came from, before she saw the little lad in short pants with his nose just reaching the bar.

"Hey, you. I said I'll have a glass of beer and a packet of fags," insisted the brat.

The barmaid saw that he was a lad of about 13.

"Do you want to get me into trouble?" she said.

"Forget the sex, just give me the beer and fags," he said.

* * *

ALTHOUGH it was a tough Outback pub, Dick the barman could cope with the evening rush because everyone drank beer. Well, everyone except the town's doctor who, as regular as clockwork, would dash in at 6.30 each evening and order an almond dacquiri.

One night, at the peak of the rush hour, Dick saw the good medic pushing his way through the crowd and realised he had run out of almonds.

357

Like any good barman he was equal to the task, snatched up some hickory nuts, crushed them, and had the drink ready by the time the doctor breasted the bar.

The doctor tasted it, tried it again, and said: "This is not an almond dacquiri Dick!"

"No, it's a hickory dacquiri, Doc!"

*       *       *

THE guest complained to the proprietor of an Outback pub that the outhouse was full of flies.

"What time did you go down there?"

"Oh, about noon," said the guest.

The licensee nodded his understanding. "You should go down about one o'clock," he said "They are all in the dining room then!"

*       *       *

"THE flies are thick," said a drinker.

"Well what would you expect out here," said the barman, "educated ones?"

*       *       *

BLOKE fronted the bar with a newt perched on his shoulder and after serving his fifth beer the barman could contain his curiosity no longer.

"You've got a newt on your shoulder," he said.

"I know," said the drinker. "His name is Tiny."

"Why Tiny?" asked the barman.

"Because he's my newt!" was the obvious answer.

*       *       *

PADDY rushed into the bar and said: "Quick, a beer before the fight starts, quick."

The barman pulled a beer and Paddy gulped it down.

"Quick, another beer before the trouble starts," he said.

The barman watched him quaff the second pot and said: "Righto, when is this row supposed to start?"

"Right now," burped Paddy, "I'm broke!"

358

PADDY ordered a pot of stout, but as soon as it was placed before him he cancelled the order and asked the barman for a pot of lager instead.

When he drank it the barman asked for the money.

Paddy was indignant. "I gave you a pot of stout for it."

"But you didn't pay for that either."

"Well I didn't drink it, did I!"

*　　*　　*

THE travelling salesman arrived at the one-pub three-dog town and fronted the bar. After a couple of drinks he said to the barman: "Is there any night life hereabouts?"

"You just missed it by a few days. She's gone to the city for a holiday."

*　　*　　*

THEN there's the Scot who drinks Scotch and Horlicks. When it is his turn to shout he is fast asleep.

*　　*　　*

A SCOT pushes his way to the bar. "I've had an attack of the Yaws," he says to the barman.

"What's Yaws?" he says.

"Double whisky," says the canny Scot.

*　　*　　*

A SCOT ordered a pot of beer and as the barman handed it over he said, "D'yer think yer canna fit a nip o' whisky in it too?"

"Certainly," said the barman.

"Then fill it ta the top wi' beer."

*　　*　　*

THERE is a pub in town that has a fifty cent entrance fee. It's to keep out the riff-raff.

*　　*　　*

BLOKE went into a pub and had a ploughman's lunch.

The ploughman became quite agitated.

*　　*　　*

PADDY fronted the bar and said: "Drinks all round, barman, and have one yourself."

Paddy was immediately the toast of the pub and after all pots were quaffed the barman gave him the bill.

"But I haven't got a cent," he said.

The angry barman grabbed him by the scruff of the neck and hurled him straight through the swinging doors onto the pavement outside.

It was a few moments before Paddy managed to stand himself up and dust himself down. He staggered back into the pub.

"Drinks all round," he proudly declared for a second time, "but not you, barman. One drink and you go bloody mad."

\* \* \*

AFTER a long overseas assignment Charlie returned to the pub he liked to call his local.

"You know," he said nostalgically to the barmaid, "it's all of ten months since I've had a drink here."

"Look," she replied, "this is my first night and I'm serving as fast as I can!"

\* \* \*

TWO brothers were leaning on the bar enjoying a drink when one pushed two bottle-tops across to the barman as payment for a round.

In response to the puzzled look on the barman's face the elder of the brothers beckoned him close and whispered: "My brother is not the full two-bob. He always pays in bottle-tops. If you can humour him for a while I will settle up before we leave."

The barman wasn't entirely happy with this arrangement, but went along with it for the rest of the afternoon.

When both brothers went to stagger out that evening he said "Hoy," and indicating the great heap of bottle-tops said: "What about settling up?"

"No worries," said the elder brother turning back and throwing a garbage bin lid on the counter. "Here, take it out of this and keep the change!"

HE was about to enter the Pig & Whistle when he was accosted by a nun who began berating him on the evils of strong drink.

He was equal to the challenge. "Unless you've tried a drop yourself, Sister, you don't know what the hell you're talking about. Don't knock it unless you've tried it."

He ranted on until he convinced her to have a taste.

"Well, only for the purpose of argument, mind. What do ladies drink?"

"Try a gin and tonic," he said.

"Okay, but I'm not going into that evil place, and I'm not drinking from their glasses." She unhooked a tin mug from her belt. "Get me some in this."

When he fronted the bar for a beer and a pannikin of gin the barman said: "Don't tell me that nun is still out there!"

* * *

THE conversation stopped as the old bloke entered the pub. He was in his pyjamas, slippers and with the aid of a walking frame shuffled towards the bar.

"I'll have three double Scotches," he whispered to the barman.

The drinks were placed in front of him. He gulped down two and just before he quaffed the third he said: "Shouldn't be drinking these really, with what I've got."

"Why?" asked the barman. "What've you got?"

"Just 15 cents," replied the old-timer.

* * *

A BLOKE with a pig under his arm approached the bar.

"Where did you get that?" asked the barman.

"I won it in a raffle," replied the pig.

## QUESTIONS

SHOULD single crabs have nippers?

   CAN a cross-eyed teacher control her pupils?

   IS it cruel to sew buttons on flies?

   IF a light sleeper sleeps with the light on, does a hard sleeper sleep with the window open?

   COULD a drinking lizard be any flatter?

   COULD a half-wit work part time for intelligence?

   INSTEAD of having ballet girls prancing around on tip-toe why don't they hire taller showgirls?

   IF the answer is "9W" what was the question?

   The question is: "Hey Fritz. Do you spell Wagner with a V?"

   IF the answer is "Washington Irvine"

   The question is: Who was the first president of the United States, Fred?"

*   *   *

WHY is 'abbreviation' such a long word?

# R

## RADIO ANNOUNCERS

THE radio announcer was delighted to hear the way in which his little son said his prayers, concluding with: "And here again, Dear God, are the headlines."

* * *

AN Aussie on a flight to Rome got talking to the fellow seated beside him and couldn't help noticing he had one heck of a stutter. He was even more astonished when his new acquaintance told him, with difficulty, that he was going for an audition as an announcer for Radio Vatican.

"How do you rate your chances?" asked the Aussie.

"Ner, ner, ner, not too good," he replied. "They will per-per probably ger-ger give the job ter-ter some ber-bloomin' Catholic!"

* * *

A RADIO announcer is one who works for the love of mike.

* * *

THE longest word in the English language is announced by disc jockeys as "Now a word from our sponsor."

## RELIGION

THE trouble with born-again Christians is that they are a worse pain in the neck the second time around.

363

THE meek had a meeting today and decided they don't want to inherit the earth.

* * *

PEOPLE who use the rhythm method of contraception are usually called Parents.

* * *

FROM the pulpit the vicar announced that one of his flock, Miss Helen Hunt, had found a purse containing money, a variety of personal items and what he believed to be a small packet of white balloons. "So whoever has lost this purse, go to Helen Hunt for it!"

* * *

AS the proud father handed the baby to the vicar at the christening font the cleric said: "And what will we call this little chap?"

"It's a girl," whispered the father. "You've got hold of my thumb!"

* * *

THERE was a knock on the door and Fred found himself being asked to become a Jehovah's Witness.

Quick on his feet, Fred replied: "I didn't even see the accident," and shut the door.

* * *

THE priest took Paddy aside. "I've been told that you went to a football match last Sunday morning instead of coming to Mass."

"No father, not true, and what's more, I've got the fish to prove it."

* * *

THE protestant minister met his friend the priest and said he dreamed about a Catholic heaven last night.

"It looked like a nice place, with plenty of pubs, bright music and people dancing about," he said.

"That's funny," said the priest. "Only last night I dreamt about a Protestant heaven. It looked nice with lots of flower beds, pretty trees and gardens."

"And what were the people doing?" asked the vicar.

"What people?" replied the priest.

\* \* \*

THE vicar's term at the parish was up and he was about to be transferred. The regular parishioners had gathered at a tea party in his honour.

"We'll really miss you," said one little old lady. "No matter who they send as a replacement he will never be as good as you."

The vicar was flattered, but he assured her his successor would be an adequate and caring pastor.

"No, no," the old-timer insisted, "it's always the same. We've had six ministers here in my time and I can assure you each one has been worse than the one before!"

\* \* \*

THE not-too-successful minister was asked by the bishop why he had entered the clergy.

"I was called," he replied.

"Are you sure," pondered the bishop, "it wasn't some other noise you heard?"

\* \* \*

A BISHOP had fallen seriously ill and was told by his doctor not to have too many visitors. But when his long-time agnostic friend called he was ushered in to the bishop's bedside.

"My Lord," said the unbeliever, "I do appreciate you seeing me when your friends have not been admitted."

"It's like this," said the bishop, "I feel confident of seeing my friends in the next life, but I was concerned that this might be my last chance of seeing you."

\* \* \*

PADDY crept around the back of the country parish presbytery and nicked one of the priest's chooks. He then promptly went to confession.

"I stole a chook, father," he began. "I know it was very wrong and I am sorry. Can I give it to you for repentence?"

"Certainly not," said the priest. "I don't want it. Return it to the man you stole it from."

"Oh, he says he doesn't want it," said Paddy.

"In that case you might as well keep it and say ten Hail Mary's."

\* \* \*

AS Rabbi Rozenbloom was passing St Patrick's, Fr O'Calleghan rushed out in an agitated state. "Izzi, you're just the man," said the priest. "Can you help me out of a tight spot?"

The priest explained that he was double booked. He had to officiate at the funeral of the local bishop but couldn't find another priest to take over the confession session.

"Surely you can stand in for me. It's only an hour."

The rabbi said he didn't know anything about confession. Jews were not into confessing anything.

"There's nothing to it," insisted the priest. "Come with me now and listen to the first few, then you can take over."

When they got to the dark confessional the rabbi sat behind the priest and listened to the procedure.

A woman came in: "Father I have sinned."

"What have you done my child?"

"I have committed adultery."

"How many times?"

"Four times father, and I sincerely repent."

"Put $2 in the poor box and say ten Hail Marys and you will receive absolution," said the priest.

Then a second woman came in.

"Father I have sinned."

"What have you done my child?"

"I have committed adultery."

"How many times?"

"Twice, Father."

"Put $1 in the poor box and say five Hail Marys, and you will be forgiven," said the priest.

As soon as the woman had left the priest whispered to the rabbi, "You have got the hang of it now, quick, take my place, I have to rush."

The rabbi settled down in the priest's position and soon enough another woman knelt at the other side of the grill.

"Father, I have sinned," she said.

"What have you done my child?"

"I have committed adultery."

"How many times?"

"Just the once, father."

"Well, you had better go and do it again. It's two for a dollar this week."

\* \* \*

"FORGIVE me Father, but I have had an obsession about stealing wood from the timber mill where I work. I have suffered with this problem for years. What shall I do?"

"That's alright my son," said the priest. "But because this sin has been perpetuated for so long I must ask you to make a novena."

"If you've got the plans Father, I've got the timber."

\* \* \*

TERESA went to confession and told the priest she had sinned three times that week. She said she had slept with Shaun on Tuesday, Paddy on Wednesday and Shamus on Friday night. "Oh Father what should I do?"

"On your way home, my child," he said. "Call in at Con the Fruiterer's, buy a lemon and suck it."

"Oh Father, will that cleanse me of my sins?"

"No. But it should take that damn smile off your face."

\* \* \*

ON Saturday nights the three lads always went out on the town together, but Shamus always made a point of going past the church first so he could duck into confession while the other two waited outside.

"It's been a week since my last confession father," said

Shamus, "and I'm sorry to say that I have sinned of the flesh once again."

"Was it that O'Flannagan hussey from the dairy?"

"No father."

"Was it the cheeky Costanzo girls in the fruit shop?"

"No father."

"Don't tell me it was the widow Murphy flauntin' her wares again?"

"No father."

"Well do your usual penance and be off with you then," said the priest.

Shamus rushed out of the church to his waiting mates. "Got at least three good tips for tonight," he said.

\* \* \*

"FATHER, yesterday I made love to my wife."

The priest explained that there was nothing wrong with that.

"But Father, I did it with... lust."

Again the priest re-assured the man that it was no sin.

"But Father, it was the middle of the day."

The priest was growing uncomfortable with the description but assured his parishioner that it was a natural act for man and wife.

"But Father, it was sheer passion. As she leant over the deep freeze I just jumped on her and we did it on the floor. Am I banned from the church?"

"Of course not," said the exasperated priest.

"Oh good. We're both banned from Safeways."

\* \* \*

LITTLE Patrick to little Isaac: "Our parish priest knows more than your rabbi."

Isaac: "That's because you tell him everything."

\* \* \*

THE vicar, the priest and the rabbi were always arguing about which was the true religion. But they were friends enough to make a pact that whoever died first the other two would each put $300 in the coffin to ensure admittance to the Pearly Gates.

It came to pass that the vicar died first. The other two attended the funeral service and as good as his word the priest approached the coffin and put in his $300. The rabbi followed, wrote a cheque for $600, put it in beside the vicar and took his $300 change.

\*     \*     \*

MY wife converted me to religion. I never believed in hell until I married her.

\*     \*     \*

IT all started in the Garden of Eden, and one day Adam was intrigued by the antics of a buck rabbit. "What's he doing?" he asked God, and was told that the rabbits were simply making love.

He saw two birds doing something similar, and upon enquiry from on high was told they were also making love.

"Why I haven't I got anybody to do that with?" he asked God, who replied that he would fix it first thing next morning.

Sure enough, when Adam awoke, there was Eve laying beside him. He took her by the hand and they ran into the bushes.

Ten minutes later Adam emerged from the bushes. "Hey God, what's a headache?"

\*     \*     \*

HELL is multi-cultural.

The Germans are the police force, the Italians the defence force, the Indonesians are in charge of housing, and the Indians run the railways. The Irish make the laws, the English are the cooks and the common language is Dutch.

\*     \*     \*

A MINOR religious sect in India worships the Goddess of the Harvest, Kali. Every morning they visit Kali's temple and make an offering; a watermelon.

369

They present the offering and then sing their sacred song: "Here's another melon Kali baby!"

* * *

A NUN raced in to mother superior's office screaming and waving her hands. "Oh, mother," she cried "we seem to have a case of hepatitis!"

"Well, my dear, bring it in," said mother superior. "I'm sick to death of Bernie Smith's Bodega."

* * *

SATURDAY night is confession night but Father O'Riley stopped Pat as he entered the church. "Pat, the church is full. Can you come back tomorrow night? You haven't committed murder since last time have you?"

"Indeed I haven't," said Pat and he turned to leave.

On the way out he met Shamus. "Go home Shamus and come back tomorrow. They are only hearing murders tonight!"

* * *

THE monastery was in financial trouble and decided to go into the fish and chip business. One night a customer rapped on the door which was opened by a monk.

"Are you the fish friar?"

"No," replied the robed figure, "I'm the chip monk!"

* * *

"I DON'T like the look of the new missionary," said one cannibal to the other.

"That's alright," said the other, "just eat the potatoes."

* * *

ISRAELI prime minister Rabin invited the Pope to a game of golf. Since the Pope had no idea of the game he convened the college of cardinals and asked their advice.

"Call Greg Norman, make him a cardinal, tell Rabin you're sick and send Cardinal Norman in your place."

Honoured by the Pope's request Greg Norman agreed to represent him.

When he returned from the game the Pope asked how he had done. "I came in second," said Norman.

"You mean Rabin beat you?"

"No, Your Holiness, Rabbi Nicklaus did."

\* \* \*

THE sermon for the evening was "Christian Perfection," and the minister was quick to point out that this was an ideal state of grace unattainable by the sinners as constituted the nondescript congregation before him. Nevertheless, in the course of his sermon he challenged anyone present to stand and proclaim they were perfect. To his astonishment a bloke in the fifth pew got to his feet.

"Do you dare claim you are perfect?" thundered the cleric.

"No, not me," replied the man, "I am standing proxy for my wife's first husband!"

\* \* \*

A COUPLE who went to the movies found themselves sitting directly behind two nuns; the ones with the large headgear.

Trying to see the screen past these obstacles the girl muttered to her boyfriend: "It would be nice to go to Scotland, there are not so many nuns there."

The boyfriend replied audibly: "What about Sweden, there were even fewer there."

One of the nuns turned around, gave the couple a sweet smile and said: "Why don't you both go to hell, you won't find any there!"

\* \* \*

THE two men dressed in black were the only occupants in a compartment on a long train journey. After a time one said, "Excuse me, but would I be right in thinking you are a Catholic priest?"

"Yes. And would you be a rabbi?"

"I am," said the first.

They had a lot of time to kill and eventually the rabbi said: "Have you ever broken a commandment?"

The priest admitted that he had "taken a woman."

After a while the priest said: "Have you ever eaten pork?"

The rabbi looked around as if to check nobody else was in the compartment, then nodded his head, "yes," he whispered.

The long silence was broken by the priest. "Sex is much better than pork isn't it!"

*　　*　　*

A JEWISH tailor was troubled the way his son had turned out and went to see his rabbi about it. "I brought him up in the faith, gave him a very expensive bar mitzvah, cost me a fortune to educate him. Then he tells me last week he has decided to be a Christian. Rabbi, can you help me, what will I do?"

"Funny thing you should bring that problem to me," said the rabbi. "Like you I brought my boy up in the faith, put him through university, cost me a fortune, then one day he comes and tells me he has decided to become a Christian."

"What did you do?" asked the tailor.

"I went to the synagogue and prayed to Almighty God for an answer."

"And what happened," pressed the tailor.

God's voice came into the synagogue as clear as a bell: "Funny thing you should bring that problem to me," he said.

*　　*　　*

OF course it was a certainty that Jesus was Jewish. He lived at home until he was 30, he went into his father's business, his mother thought he was divine, and he thought she was a virgin.

*　　*　　*

WHY wasn't Christ born in Australia?

Well, where would you find a virgin, and where would you find three wise men?

*　　*　　*

ACTUALLY there were four wise men. While following the star on the way to the manger, one of them said he knew a short cut.

THE city council had just taken delivery of the new mayoral car and called on the three denominations to consecrate it at a special ceremony.

The priest chanted a blessing and sprinkled it with holy water. The parson chanted a blessing and waved the cross over it. The rabbi chanted a blessing, went round the back and cut an inch off the exhaust pipe.

\* \* \*

THE minister pranged his brand new car when a woman stopped to check her make-up in the rear-vision mirror. It was only the car's first time on the road and the minister got really angry.

He got out and roared at the woman: "Why don't you go forth and multiply!"

\* \* \*

THE priest called on the village belle Mary O'Shaunessy who was in hospital after falling off the stage during her dance act for the church fete. "I prayed for you last night," he said.

"No need," she replied, "I'm in the phone book."

\* \* \*

MOTHER Superior rapped the desk with her cane and asked the Grade IV girls what they wanted to be when they grew up.

One 13-year-old put up her hand and said: "I want to be a prostitute."

Mother Superior fainted with shock. When she was revived and had composed herself she asked the same girl: "What did you say you wanted to be?"

"A prostitute," affirmed the youngster.

"Oh, thank goodness, I thought for a moment you said you wanted to be a Protestant."

\* \* \*

THE vicar walked around to the back of the church and saw three boys sitting on the ground with a handful of coins at their feet. "What might you boys be doing?" he enquired.

"We're having a competition," explained one. "Whoever tells the biggest lie gets the money."

The vicar was visibly shocked. "When I was a boy," he said, "I never told untruths."

They said "Okay, you win," and gave him the money.

* * *

IT was one of those silent orders where the only utterances allowed were the morning and evening rituals to greet the head monk. "Good Morning Head Monk" they would chant at breakfast and "Good Evening Head Monk" just before retiring.

After 15 years this ritual was getting on Brother Paddy's wick and causing rebellion to swell within him. Finally he planned a revolt.

Next day, when the brethren chanted "Good Morning Head Monk," he would deliberately chant "Evening!"

The prospect nearly sent his rocks off. He was all of a tremble at the breakfast table and when the head monk entered he stood with the rest of them and in the chorus of "Good Morning Head Monk" Paddy threw in his rebellious "Evening!"

The head monk was very perceptive. There was an awesome silence until his monotone baritone loudly proclaimed: "Someone Chanted Evening!"

* * *

AGAIN it was one of those monastic orders where the monks were silent, except on the day of their patron saint, St Titus. The first year Brother Basil asked for another blanket. The second year he asked if he could have porridge instead of wheaties. The third year he asked if he could have sugar in his tea. The fourth year he asked if he could leave the order.

"You might as well," said the head monk, "You've done nothing but winge since you've been here."

* * *

GOD spent a lot of time hacking out the commandments on one tablet of stone then he offered it to the first tribe he saw. They happened to be Germans, and after studying the bit about "Thou Shalt Not Kill," decided it was not their cup of tea. God offered them to the French. They took one look and said "What's all this ban on adultery. That's not for us," so they refused.

God then offered them to the Jews.

"How much?" said Moses.

"They are free," said God.

"Okay, we'll take two."

\* \* \*

TRAVEL seems to induce confession, so when three priests found themselves in the same compartment of a train on a long journey to a eucharistic council, they began to bare their souls and admit to certain sins.

"It's women with me," said the first. "I find them very hard to resist and I have fallen several times."

"It's the grog with me," said the second. "Struggle as I may there have been times when the proceeds of the poor box have gone on Demon Drink."

The third priest was quiet. "I suppose you succumb to gambling," prompted his colleagues.

"No," he said. "My problem is gossip. I am a blabber-mouth and I can hardly wait to get off this train."

\* \* \*

A DRUNK sat opposite a priest on the train and studied him for ten minutes. Finally he said, "Tell me, yer worship. Why do you wear your collar back to front?"

"Because I am a father," said the priest.

"But I'm a father too," said the drunk.

"No, I am a father to hundreds in my parish."

"Then maybe it's your trousers you should be wearing back to front," said the drunk.

\* \* \*

LEANING on the bar, two drinkers were arguing about religion. "What do you know about the Lord's Prayer," said one. "I'll bet you ten cents you don't know the first line."

375

"You're on," said the other, and put his ten cents on the line.

"Now I lay me down to sleep," proudly recited the first.

"You win," said his mate. "I didn't think you knew it!"

* * *

A SWAGGIE happened to call at the vicarage, on the bite for a hand-out.

"I want to ask you one question," said the vicar when he had heard the man's hardluck story. "Do you take alcoholic drinks?"

"Before I answer that," said the swaggie thoughtfully, "is that in the nature of an enquiry or an invitation."

* * *

THE vicar had not seen young Johnny at Sunday school, so when he found the lad beside a country road minding his dad's cattle he thought it an appropriate time to deliver an impromptu sermon. "They are fine bullocks, Johnny, do you know who made them?"

"Dad did," replied Johnny.

"Oh no," the vicar smiled, "God made those bullocks."

Johnny shook his head. "God made them bulls. Dad made them bullocks."

* * *

AN Aussie on holiday in Ireland was given a piece of advice by his Irish wife before the aircraft landed at Shannon Airport. She told him not to tell religious jokes or to be critical of Catholics.

He was in a pub the very next night playing a darts match with the locals when a television bulletin reported that the Pope was sick, and near death. The locals all gathered around the television set.

"C'mon you fellas, to heck with the Pope let's get on with the game," he said.

When he woke up in hospital with his wife sitting beside him he said, "Nobody told me the Pope was a Catholic."

THE priest, the vicar and the rabbi were discussing how they divided the collection between God's work and themselves.

"We lean more towards the fundamentalist side," said the rabbi. "I take the money outside and literally fling it up to heaven and what God wants he keeps, what falls back on the ground, I keep."

*   *   *

THE district inspector of Catholic Primary Schools called at St Patrick's and decided to put Grade V to the test with some basic questions on the faith.

When he came to young Johnny he asked: "Who knocked down the Walls of Jericho?"

"It wasn't me," was the instant reply.

The inspector was taken aback. Johnny's parents obviously needed a word about their responsibility in religious instruction so he noted the address and knocked on the door that evening.

When Johnny's Mum opened the door the inspector introduced himself and said: "When I asked your boy who knocked down the Walls of Jericho, his answer was that it wasn't him." he said.

In a defiant pose she answered: "If my Johnny said he didn't do it then he didn't do it."

This was too much for the inspector and he asked to see the man of the house. Paddy was in bed, looking for work, but when the inspector revealed the purpose of his visit Paddy reached for his trousers. "Okay, okay, how much did this bloomin' wall cost anyway?"

*   *   *

PUZZLED about his first lesson on evolution young Joey arrived home and said: "Mum, is it really true that I am a descendant of apes, monkeys and gorillas?"

"I don't really know, darling," she replied, "I never knew any of your father's family."

377

A RICH tourist who had come to Vatican in hope of seeing the Pope was estatic when the Pontif came into the crowd near him and placed his hands on the shoulders of a derelict. The tourist was amazed to see the Pope do the same thing the following day, so he approached the tramp and offered him $100 to swap clothes, to which the down-and-outer eagerly agreed.

Next day, dressed in the tramp's smelly rags the tourist was delighted to see the Pope turn and approach him. With both hands on his shoulders the Pope bent forward and whispered: "I've told you to push off twice. Now beat it!"

\* \* \*

THERE was a young lady called Alice
Who peed in the presbytery's chalice
The padre agreed
'Twas done out of need
And not out of Protestant malice.

\* \* \*

A RENOWNED archaeologist named Nostle
Discovered a fantastic fossil
He knew from its bend
And the knob on the end
'Twas the peter of Paul the Apostle.

\* \* \*

THE eternal question was being argued by a theologian and a philosopher.

The theologian defined a philosopher as being like a blind man in a darkened room looking for a black cat that wasn't there.

"That's as may be," said the philosopher, "but the theologian would have found it."

\* \* \*

THE vicar was the lone survivor of a shipwreck and as he staggered ashore he found himself surrounded by hundreds of spear-wielding warriors.

"Oh God! I'm finished," he cried.

"No you are not," thundered a voice from on high.

"Who's that?" asked the vicar.

"It's God. Now listen carefully. Grab that spear from the thin native next to you and plunge it into the heart of the chief."

Although terrified the vicar did exactly as he was told, and as the chief collapsed to the ground the voice boomed out once more: "NOW you are finished."

# RESTAURANTS
See WAITERS

THE couple had just finished dinner and the waiter was pouring a third glass of port when he noticed the gentleman slide off his chair and disappear.

"Excuse me madam," he said. "Your husband is under the table."

"No he's not," she replied white-faced. "My husband has just come through the door!"

*    *    *

THERE were only two restaurants in the little tourist village, one opposite the other. The visitor stopped a local and asked which served the best meals.

"Let me put it this way," he replied. "Whichever one you go into, you will have wished you had gone to the other."

*    *    *

THE diner called the waiter: "I would like to report this meal to the Bureau of Missing Portions."

*    *    *

THE food was so bad at this place the mice used to send out for take-away.

*    *    *

THE estate agent said it was not the right location for a Chinese restaurant.

"They'd be flogging a dead horse."

HE was in a hurry. "I'll have a crocodile sandwich. And make it snappy."

* * *

"A GLASS of vin rouge, please Ethel."
   "Certainly sir, red or white?"

* * *

"WHAT'S that?" said the stuffy matron looking at the morsel on the plate set before her.
   "It's pressed tongue," said the waiter.
   "Yuk! I could never eat anything that came out of a beast's mouth," she said. "Bring me a boiled egg!"

* * *

FRED got into trouble when he took his girlfriend to a restaurant. They ordered soup, and when the waiter brought it his girlfriend spotted a bug in it. She screamed and said: "Waiter, remove this insect."
   The waiter threw Fred down the front stairs.

* * *

SOUP du jour, $2.
Soup de yesterday, $1.
Swiss cheese with holes, 50 cents.
Extra serve of holes, 25 cents.

* * *

SIGN: Customers who pay for their meal then leave without eating will be prosecuted.

* * *

THUMP and thump the old sauce bottle
   First none'l come, And then the lott'l.

* * *

"I'LL have some Spinoti Vertimicelli."
   "Where did you see that?"
   "On the menu."
   "Oh, that's the name of the proprietor."

* * *

SHE was such a noisy eater that when she started on her soup three couples got up to dance.

* * *

THE fat lady had an enormous steak on her plate. Her

380

husband took one look at it and said. "Surely you are not going to eat that alone?"

"Of course not. I've just ordered some potatoes."

*　　*　　*

FRED was the type of bloke who always let his friends pick up the dinner bill. He had an impediment in his reach.

*　　*　　*

TWO crayfish were in the restaurant's aquarium. It seemed this would be their last night so the male cray put the hard word on the female.

She said: "Okay, but will you still respect me in the mornay?"

*　　*　　*

SIGN in a restaurant window: "Kitchen hand wanted, to wash dishes, and two waitresses."

*　　*　　*

THE commercial traveller entered the dining room of the hotel and gave the waiter a complicated order.

"I want two fried eggs so over-done they would chew like tennis balls, two slices of burnt toast, some charred bacon and a cup of cold coffee that tastes like dishwater and don't forget to slop it into the saucer."

The waiter scratched his head. "That's a tall order, I don't know if I can manage that."

"Oh?" said the traveller. "You didn't seem to have any trouble yesterday."

(There is another punchline to this. The traveller says he is homesick and misses his wife's cooking).

*　　*　　*

IT was a roadside cafe and the traveller asked for the menu. It read: Ham sandwiches, bacon, roast pork, pigs feet, pork chops or pork sausage."

"Could I have a glass of water first?" he asked.

"Sure," said the proprietor, "but we only have bore water out here."

"Blimey, you don't waste much of that pig do you," said the traveller.

TWO society dames settled down for a cup of coffee and when the waitress delivered the drinks she also brought a plate with two cakes; one was large, the other small.

"After you," said one socialite offering her friend the plate.

"No, after you."

"No, but I insist," said the first.

"No, you take first pick," said the other.

Eventually, one broke the stalemate by taking one of the cakes. The big one.

The other was upset. "Oh, you helped yourself first and took the big cake," she pouted.

"So, and if you had chosen first, which one would you have taken?"

"The smaller one of course."

"Well, what are you complaining about, that's what you've got!"

*     *     *

IT was such a high class restaurant they could provide gravy that would match your vest.

*     *     *

WHAT'S worse than eating shepherd's pie in a restaurant where you don't know what's gone into it?

Eating it at home where you do know what's gone into it.

*     *     *

THIS restaurant boasted that it could provide any dish the customer could order, no matter how alien or rare. If the chef couldn't produce the dish, then an alternative meal was on the house.

Consequently they did good business with smart alecs ordering filleted bee's knees marinated in port sauce, or roast goanna tails in curry, surrounded by Tibetan cabbage on rice.

But one evening the order was for braised elephant's kidneys on toast. A simple demand, but as ten minutes stretched to 20 the chef finally came out to apologise.

Due to an earlier rush on crocodile knuckle sandwiches they were completely out of bread.

*   *   *

MARY had a little lamb
A lobster and some prunes
A glass of wine, a piece of pie
A plate of macaroons
She gobbled down a sponge cake
And what else we don't know
But when they carried Mary out
Her face was white as snow.

## ROMANCE

WHEN she asked him why he had suddenly stopped loving her, he said he had a train to catch.

*   *   *

EVE: "Do you love me?"
ADAM: "Who else?"

*   *   *

HE told his girl of course he knew where the erogenous zone was. He got booked for parking in one yesterday.

*   *   *

ON their wedding night he declared his love for her. He said he would swim the deepest river, cross the widest desert and climb the tallest mountain.

She divorced him. He was never home.

*   *   *

IN the warm summer night the young couple lay in close embrace in the canoe as it gently drifted out on the shimmering lake. She looked up at him and asked: "Will you love me always?"

"Of course my darling, which way will we try first?"

*   *   *

IT was only their second night out but he had fallen deeply in love with her after they spent the entire night in his flat. To him it was the real thing.

"Am I the first man you ever made love with?" he asked.

She studied him reflectively. "You might be. Although, you're face looks rather familiar!"

*     *     *

IT was one of those enchanting evenings when the lights were dim and the music softly sentimental. They sat in a corner and he gazed into her eyes.

"Drink does a lot for you," he murmured. "It makes you look beautiful, appealing, divine..."

"But I haven't been drinking," she protested.

"I know," he whispered, "but I have."

*     *     *

HE noticed her bedroom was stacked high with teddy bears and other toy animals, but he was more intent on the job in hand.

After they had made love he asked how it had been for her.

"Yeah, you were alright," she said. "You can have anything on the bottom shelf."

# ROYALS

WHEN Prince Philip visited Korumburra to open a butter factory he looked resplendent in his naval uniform, except for the fur hat.

A local reporter, suspecting there might be a story attached to it, waited for the appropriate moment and asked: "Why the fur hat?"

"Well, I phoned Mummy last night," began the Prince, "and she asked me what I was doing today. I said I was going to Korumburra and she said "Where the fox hat?"

# S

## SALES

SALES resistance, of course, is the triumph of mind over patter.

* * *

"THERE'S a salesman outside with a young lady."

"Tell him I'll take one."

* * *

"HOW did the new salesman go today?"

"He got two orders. One to get out, and one to stay out."

* * *

FROM the For Sale section of the newspaper: "Home Computer, as new. Never been figured out."

* * *

A MELBOURNE youth wanted to buy a motor cycle. "It must be the fastest machine you've got," he demanded.

The salesman said he had just the bike, but its true speed could only be demonstrated at night when the roads were clear. "Come back tonight, at midnight, and I'll guarantee we can be in Geelong in 45 minutes," he said.

The youth thought for a minute. "No thanks."

"Why not. It's very fast."

"It may be, but who wants to be in Geelong at a quarter-to-one in the morning?"

"DON'T you know you can't sell second-hand cars without a licence?" said the inspector.

"Thanks, I knew I wasn't selling any, but I didn't know the reason."

* * *

AN attractive salesgirl approached a young man in a department store and said: "What would you like, sir?"

"What would I like?" he repeated. "Why I would like to take you out of here, take you to my pad, mix a nice cocktail, take you in my arms and make passionate love to you. That's what I'd like. But what I NEED is a pair of socks."

* * *

A TRAVELLER noted that the small corner store in the country town had large bags of salt stacked high around the verandah. When he went in to buy some cigarettes he saw more bags of salt stacked so high they reached the ceiling. After he paid for his cigarettes he said, "You must sell a lot of salt."

"To tell you the truth, I hardly sell any," said the storekeeper. "But the wholesale rep who calls here, boy can he sell salt."

* * *

SID was told if he didn't sell more toothbrushes he would be fired. One month later his sales record had soared and the manager called him in to explain the dramatic turnaround.

Sid explained that he got sick of calling on pharmacies. He said he set up a little table at Flinders St Station with some dry biscuits and a new dip.

"Try my dip," he would say, and a constant stream of people did so. When they enquired about the ingredients of the dip Sid told them: "Garlic and chook shit!"

They would go "Aaaargh!" and spit it out.

Then Sid would say: "Would you like to buy a toothbrush?"

IT was the old story of a salesman finding himself stranded in the country and knocking on the door of the only pub in town.

"Well, we don't have a spare room," said the proprietor, "but you are welcome to share with the little red-headed school teacher if you like."

The salesman could hardly contain his excitement. "Oh thanks. I will be a real gentleman."

"That's good," said the farmer. "So's the little red-headed school teacher!"

* * *

ONCE again the salesman found himself knocking on a farmhouse door seeking a bed for the night.

"Sure," said the farmer, "but we only have one spare bed and you will have to share that with Cecil, my son."

The salesman turned and headed for his car. "Crikey, how did I get into the wrong joke?"

* * *

HARRY and Sam were travelling together when their car broke down in the country. They approached the farmhouse and were well received by Widow Mary who fed them well and put them up for the night.

It was about nine months later when Harry rang Sam.

"Remember the night the car broke down out in the country?" he asked. "You didn't by any chance slip into the widow's bedroom did you?"

Sam admitted he did. "And you didn't by any chance use my name did you?"

Sam admitted that he did, and said he was sorry.

"Don't worry about it Sam," said Harry. "I've just got a letter from a legal firm that says she has died and left me the farm."

* * *

THIS salesman was travelling late at night when his car blew a tyre and he realised he didn't have a jack. It was miles from anywhere, but across the field he could see a farmhouse in silhouette against the rising moon.

"He could lend me a jack," mused the salesman as he set off towards the farm.

As he stumbled across the paddocks in the dark he wondered if farmers still had the hospitality for which they were renowned.

"It's late," he thought. "He probably won't be too pleased about being woken up. He has probably had a hard day in the field and was looking forward to a bit of rest."

He approached the farmhouse and knocked on the door.

While he waited his thoughts continued: "The poor bloke is most likely getting out of bed now. His wife could be nagging him. The jack's probably out in the cold garage. He will be upset. He could even put the dogs onto me."

When the farmer opened the door the traveller said: "To hell with your jack!"

\* \* \*

TOLD to accompany the firm's top salesman on his round to learn the ropes the rookie noticed that before entering a prospective client's office the super salesman would always make the sign of the cross, and inevitably make a sale.

"I didn't know you had to be a Catholic," said the rookie.

"I'm not," replied his mentor. "But never tackle a client without checking your glasses, your wallet, your pen, and your zipper!"

\* \* \*

THE travelling salesman sent a telegram to his wife: "Coming home Friday."

When he arrived home he was alarmed to find a man in bed with his wife. He went berserk, but was restrained by his mother-in-law. She urged him to keep calm and not to commit any violent and hasty action he would, in time, regret. "Leave it to me," she said. "There must be an explanation."

Next day she had her explanation. "I have gone into the matter thoroughly, and like I told you, there is a reason for your wife's behaviour. There was a postal strike on Friday and she didn't get the telegram!"

\* \* \*

THEY just buried a salesman named Cripps
He married, on one of his trips
A widow named Block
Then died of the shock
When he found there were nine little chips.

# SCHOOLS
See EDUCATION, TEACHERS

JOHNNY told his dad: "There's going to be a small meeting of the Parent Teacher Association at the school tomorrow morning.

"What's a small meeting?" asked his dad.

"Just you, me and the headmaster," said the lad.

\* \* \*

TEACHER: "Name two pronouns?"

Johnny: "Who? Me?"

\* \* \*

WHEN I was a kid I went to an immoral school. It had no principle and it had no class.

\* \* \*

"STAND up all the little boys and girls who want to go to heaven," said the Sunday School teacher.

They all stood except little Fred.

"Don't you want to go to heaven," she asked Fred.

"Not yet, Miss," he said.

\* \* \*

THE six-year-old was a study of concentration as she laboured over her drawing. "What will your picture be, Angela?" said the teacher.

"I'm drawing God," she said.

"That's a difficult subject," said teacher. "Nobody knows what he looks like."

"They will when I'm finished," said the youngster.

* * *

IT was Monday morning and Mum was having a tough time preparing a rebellious son for another week at school.

"Nobody likes me," he groaned. "Teachers don't like me. The kids don't like me. I just don't want to go anymore," he complained.

"Pull yourself together," said his mother. "School can be tough, but at 40 years of age and as principal of the school you've just got to go."

* * *

THE demure co-ed said to her tutor: "I would do anything to pass my exams."

"Anything?" he queried.

"Yes, anything."

"Well try studying," he said.

* * *

"DO you know your alphabet?"

"Yes."

"What comes after G?"

"Whizz."

"Right, and what comes after whizz?"

"Bang."

"Good boy."

* * *

ONCE I won a prize for arithmetic. The teacher asked what was 20 multiplied by four. I put up my hand first and said "thirty-four." I got the prize for being closest.

* * *

"JOHNNY, how much is three times three?"

"Nine, Miss."

"That's pretty good."

"Pretty good. It's bloody perfect."

"THAT essay on the dog is exactly word for word, the same as your brother's."

"Of course sir, it's the same dog."

* * *

O'GRADY was asked how many honours he received in his leaving certificate.

"Three," he said proudly. "Pure mathematics, and applied mathematics."

* * *

THERE are three kinds of people in this world: Those who can count and those who can't.

* * *

THE kids at our school were so tough the teacher used to play hookey.

* * *

THE voice over the phone said; "Young Tommy won't be at school today, he is very sick."

"Who is speaking?" said the principal.

"My father," said the caller.

* * *

YOUNG Freddy was on his feet as soon as the teacher entered the room. "Do you think it is right to punish people for things they haven't done?" he asked her.

"Certainly not," she replied.

"That's good. Because I haven't done my homework."

* * *

TEACHER: "What is a comet?"

Johnny: "A star with a tail."

Teacher: "Name one."

Johnny: "Mickey Mouse."

* * *

TEACHER: "Which month has 28 days?"

Johnny: "They all have."

* * *

OVER a row of hooks in the cloakroom was a sign which said: "These hooks are for teachers only."

✓ Underneath, some bright spark had added: "They may also be used for hats and coats."

* * *

THE young schoolteacher had been assigned to a country school for three years before her mother had a chance to visit her.

Mum noticed that most of the men in town seemed to know her daughter.

"Oh they are probably fathers of some of my children," explained the teacher.

* * *

✓ THE school inspector was sent out into the country to check on the standard of education in the bush school.

His first question to the class, "Who knocked down the Walls of Jericho?" was met with an embarrassing and fidgety silence.

"Can't you tell me?" he said pointing to young Murphy.

"It wasn't me, honest sir," was the only response.

Disappointed at the low standard of the class the inspector went to the headmaster. "I asked a young lad in your school who knocked down the Walls of Jericho and he said it wasn't him."

"The little scally-wag," said the headmaster. "I'll bet it was him all the time."

Staggered at this response the inspector sought out the president of the Parents and Teachers' Association to report the sad state of affairs.

"Well," said the president, "young Murphy comes from an honest family and you can take it from me that if he says he didn't knock them down, then he is bloody-well telling the truth."

Finally, in despair the inspector reported the matter to the Department of Education and a week later received the following reply:

"Dear Sir. With regard to your letter regarding the Walls of Jericho, we are obliged to inform you that this matter does not come within our jurisdiction. We suggest you contact the Board of Works."

*     *     *

THE teacher was getting to know the kids.

"What does your father do, Johnny?"

"He's a train driver, Miss."

And what does your father do, Sammy?"

"He's a policeman, Miss."

"And what about your father, Freddy?"

"He's dead, Miss."

"Oh. And what did he do before he died?"

"He clutched his throat, let out a groan and fell on the floor."

## SEDUCTION

HE wined and dined her before they went to the theatre.

"Thanks for a beautiful evening," she said when he had driven her home.

"Ah, but the night's not over," he said, pouring her a glass of champagne. And as she sipped the drink he pushed two white tablets towards her.

"Aren't these aspirins?" she asked.

"Indeed they are," he replied.

"But I haven't got a headache."

"Good," he said. "Then let's go to bed."

## SHEPHERDS

THE locals in the village pub watched the stranger with suspicion because it was rumoured he was a taxman. Finally, they elected one of their number to check him out.

The appointed one moved along the bar and engaged him in conversation. "You're not from these parts?" he began.

"No," said the stranger.

The local continued with the small talk for a time and then asked what the stranger did for a living.

"I'm a taxidermist," he said.

"Oh yeah," said the local. "And what have you been doing around here?"

"Had a marvellous time really," said the stranger. "Yesterday I stuffed a prize sheep dog, this morning I mounted Farmer Brown's goat and tomorrow I am going to have a go at his sow."

At this the local retreated slowly along the bar to where his mates were eager for his report.

"He tried to tell me he was a taxi driver, but I've figured him out. He's really a shepherd like us, on holiday."

## SHOPPERS

FRED was talking to his mate in the pub.

"The wife is shopping crazy. She will buy absolutely anything marked down. Yesterday she came home with an escalator."

\* \* \*

HIS wife was a kleptomaniac. But her sister was worse. She used to walk into stores backwards and leave things on the counter.

\* \* \*

"WHERE can I get some talcum powder?" she asked the supervisor.

"Walk this way, madam" he said.

"If I could walk that way I wouldn't need the talcum powder," she answered.

\* \* \*

WHEN he claimed his money back under their "satisfaction or money refunded guarantee," they said they were perfectly satisfied with his money.

MISS Lottzabazooma bought a dress. It was marked down 50%, and that's how she wears it.

* * *

THE advertisement for a kitchen gadget said it was so marvellous it would cut the housework in half. So she bought two.

* * *

"THANKS for your patience in showing me all that linen, but I am not buying anything myself. I am looking for my neighbour."

"Well, do you think she may be in that last bolt of pink on the top shelf?"

* * *

SHE walked into the delicatessen and selected a chicken. She prodded and poked it. She lifted one wing and sniffed underneath, lifted the other wing and did the same. Finally she looked at the chicken's rear end and gave it another sniff. "This chicken is not fresh," she declared.

"Lady," said the shopkeeper, "do you think you could pass the same test?"

## SHOWBIZ

IT has been attributed to the great actress Katherine Hepburn that there wasn't much to acting. "After all," she said, "Shirley Temple could do it at the age of four."

* * *

TWO sailors spent the evening getting drunk then decided to go to a variety show. Half way through the program one sailor needed to go to the toilet. On asking directions from the usherette she told him, "Go left, then to the end of the passage on the right, left again and straight ahead."

A little the worse for wear the sailor followed the directions with some difficulty, relieved himself and eventually found his way back to his seat.

"You missed the best act," whispered his mate.

"While you were out a sailor came on stage and pissed into the orchestra pit."

*　　*　　*

A VENTRILOQUIST with the usual dummy on his lap was making several offensive jokes at the expense of the Irish. Finally, Paddy could take it no longer.

"Hey, you!" he shouted. "I object to you making fun of my countrymen."

"I'm sorry," said the ventriloquist. "I meant no offence."

"I'm not talking to you," said Paddy. "I'm talking to that cheeky little bastard on your lap."

*　　*　　*

HE will never forget his first Royal Command performance.

The Queen told him to shut up.

*　　*　　*

"YOU can't resign," said the circus manager to the human cannonball. "Where would I get another man of your calibre?"

*　　*　　*

OLD actors never die, they just get smaller parts.

*　　*　　*

THE ventriloquist was so bad his lips were moving when he wasn't saying anything.

*　　*　　*

THE ventriloquist went into a pub and asked for a gottle of gear. Then he drank it without moving his lips.

*　　*　　*

CONCEITED actor: "Have you seen my latest show?"

"I never miss it. I've never seen it and I never miss it."

*　　*　　*

"DID the new show have a happy ending?"

"Sure, everybody was delighted it was over."

*　　*　　*

THE show closed after its first night. A foul play was suspected.

"THIS is an education show," said the comic. "When you leave you will say: 'That taught me a lesson'!"

*    *    *

IT was a sneak preview. After 15 minutes everybody sneaked out.

*    *    *

HOLLYWOOD is the only place where the brides keep the bouquets and throw away the grooms.

*    *    *

HER adoration of the actor was obvious. "When will your life story be published," she asked, "I would love to read it."

"Oh, not yet," he said, "My life story will be written posthumously."

"Well, I do hope it is soon," she gushed.

*    *    *

THE actor had a hard time deciding whether to marry the chorus girl, who was very pretty, but a little scatty, or his leading lady, who was not so beautiful, but had a magnificent singing voice.

It was a close decision, but he went for quality and married the soprano.

The morning after the honeymoon he took a good hard look at his bride. Then he nudged her and said, "For Goodness sake, sing!"

*    *    *

IN Hollywood parents have to edit the fairytales they tell their children: "Once upon a time there were three bears. Daddy Bear, Mummy Bear, and a baby bear by a previous marriage."

*    *    *

WHEN the much married actress finally died her friends clubbed together for a fitting funeral and a tomb stone with the fitting epitaph: "At last she sleeps alone."

*    *    *

THIS week's movie trailer: "You yelled when you saw

"Psycho," you screamed when you saw "Cape Fear," and you literally shrieked when you saw "Vampire Wolves." So now a word from the manager: Why do you make so much bloody noise at the pictures?"

* * *

A PEDANTIC theatrical producer decided to direct his own wedding. He insisted on two rehearsals, and after the second he called for someone to replace the leading female role.

* * *

A GROUP of showgirls had been entertaining the troops at a remote army camp. After their performance the major asked: "Would you girls prefer to mess with the officers or the troops?"

"Makes no difference to us," said one shapely blonde, "but we've just got to have something to eat first."

* * *

TWO nuns had gone to the circus, but after the show they were dismayed to find heavy rain had created a deep puddle between the bigtop and their bus stop. They didn't want to get their habits or their shoes wet.

Two clowns came to their rescue and offered to piggy-back them across the water.

Halfway across one clown stopped and said to his mate: "Do you realise that this is virgin on the ridiculous?"

* * *

PADDY dragged a shaggy mongrel into the talent scout's office and announced, "This is the best dog act you're ever likely t' see. This dog can count, and I trained him m'self."

The agent gave the pair a dubious stare.

"Okay, I'll prove it," said Paddy, and holding a commanding finger to the dog said, "Right Nigel, what's two and two?"

The dog went "woof, woof." Then there was a pause until Paddy said, "C'mon Nigel, you can do it." There was another "woof" then a long pause and another "woof."

"C'mon Nigel," said Paddy. "Just one more."

*    *    *

BERT said he had two tickets for the Elton John show.

"Don't want to go, he's awful," said Fred.

"But you've never heard him."

"I have heard a bloke at the pub imitate him," said Fred, "and he's damned awful."

*    *    *

ONE actress complained to her friend that she was so tired. "I didn't get to sleep until after three," she said.

"No wonder you are tired," said her friend, "two is all I need."

*    *    *

THE young actor was excited at getting a job and rushed home to tell his father: "Guess what, Dad, I play a man who has been married for 30 years."

"No matter, son. Let's hope you will eventually get a speaking part!"

*    *    *

HE had been the clumsiest dancer in the chorus line and when he fell into the orchestra pit he was carted off to hospital.

Like everybody in show business he was worried about being replaced in his absence. "Oh don't worry about that," said his mate on a visit to the ward. "Everybody has been talking about you. Why only yesterday the director said, 'Whatever happened to old whats-is-name'!"

*    *    *

AT the reunion of Actors Equity members one old thespian who had the reputation of being an utter bore looked around the room and said, "How many great actors do you think there are in this room?"

"One less than you think," came the reply.

THEY were dancing together at the Arts Fancy Dress Ball. "Can I drive you home?" he leered.

"Of course," she said. "What kind of a car have you got?"

"I don't have a car," he said. "But I've got a whip."

\* \* \*

A YOUNG trapeze artist well stacked
Is faced by a very sad fact
Imagine the pain
When time and again
He catches his wife in the act.

\* \* \*

PADDY had a good repertoire of jokes and was always making his mates roar with mirth.

"You should go on the stage, Paddy," they said.

"No way," said Paddy. "People would laugh at me."

\* \* \*

ACTORS' Equity's surveillance officer had been following Dan Duo's Dog Show around the country circuit for some time. He suspected there was something phoney about a cocker spaniel playing the piano while a fox terrier sang assorted excerpts from Gilbert and Sullivan.

And sure enough he caught them out.

At the next show he rushed onto the stage to expose them. "The fox terrier can't sing a damned note," he told the audience, "the cocker spaniel is a ventriloquist!"

\* \* \*

INSTEAD of getting ballet dancers to prance around on tiptoe, why don't they get taller showgirls?

\* \* \*

THE man had sought an audition with a prominent theatrical agent who was pressed for time and when the newcomer said he was a bird impersonator he dismissed him with some irritation.

"Bird imitators are more common than pop singers," said the agent. "I've got no time to hear you now. Just give me your name and leave your number."

The man said his name was Willie Warbler, took a numbered ring off his left leg and dropped it on the desk, laid an egg, cacked on the window sill and flew away.

\* \* \*

SHE had egged him on to be an actor, and his very first audience egged him off.

\* \* \*

HIS mother would be most upset if she knew he was an actor. She still thinks he is running dope from Bangkok.

\* \* \*

THE definition of a Shakespearean actor is tall, dark and some ham.

Definition of a conceited actor is Ham and Ego.

\* \* \*

THERE was a young actor named Bates
Who danced the fandango on skates
But he fell on his cutlass
Which rendered him nutless
And practically useless on dates.

# SIGNS

ENGLISH speaking travellers, particularly travel writers, should forgive the well-meaning attempts to anglicise official notices in foreign lands. Instead, I've chuckled and written them down. Indians have produced more than their share of wonderful signs and are the source of the majority listed below:

\* \* \*

NOTICE on a Kashmir houseboat, where drinking water is always regarded with suspicion: "Clients should disregard worries about the water on this boat. It has been personally passed by the proprietor."

\* \* \*

SIGN in an Indian maternity hospital: "Visitors. Husbands only. One per patient."

SIGN in a Bombay beauty parlour: EARS PIERCED WHILE YOU WAIT.

\* \* \*

SIGN on an Irish pub door: "Gone to lunch, back in an hour. PS: Already gone 15 minutes!"

\* \* \*

SIGN on a Melbourne pub: "Good clean entertainment, every night except Monday."

\* \* \*

PLAYERS picked for the darts team will be pinned to the notice board on Thursday.

\* \* \*

SIGN beside the sandwiches on the bar said: "Do not touch the food."

\* \* \*

"TRY our home-made pies. You'll never get better."

\* \* \*

IN several pubs: "We have an agreement with the bank. They don't serve beer and we don't cash cheques."

\* \* \*

IN a Scottish pub: Happy Hour, 5-30 pm until 6 pm.

\* \* \*

LADIES are requested not to have children in the bar.

\* \* \*

DON'T drink if you're driving. There's no cure for the mourning after.

\* \* \*

IF you are driving, be sure you have a car.

\* \* \*

DON'T drive yourself to drink. Get a chauffeur.

\* \* \*

ONE for the road could be the pint of no return.

\* \* \*

PLEASE do not leave while the bar is in motion.

\* \* \*

THIRST come. Thirst served.

OUTSIDE the Registry Office: Marry Now, Pay Later!

\* \* \*

SIGN outside the church: "Next week's preacher will be pinned on the notice board."

\* \* \*

DIRECTIONS on a jam jar: "To open lid, pierce with knife to release vacuum, then push off."

\* \* \*

PATRONS WHO CONSIDER OUR STAFF UNCIVIL SHOULD SEE MANAGER. — New Delhi restaurant.

\* \* \*

CUSTOMERS GIVING ORDERS WILL BE PROMPTLY EXECUTED. — New Delhi restaurant.

\* \* \*

The Germans have theirs too: PATRONS WHO REQUIRE BATHING, PLEASE NOTICE THE CHAMBERMAID.

\* \* \*

IN CASE OF FIRE, PLEASE DO YOUR BEST TO ALARM THE PORTER.

\* \* \*

AND one from a British tourist brochure: These self-contained apartments are excellently situated near the Torquay sea front. Practically on the level.

\* \* \*

THE Houses of Parliament in Budapest are magnificent structures fronting the Danube, but as our Hungarian guide put it: "The buildings are best viewed from the backside."

\* \* \*

TO avoid burning your hands with hot water feel the water first before putting your hands in.

\* \* \*

"INSTANT hot water, in two minutes."

\* \* \*

PASSENGERS HIT BY CANCELLED TRAINS — Leader Newspapers, Victoria.

FROM Flinders Street railway station, Melbourne: TOILETS OUT OF ORDER, please use platform 7–8.

* * *

PADDY had a sign under his arm which read LONG VEHICLE. A cop stopped him and asked him where he got it. Paddy replied: "It fell off the back of a truck."

* * *

SIGN in a Fitzroy fruit shop: "God help those who help themselves!"

* * *

SIGN in a book shop read: "Browsers welcome, both high browse and low browse."

* * *

SIGN in an Albury Returned Servicemen's Club says: "Don't thump the machines, look for an attendant!"

* * *

SIGN on a photocopy machine: "The typists' reproduction equipment is not to be interferred with without prior permission of the manager."

* * *

ON the barber shop window: HAIR CUT, WHILE YOU WAIT.

* * *

LARGE sign on the door of an Australian church: "This is the House of God, and these are the Gates of Heaven." And below in smaller print: "This door is locked between the hours of 6 pm and 10 am."

* * *

"BOAT for sale, one owner, green in colour."

* * *

OUT to lunch. If not back by five, out to dinner also.

* * *

SIGN outside a funeral parlour: "Parking for clients only!"

* * *

WANTED. Man to wash dishes and two waitresses.

PRICES subject to change, according to customer's attitude.

* * *

SIGN at a creek: "When this sign is under water the crossing is dangerous."

* * *

SIGN in a pub: "If you are drinking to forget, please pay for your drinks in advance."

* * *

PLEASE do not insult our bartenders. Customers we can get.

## SMOKING

CANCER cures smoking.

* * *

SMOKING shortens your cigarettes.

* * *

HE has read so much about the effects of smoking that he has finally given up reading.

* * *

IT took a lot of will power, but finally he has given up trying to give up smoking.

* * *

"WILL you give up smoking for me?" she said.
    "Who says I've been smoking for you?" he said.

* * *

"GIVE me a cigarette, Fred."
    "But I thought you had given up smoking."
    "Well, I've reached the first stage. I've stopped buying them."

* * *

"HOW many fags do you smoke a day?"
    "Any given amount."

* * *

ASKED why he smoked 100 cigarettes a day, Fred replied: "Coughing is the only exercise I get."

FRED and Harry formed Smokers Anonymous. When one of them feels like a cigarette he rings the other and they get drunk instead.

\* \* \*

DON'T smoke in bed, for the ashes which fall on the floor may be your own.

\* \* \*

AND one for the smokers: And old bloke from the bush settled himself into the train compartment and began to light up his pipe, much to the obvious disgust of the only other occupant, an elderly woman.

"Do you know," she said, with all the disapproval she could muster, "my husband is 65 and he has never once put a pipe in his mouth."

The old-timer pondered this for a moment and replied, "I'm just on 70, and I've never put it anywhere else."

## SONGS

SHE used to go out with the landlord, but now she goes with the lease.

\* \* \*

YOU can lead a horse to water, but you can't lead a whore to culture.

\* \* \*

SHE wore a string of love beads and I knew I could count on her.

\* \* \*

THE volcano song: "Larva Come Back to Me."

\* \* \*

DRINK to me Only with Thine Eyes, cos I need all the Scotch myself.

\* \* \*

I'LL be Seizing You, in all the old familiar places.

IF you were the only girl in the world, well okay, but as you're not, forget it.

## SPEECHES

THE MC is the bloke who introduces people who need no introduction.

\* \* \*

HE was testing the microphone. "Can you hear me in that back corner?"

"Yes," came a reply, "and I will gladly change places with somebody who can't."

\* \* \*

I DON'T mind people looking at their watches when I'm making a speech, but it is damned disconcerting to see them shaking them to see if they are still going.

\* \* \*

SO many people start with the words, "I am not really a speech-maker." Then they spend the next half hour proving it.

\* \* \*

THE vicar asked the pert young widow to give a little talk to the Temperance Society because he said the men liked her short addresses.

\* \* \*

EVERY rose has its thorn
   That's the catch life teaches
   There hasn't been a free lunch yet
   Without those boring speeches.

## SPINSTERS

SHE called at the police station to complain about the young man next door. "It's not safe to go out on the street," she said. "He's always sitting on his front porch whistling dirty songs!"

MISS Prim had phoned the local police station several times to complain about the man next door who walked around his apartment completely nude. Finally the sergeant called around. "But you can't even see his window from here," he said.

"Try standing on that kitchen chair and looking through the skylight," she said.

*　　*　　*

TWO elderly spinsters were sitting on the front porch of their country house convincing each other they had made the right choice in life when a rooster chased a flurried hen past them. The hen took evasive action, running around the house three times, then dashed onto the road, straight into the path of an oncoming car.

"See that," said one spinster, "she'd prefer to die."

*　　*　　*

SPINSTER Brown rang the police to say she had captured a man climbing into her bedroom window, and that they could call around for him next morning.

## SPORT
See FOOTBALL, TENNIS, CRICKET

"I'M a little stiff from Badminton."
"I don't care where you come from."

*　　*　　*

SHE thought lacrosse was something you found in la church.

*　　*　　*

BOXING is like marriage. The preliminaries are often better than the main event.

*　　*　　*

AN Englishman, an Irishman and a Scot were sentenced to share a prison cell. The Englishman produced a pack of cards.

"At least we can pass the time playing poker."

The Scot said he liked music and would while away the time playing his mouth organ.

The Irishman smiled and said he had something better than either of his mates and produced a packet of Tampax. "It says on the packet that you can go riding, swimming, skiing, and play tennis with these."

## SQUELCH

WHEN a reporter asked New Zealand's ex-prime minster David Lange if he was concerned about the exodus of New Zealanders to Australia the PM replied, "Not at all. I think it is bound to raise the IQ of both countries."

\* \* \*

HE saw himself as a maker and shaker, but he was having trouble clinching the deal with two executives he had tried to impress over lunch.

He saw Bob Ansett pass by on the way to the gents, and quickly excused himself to follow. He lined up beside Bob and introduced himself. "My name's Peter. I have been a fan of yours for a long time, Bob. I admire your corporate image. Could you do me one great favour, little cost to you, but forever appreciated by me, if you just say hello to me as you pass my table. It would help me clinch the deal."

"Not at all," said Bob Ansett.

Sure enough, our yuppie had got settled and had resumed his spiel when Bob Ansett came by and said, "Hi Peter, how's it going?"

"Push off, Bob. Can't you see I'm talking business!"

\* \* \*

THE local State School decided to challenge the toffs at the Grammar School to a game of football. The date was arranged and the State School boys decided to adopt a gentlemanly stance and send the college a telegram which read: "May the best team win."

The college sent a telegram in reply which read: "May the better team win."

* * *

THE train was rattling towards a long tunnel and in one compartment sat an Englishman, an Irishman, a pretty young woman and a little old lady.

The train entered the tunnel and all went black. There was a loud kiss followed at once by an even louder smack.

When the train emerged from the tunnel the four occupants were still in their seats and busy with their own thoughts about what happened.

The pretty young woman was thinking: "Why would that Irishman want to kiss an old lady?"

The old lady was thinking: "What a hussy sitting there as if nothing had happened when I know that Englishman kissed her."

The Englishman was thinking: "I didn't do a damned thing, so why should I get my face slapped?"

And the Irishman was thinking: "How about that! I kiss my own hand, smack an Englishman in the mouth and get away with it!"

* * *

PADDY O'Leary boarded a train and found himself sharing a compartment with a snobby Englishman and his large dog.

"And what koind o' dog be that?" he asked the Pommie.

"It's a cross between an ape and an Irishman," was the surly reply.

"You mean it's related to both of us," said Paddy.

* * *

THE drunk boards the train and plonks himself down beside a priest and begins to read the paper.

He looks up after a bit and says: "Tell me father, what causes arthritis?"

It was just the opening the priest wanted. "I will tell you what causes arthritis my man," he said with passion.

"It's immoral living, too much drinking and smoking and no doubt sins of the flesh. How long have you had it?"

"Oh it's not me, father," said the drunk. "It says here the Pope's got it."

* * *

A NEWLY commissioned army lieutenant was standing outside a public phone box sorting through some coins. He stopped a passing soldier to ask if he had change of a dollar.

"I think so, mate," said the trooper diving his hand into his pocket.

"Just a minute, that's no way to address an officer," snapped the young lieutenant. "Let's try that again shall we. Do you have change of a dollar?"

The trooper snapped to attention and saluted. "No, sir!"

* * *

SHE was the self-appointed supervisor of village morals and accused a workman of having reverted to drink because with her own eyes she had seen his car parked outside the local pub.

The accused made no defence, but that night he parked his car outside her house, and left it there all night.

* * *

AS he arrived home from the pub he noticed his wife ironing her bra and couldn't refrain from commenting, "I don't know why you bother with that, dear, you've nothing to put in it."

She continued ironing and casually remarked, "I often think the same thing when I'm ironing your underpants."

* * *

AFTER 25 years of marriage a couple decided on an amicable divorce. To celebrate the granting of the decree they had dinner together. After the third glass of champagne the husband said, "There's something I have always wanted to ask you, but I didn't have the nerve. Now it can't possibly worry me."

"What's that?" said his immediate ex-wife.

"Why is it that five out of our six children have black hair and Tommy is so blonde."

She didn't answer. "Come on, you can tell me now," he insisted. "Whose child is Tommy?"

Finally she acquiesced. "Well, if you really want to know, Tommy is your child."

\* \* \*

A NUN had just beaten three young men to the last table in the railway cafeteria. They sat down beside her and decided to embarrass her with a conversation which would force her to leave.

"Your Mum and Dad get married yet?" said one to his mate.

"No. What about yours?"

"No. Not interested in that church stuff."

This went on for awhile until the nun said: "Excuse me, would one of you bastards pass me the salt?"

## STINGY
### AS IN CHEAP, MEAN OR PARSIMONIOUS

JOCK McTavish went to the Op Shop to buy a suitcase for his holiday. He found one at a reduced price. The manager asked if he wanted it wrapped. "Nae mon. Just put the brown paper and string inside."

\* \* \*

HE took all his money out of the bank for a holiday. After it rested in his pocket for a week he put it all back.

\* \* \*

WHEN the police put a price on his head he gave himself up.

\* \* \*

IF Jock and Sandy were alone in a bar together they would die of thirst.

THE first time Jock used the free air at the service station he blew out four tyres.

*     *     *

HE wouldn't shout if a shark bit him.

*     *     *

SHE said she would never go to a restaurant with Jock again. "He reads the menu from right to left," she said.

*     *     *

HER husband seldom bought her anything. He was a man of rare gifts.

*     *     *

HE took his kids to the beach and bought them an ice-cream, but they still squabbled and fought. They wanted one each.

... or, JOCK had promised to buy his mates a beer. Eventually he did, but they were still dissatisfied. They wanted one each.

*     *     *

JOCK was so mean that when he found a bottle of indigestion mixture, he ate a jar of pickles.

*     *     *

JOCK was down in the dumps and his office mate wondered why, because he left the pub the previous evening with a lovely blonde on his arm.

"What happened?"

Jock said he took the blonde to dinner, bought her chocolates and champagne and they went back to his flat for the night.

"Well why so gloomy?"

"I spent a fortune," said Jock, "and another bloke has just told me I could have got the same result with a couple of beers and a packet of potato chips."

*     *     *

NEXT night he hailed a cab to go home with his new girlfriend. She was so ravishingly beautiful he could hardly keep his eyes on the meter.

413

THE Salvation Army lass approached Jock and asked him for a dollar for the Lord.

"How old are ye?" said Jock.

"I'm nineteen," said the lass.

"Well, I'm 75 and I'll be seeing the Lord before you do, so I will slip him the dollar myself."

*　　*　　*

HE had been mean and stingy all his life so when he finally arrived at the Pearly Gates St Peter asked for his report card. "I once gave a dollar to a widow who was turned out of her house, and I once gave two dollars to an orphan who had just lost his parents."

God overheard it and said to St Peter: "Give him his three dollars back and tell him to go to Hell."

*　　*　　*

AN old farmer and his son had scratched out a living on their farm for 30 years. One day the son came home yelling for joy that he had won the $500,000 first prize in the lottery.

"Here Dad, here's your share," and he slapped a hundred dollar note on the table.

The old man looked at it a while. "When I was young," he said, "I never had time to smoke, drink or gamble because working this farm took all my time. In fact, I never had time to marry your Ma."

The young man considered this. "Well that's a nice state of affairs," he complained. "Of course you know what that makes me?"

"Yeah," said the old man, "and a bloody mean one at that."

*　　*　　*

TWO Scots established a business and at the end of the financial year they tried to balance the books, but no matter how many times they went through the accounts and receipts they were constantly $23.50 short.

Finally Jock confronted his partner: "Tell me the truth Angus. Have you been keeping a woman?"

PADDY had two stingy mates, Jock and Isaac. So he was surprised when they reluctantly agreed to take him out for his birthday. At the end of the meal he waited with some anxiety to see which one offered to pay.

"I'll take care of the bill," piped up Jock when the waiter approached.

Paddy went home that night amazed at Jock's generosity, until he read the newspaper headline next morning: Jewish Ventriloquist Strangled by Crazed Scotsman.

*    *    *

WE went round to a party at Jock's place where the water flowed like champagne.

## SWEARING

WHEN he boarded the country train he explained he was tired and asked the conductor if he could be woken at Junction Town.

"Don't worry if I swear a lot," said the passenger. "I am a notorious grump when I get woken up."

"No worries," said the conductor.

It was dark when the train stopped and the conductor finally gave the passenger a shake.

"What the hell's this?" roared the passenger realising he was at the terminus. "I told you to wake me at Junction Town you godforsaken son of a no-good bastard."

The conductor listened to the long string of abuse and finally muttered: "Yes, you can sure swear a lot. But not as much as the bloke we put off at Junction Town."

*    *    *

YOUNG Basil had moved to town from the country and had settled in at the suburban primary school fairly well; except for his constant swearing. It was "bloody" this and "bloody" that until he was sent home with a note:

"If this boy won't stop swearing he will not be allowed to school anymore."

His father gave him a bloody hiding and sent him back next day with a note to say he wouldn't bloody well swear again.

The teacher was impressed and sent home another note. "Basil has been so good he can come to the school picnic on Saturday week."

When the big day came, little Basil set off for the picnic, with a caution and yet another note. "If he swears again, please send the little bugger straight home."

In less than an hour Basil was back, weeping his eyes out, and copped another hiding from his father for swearing.

"I didn't swear," he protested. "You sent me off on the wrong bloody Saturday. The bloody picnic is not until next bloody week!"

* * *

TWO young brothers were sent home from their country school with a note to say they had been suspended for the afternoon for swearing.

Their father gave them a hiding, a lecture and sent them to bed without dinner.

Next morning as they sat down for breakfast their father, in a more conciliatory mood, asked what they would like for breakfast.

The first one said: "I'll have some of those bloody cornflakes." He received an immediate thrashing from his father and was sent back to bed for the day.

The father then asked the second boy what he would like for breakfast.

"I don't know," he said. "But it won't be bloody cornflakes, that's for sure."

* * *

BECAUSE he had been heard swearing, young Billie had been put across his father's knee and given a few good whacks. "Now son," said his Dad, "tell me why I punished you."

The kid threw up his hands in despair. "That does it. First you belt shit out of me and now you don't know why you bloody-well did it!"

# T

## TACT

TACT is the ability to describe others as they see themselves.

* * *

A SALESMAN with a phenomenal record finally revealed his secret to the new sales recruits. He said he put it down to the first seven words he invariably uttered when a woman answered his knock on a door: "Miss, may I speak to your mother?"

* * *

THE patient told his psychiatrist, "I don't seem to be able to mix with people. I have no friends. When I talk to people they soon walk away. Do you think you can help me you money-grabbing parasite and incompetent shrink?"

* * *

"HERE is a photo of my new bride."
  "Gosh. She must be very wealthy."

## TAXATION

WHOEVER said you couldn't be wounded by a blank obviously hasn't received a taxation form.

* * *

A CLOUDFUL of clergymen arrived at the Pearly Gates

and were gathered around the reception desk booking in when suddenly a fanfare of trumpets signalled a late arrival and St Peter called for the clergy to stand aside.

The new arrival was the taxman and he was ushered straight in on the red carpet.

The clergy were amazed and demanded to know why the preferred treatment.

"Because that bloke," said St Peter, "has put the fear of God into more people than the lot of you put together."

*     *     *

THE new tax inspector was intrigued to find that for many years Mr Abraham Finklestein had consistently claimed deductions for substantial amounts to charity.

The inspector became downright suspicious when he found that these annual donations were being made to St Mary's Catholic Church, and that Mr Finklestein could produce hundreds of cancelled cheques going back for years, all made out to the church, and each endorsed by the priest.

The inspector decided to question Fr. O'Malley over Mr Finklestein's generosity.

"Generosity?" said the priest. "Yes I know Finklestein well, but he is hardly generous."

"But we have his cancelled cheques going back over years," said the tax man.

"Oh those," said the priest. "Indeed he helps us there. We take up a big collection each mass, and as the banks are closed on Sundays, Mr Finklestein will always give us a cheque for it to save us worrying about the cash over the weekend."

## TAXIS

"IT's not so much the work I enjoy," said the cabbie, "it's the people I run into."

THE pompous English colonel arrived in New York and hailed a cab. "Take me to Christ's Church," he said.

About ten minutes' later the cab stopped outside St Patrick's cathedral.

"That's not Christ's Church," protested the colonel.

"If He's in town He's in that one," said O'Flaherty.

\* \* \*

THE surly businessman jumped into the cab.

"Where to?" said the cabbie.

"Mind your own business," he replied.

\* \* \*

SHE was only a cab driver's daughter but you sure auto meter.

\* \* \*

BUT he finally gave the job up. He didn't like people talking behind his back.

\* \* \*

FRED took a cab to the drive-in. The movie cost him $120.

\* \* \*

THERE were no serious injuries in an accident on the highway when a car collided with a taxi. The couple in the car escaped unhurt, but the 16 Scotsmen in the taxi were treated for shock, as they had paid for the trip in advance.

\* \* \*

JOCK picked up a lovely young woman in the pub and hailed a cab to take her home. He was so infatuated with her he could hardly keep his eyes on the meter.

\* \* \*

CHAP phoned the taxi company to complain that a cab he ordered had not arrived at the specific time.

"I told you when I made the booking that I had to be at the airport at a certain time," he complained.

"Don't worry, it will be there soon," said the girl. "Anyway, your plane is bound to be a few minutes late."

"You're damned right it will," complained the man. "I'm the pilot!"

*　　*　　*

THE passenger got a hell of a shock when the cab driver accelerated and raced through an intersection against the red lights. "Hey, go easy, where the heck did you get your licence?"

"Relax," said the cabbie. "My brother taught me to drive and he taught me how to run red lights."

The lights were red at the next intersection and to the passenger's horror he raced through again. It was not until he approached the fifth set of lights that they suddenly turned green and the cabbie nearly stood the taxi on end as it screeched to a stop.

"I don't understand, that's a green light," said the passenger.

"I know that, mate," said the cabbie looking both ways, "but my brother drives around this neighbourhood."

*　　*　　*

THE cabbie's careless driving was a worry to the expectant mother. "Be careful," she said, "I'm expecting my fifth child."

"And you're telling ME to be careful?" he asked.

*　　*　　*

IN a taxi on the way to the maternity hospital the 19-year-old wife complained she was in pain and terrified. Her 20-year-old husband put a comforting arm around her and asked: "Darling, are you sure you want to go through with this?"

*　　*　　*

HE lay under the cab tinkering with the motor and groping for spanners and tools when his attractive fare said: "Do you want a screwdriver?"

"Not now, Miss, but as soon as I fix this I'll be in it."

## TEACHERS
See EDUCATION, SCHOOLS

A STRAPPING young farm hand was sent to the station to pick up the new school teacher who turned out to be an attractive young woman.

On the way back to the farm she noticed a stallion mounting a mare. "How do they know when to do that?" she enquired.

The young man explained that it was a sense of smell.

In the very next paddock a bull was enjoying himself on a cow.

"Again, it is a sense of smell," explained the country boy, "just like that ram and ewe over there."

He unloaded her luggage at the farmhouse and turned to go. "See you later," he said.

"Thanks," she replied, "And do come over when your cold gets better."


## TEENAGERS

"MY son is going through one of those awkward stages, changing from a hooligan to a layabout."

\*　　\*　　\*

ADOLESENCE is that stage between infancy and adultery.

\*　　\*　　\*

TEENAGERS are very much alike in many disrespects.

\*　　\*　　\*

TEENAGE girls are between pigtails and cocktails.

\*　　\*　　\*

TEENAGE boys complain there is nothing to do and then stay out all night doing it.

\*　　\*　　\*

TEENAGERS express a burning desire to be different from anyone else, then dress exactly alike.

TEENAGERS think curbing their emotions means parking by the roadside.

*     *     *

WHEN he knocked on the door for his first date her father opened it and shouted back into the house, "Joanne, there's something here to see you."

*     *     *

MUM heard her daughter come home an hour ago, but she hadn't heard the new boyfriend leave, so she tiptoed down the stairs. She heard a giggle in the darkened lounge room. She switched on the light to find the couple in a passionate embrace on the couch.

"Well I never," she gasped.

"Oh, c'mon Mum, you must have," said the daughter.

# TENNIS

TENNIS was the trendy thing to do, so the Yuppie fronted the local sports store and asked to be kitted up. The proprietor sold him tennis shoes for $300 a pair, shorts for $200 a pair, a can of balls for $60 and shirts at $150 each.

"Oh, and I'll need a racquet," said the Yuppie.

So the proprietor sold him a half share in the store.

# TIME

TODAY is Tomorrow's Yesterday.

*     *     *

TIME is nature's way of preventing everything happening at once.

*     *     *

THINGS are getting so bad so quickly that the Good Old Days seem only a week old.

*     *     *

"WHEN I am with my girlfriend, time stands still."

"No wonder. She's got a face that would stop a clock."

DON'T give me a watch for Christmas. I've already got one. And I can assure you a man with one watch knows what time it is, while a man with two would never be sure.

\* \* \*

MABEL told him: "Your father can stay longer in an hour than others can stay in a bloomin' fortnight."

## TOASTS

THE purpose of most public speaking is to propose a toast. While the speech is designed to put everyone at ease and remind those who started drinking early why they are present, the patter merely paves the way towards the toast. So always have a few up your sleeve.

Toasts are also a wonderful ploy for having another drink and most of the Irish examples listed here are the result of a memorable night in a Dublin pub called the Limerick Arms.

A starter to claim the attention of those present is to stand and pronounce in a loud voice: "Fornication." And when that stops the conversation, continue with "Fornication like this we need champagne for the toast..."

\* \* \*

HERE'S to abstinence — provided it's in moderation.

\* \* \*

MAY we all get to heaven half an hour before the devil knows we're dead.

\* \* \*

MAY the skin of your bum never cover a drum.

\* \* \*

MAY you live as long as you want, and may you never want as long as you live.

\* \* \*

MAY you live a hundred years, and another month to repent.

MAY we never put our finger in another man's pie.

*       *       *

MAY you never have to eat your hat.

*       *       *

May the frost never afflict your spuds.

*       *       *

MAY the Blue Bird of Happiness crap down your chimney.

*       *       *

MAY we drink to the thirst which is yet to come.

*       *       *

MAY we all be alive this time, twelve months.

*       *       *

MAY you slide down the bannister of life, with nary a splinter.

*       *       *

MAY your luck be like the capital of Ireland, always Dublin!

*       *       *

MAY the fleas of a thousand camels infest the underpants of our enemies.

*       *       *

MAY their chooks turn into emus and kick down their dunny door.

*       *       *

HERE'S to the wowsers, whose abstinence gives us all the more to drink.

*       *       *

THERE'S many a toast, if I could think of it
    Damned if I can, so let's drink to it.

*       *       *

TO our wives and sweethearts. May they never meet.

*       *       *

LET'S drink to the soup. May it be seen and not heard.

*       *       *

HERE'S to the girl who lives on the hill
    She won't be in it, but her sister will
    Here's to her sister, then.

HERE'S to the happiest days of my life,
    Spent in the arms of another man's wife,
    My mother's.

*       *       *

HERE'S to your eyes, and mine
    Here's to your lips, and mine
    The former have met
    The latter not yet
    So here's to that moment, sublime.

*       *       *

HERE'S to us
    May we live a long life
    And here's mud in your eye
    While I wink at your wife.

*       *       *

HERE'S to Miss Prim
    For her life held no terrors
    Born a virgin, died a virgin
    No hits, no runs, no errors.

*       *       *

TO the office bore: May he give us a few brilliant flashes
of silence.

*       *       *

REMEMBER the poor. It costs nothing.

*       *       *

MUSICIANS' TOAST: May your organ never quit while
you are half way through your favourite piece.

*       *       *

I DRINK to your health when I'm with you
    I drink to your health when alone
    I drink to your health so often
    I'm becoming concerned at my own.

*       *       *

MAY you live as long as you want to
    And want to, as long as you live.

426

MAY we kiss who we please
    And please who we kiss.

* * *

IF I'm asleep when you want me. Wake me.
    And if I don't want to. Make me.

* * *

HERE'S to the bloke down the lane
    He courted a girl, all in vain
    She swore when he kissed her
    So he slept with her sister
    Again and again and again.

* * *

AND one to the author: May he live to be as old as his jokes.

* * *

A SURPRISE toast at a wedding goes this way:
    "And finally, may the happy couple lie, steal and cheat. (Pause, then explain). May they lie in each other's arms, may they steal away for a blissful honeymoon, adn may they cheat time to live as long as possible."

## TOUGH TIMES

IT'S tough when you call Suicide Prevention and they put you on hold.

* * *

IT'S tough luck when your car horn accidentally blasts off and remains jammed, while you're driving behind a group of Hell's Angels.

* * *

TIMES are so tough the local council has created a job for a painter. Signs that read "Keep off the grass" are to be re-painted, "Don't eat the grass."

* * *

MISTER, will you give me a dollar for my sick wife?
    Sorry old man, but I've already got one.

COULD you give a poor bloke a bite?

Sorry my man, I don't bite myself, but I'll call the dog.

* * *

HERE'S fifty cents then. How did you get so destitute in the first place?

Like you sir, giving away vast sums to the poor and needy.

* * *

WILL you give me a dollar for a sandwich?

Let's see the sandwich.

* * *

THE cook came to the door of the country pub: "Aren't you the same bloke I gave a pie to yesterday?"

"Yes, but I hardly expected to find the same cook here today."

* * *

THINGS were so tough in our family my parents couldn't afford to have children. Our neighbours had to have me.

We were so poor I didn't have my 21st birthday until I was 35.

* * *

THINGS get so bad so fast in these times, it seems the good old days were only a week ago.

# TRADESMEN

MANY electricians make light work.

* * *

JAKE signed on as a builder's labourer and set to work with a pick and shovel. After three days' toil he fronted the boss and asked for his week's wages in advance.

"Hang on, you've only done half a week's work," protested the boss.

But Jake had the answer. "I trusted you for the first half, now you trust me for the other!"

AFTER announcing his retirement, it was the postman's last day in the neighbourhood and most householders were giving him little presents. But he got the shock of his life when Mrs Smith took him upstairs, stripped off and took him to bed.

Afterwards she made him a cup of coffee, a hot breakfast and then pressed a dollar into his hand. The postman couldn't believe it and upon leaving asked for an explanation.

"It was my husband's idea, although he was a little preoccupied at the time," she said. "I told him you were retiring and I insisted we do something for you. He said, 'Oh, stuff the postman. Give him a dollar and a cup of coffee'."

"The breakfast was my own idea," she said.

\* \* \*

AN Irish handyman went down to the hardware store for some bolts.

"How long do you want them?" enquired the salesman.

"Well, to tell you the truth," replied the handyman, "I was sort of hoping to keep them."

\* \* \*

THE plumber finally arrived. "How have you managed?"

"Not too badly," said the housewife, "while we were waiting for you I've taught the kids how to swim."

\* \* \*

TWO plumbers were working in the street trying to unblock a drain when an angry gent came out of the house opposite.

"Go easy with that long wire you're poking about with, boys," he said. "You've had my missus leap off the toilet seat three times!"

\* \* \*

IT was many years ago since the embarrassing day that a young woman, with a baby in her arms, entered his butcher shop and confronted him with the news that the baby was his, and what was he going to do about it?

Finally, he capitulated. He promised to provide her with free meat until the boy was 16. She agreed.

He had been ticking the years off on his calendar and one day, the teenager who had been collecting the meat each week, came in to the shop and said: "I'll be sixteen tomorrow."

"I know," said the butcher with a smile, "I've been counting too, and tell your mother when you take this parcel of meat home that it is the last free meat she will get, and watch the expression on her face."

When the boy arrived home he told his mother. The woman nodded and said, "Son, go back to the butcher and tell him I have also had free bread, free milk and free groceries for the past 16 years and watch the expression on his face!"

\* \* \*

THE apprentice draftsman had just drawn his first construction plan and laid it out before his boss. "I think that's near enough," he said.

"Near enough is not good enough," said the boss pushing the plans away. "It's got to be perfect. Do it again."

The apprentice knuckled down at the drawing board for another two hours and finally presented them to the boss again.

"It's perfect now," said the lad.

"Well that's near enough," said the boss.

\* \* \*

IT was the day Fred was released from prison and they handed back his suit. He put his hand in the pocket and found a ticket for his shoe repairs. Although he thought the shoes would be out of style he decided on a whim to pick them up.

"It's been ten years and you may not remember them," said Fred producing the ticket, "but they were brown brogues to be half-soled and heeled."

"No worries, I remember them," said the shoe-repairer. "They will be ready on Tuesday."

\* \* \*

THE lawyer's brand-new television set was on the blink so he called for the maintenance man who duly arrived, pulled the set away from the wall replaced a fuse and put his hand out for $72.

"What," said the lawyer. "That's outrageous. $72 for five minutes' work? I am a lawyer and I don't get that much money."

"Neither did I when I was a lawyer," said the maintenance man.

\* \* \*

THEY called the maintenance man when the washing machine broke down. He duly arrived, pulled the machine out from the wall, studied it a few minutes, then got a large hammer and gave it a mighty whack.

It started straight away.

He then handed the couple a bill for $50.

"Fifty bucks?" said the husband. "All you did was whack it with a hammer."

"It is all itemised on the bill," said the tradesman. "Hitting the machine with the hammer is $2. Knowing exactly where to hit it is $48."

\* \* \*

WHEN the doctor rang the plumber to complain that the toilet cistern had developed a fault the weary plumber reminded him that it was 2.30 in the morning.

"So what," said the doctor. "I get called out at all hours. I have a problem which needs fixing, so what does the time of day or night have to do with it?"

Ten minutes later the plumber arrived on the doorstep and was shown to the bathroom. He lifted the lid of the toilet, threw in two aspirins and flushed it.

"If it hasn't improved by the morning ring me again," he said.

# TRAINS

A GROUP of people on the train were discussing why the railway was losing money.

"Hopeless management," said one old gent.

"Too many lazy employees," said the woman by the window.

"It's the union," said another.

A fourth was about to give his opinion as the train stopped at a station and an inspector got on board, and they all jumped out.

\* \* \*

OLD Fred and his son were down from the bush and enjoying a ride on a train when a priest hobbled into their compartment on crutches.

"Slipped in the bathtub," he explained.

When the priest got out at the next station the son said: "What's a bathtub, Dad?"

"Dunno," said Fred, "I'm not a Catholic."

\* \* \*

THE middle-aged couple had just settled in the compartment for a long rail journey. As the train pulled out of the station he asked: "Comfortable dear, is the seat soft?"

"Yes," she said.

"Not feeling any draught?"

"No."

"No vibrations or shaking?"

"No."

"Right then," he said, "let's change places."

\* \* \*

EACH time the train stopped at a station the little old man would get up, walk to the door, look out and say "Oh Damn!"

Every station it was the same until the bloke opposite, exasperated by this behaviour asked him what was wrong.

"I'm on the wrong damned train!"

FOUR people were in the same compartment on a long train journey; a young woman, a priest, a businessman and a drunk.

All had been quiet for an hour or two until the young woman suddenly began to sob. The priest bent over to console her. "Tell me why you are crying," he said.

The girl sniffed and said: "I have just learnt that I am illegitimate."

The priest replied, "That's no sin. As a matter of fact I am illegitimate myself."

Then the businessman spoke up. "Excuse me, I couldn't help overhearing, but I must tell you that I am a self-made man. I own several businesses, in fact I am a millionaire, yet I am illegitimate too."

The drunk took out a cigarette and asked: "Any of you bastards got a light?"

\* \* \*

IT was the new Very Fast Train and halfway through the journey there was a violent vibration. "What was the trouble back there?" asked a passenger, "I thought this was supposed to be a smooth ride."

"Sorry sir," said the porter. "We ran over a politician."

"Goodness. What was he doing on the tracks?"

"Oh, he wasn't on the tracks Sir, but we got him."

# TRAVEL

SOME people travel for a change and a rest; only to find the hotel takes the change and the taxi takes the rest.

\* \* \*

TRAVEL advice: Don't put all your bags in one exit.

\* \* \*

"MR Wong! Mr Wong!" cried the distraught tourist, "the monkeys have run away with my travellers' cheques!"

"Ah, what sort were they?"

"Brown ones with red backsides!"

THE best time to visit Paris is between your 18th and 25th birthdays.

* * *

TRAVEL advice: Take twice the money you've got and unpack half the clothes.

* * *

I'VE just come back from a pleasure trip. I drove the in-laws to the airport.

* * *

"CARRY your bag, sir?"

"No, let her walk."

* * *

THE woman was booking a holiday for her husband. The travel agent asked her if she had any destination in mind.

"Anywhere in the Bermuda Triangle," she said.

* * *

SEASONED couple at the airlines reservations counter: "Two tickets to wherever our luggage is going."

* * *

YOUNG bloke went to the doctor for a check-up. "You need to relax more," said the doc. "You need to get away from it all for a while. Could you go abroad?"

"Sure could," replied the patient. "What's she like?"

* * *

FIRST snob: "I understand you are not going to Paris this year?"

Second snob: "No, it is London we are not going to this year."

* * *

EUROPE is so wonderful. If you ever go there, don't miss it.

* * *

REMEMBER, it is easier to find a travelling companion than to get rid of one.

* * *

I MET my wife in Acapulco. She was looking for a vacation and I was the last resort.

A RESORT is where the locals live off your holiday until next summer.

★    ★    ★

I WENT to a travel agent and asked where I could go for $50. He told me.

★    ★    ★

"WHEN you sailed around Italy, did you touch Florence?"

"No, her husband never let her out of his sight."

★    ★    ★

MURPHY opened a pub on the moon. But it had no atmosphere.

★    ★    ★

JOCK thought Niagara Falls was a terrible waste of water.

★    ★    ★

SHE was on the phone from the Riviera. "The holiday is wonderful darling, I feel like a new woman."

"So do I. Stay there another week."

★    ★    ★

A YOUNG Aussie was enjoying his first night in Rome drinking cappuccino at a pavement cafe when a pretty girl sat beside him.

"Hello," he said. "Do you understand English?"

"Only a little," she answered.

"How much?" he asked.

"Fifty dollars," she replied.

★    ★    ★

AN older Aussie, a wealthy man who had made his money in the furniture business, was also in Rome, and alone at the same cappuccino bar, when a young woman smiled at him, and naturally he returned the smile.

She was soon by his side. He said hullo, but she shrugged her shoulders to indicate she couldn't speak English.

He took a pen and paper from his pocket and drew a glass of wine with a question mark. She nodded and

435

they had a drink. He drew a taxi with a question mark. She nodded and they soon had a tour of the city by cab.

He then drew a table for two which had the desired result, and after a splendid meal with two bottles of vino she reached for the pen and paper. She drew a four poster bed with a question mark.

"How perceptive of you," laughed our hero. "I am astounded. How did you know I was in the furniture business?"

\*　　　\*　　　\*

SHE insisted on taking innumerable outfits with her, and they arrived at the airport loaded with luggage.

"I wish," said the husband thoughtfully, "we had bought the piano."

"No need to be sarcastic," said the wife, "it's not a bit funny."

"I'm not trying to be funny," he said, "I've left the tickets on it."

\*　　　\*　　　\*

THE American was bumping about in the rear of the bus. "How far is it to Alice Springs then?" he asked.

"About a thousand kilometres as the crow flies."

"Hell. Why do we have to follow a dog-gone crow?"

\*　　　\*　　　\*

FRED says travel broadens the mind. A trip to the Holy Land taught him a lot about the bible. "They took me to see Dan and Beersheeba, and I found they were two villages," he said.

"I always thought they were man and wife, like Sodom and Gomorrah."

\*　　　\*　　　\*

THE coach was travelling through Dublin when the guide announced: "We are now passing the biggest pub in Ireland."

An Aussie voice at the back of the bus said: "Why?"

HE had a bent for pornographic literature, and he was in a taxi leaving Hongkong for the airport when the cab stopped outside a bookshop. There it was, a large volume in the window titled "How to Woo."

He told the cab driver to wait, dashed into the shop, asked the attendant to wrap it in brown paper, and bought it.

Not until he was comfortably seated on the flight home did he tentatively open the wrapper and learn that he had bought volume two of the Hongkong phone directory.

\* \* \*

YOUNG chap boarded the Ansett flight at Cairns and the hostess noticed a newspaper parcel under his arm. "Mudcrabs," he explained. "I'm taking them back to Melbourne for a gourmet meal tonight."

"Then in that case they would be best placed in the fridge," said the hostess, stowing them away appropriately.

The flight landed on time and as the aircraft taxied across the tarmac the passengers were welcomed to Melbourne, told to remain seated until the aircraft came to a halt ... "And would the gentleman who gave me the crabs in Cairns please identify himself?"

\* \* \*

PADDY, the left-handed barman had been pulling beers for 25 years in the same pub. "Why don't you travel and broaden your mind?" he was told repeatedly.

Finally he took the advice and booked a week's holiday in the Canary Islands.

When he returned he was a changed and knowledgeable man. "Well what did you learn?" asked the regulars. "I can tell you this," he said as they all leaned forward for his pearl of wisdom.

"There are no canaries in the Canary Islands."

A year passed and Paddy once more took his annual

leave abroad. This time his travel agent suggested the Virgin Islands.

"Well what did you learn this time, Paddy?" asked the regulars when he returned from his second world odyssey.

"I can tell you this," he said as they all leaned forward. "There are no canaries on the Virgin Islands, either!"

* * *

DEAR diary. This is day one of my first holiday on a cruise ship.

Day two. While the cruise is nice there is an awful lot of men, including the stewards, making passes at me.

Day three. I have been invited to sit at the captain's table.

Day four. The captain made an improper suggestion last night. I refused.

Day five. The captain says that unless I agree, he will sink the ship.

Day six. Last night I saved the lives of 965 people.

* * *

"THEY say that London is the foggiest place in the world, but I have been to a town where the fog was much thicker."

"Where was that?"

"Don't know. It was too foggy to tell."

* * *

HE is a mental traveller. His mind wanders.

* * *

SIAMESE twins were having a terrible argument about where to go for their next holidays. "We're going to America," stamped the one on the left. "I want to drive for a change!"

* * *

"I WOULDN'T go to America if you paid me," said Fred.

"Why?"

"Cos they drive on the wrong side of the road."

438

"What's wrong with that?"

"I tried it the other night," said Fred. "It's bloody dangerous!"

&ast; &ast; &ast;

TOURIST: "Have you lived here all your life?"

Local: "Not yet!"

&ast; &ast; &ast;

A HUNGRY back-packer in a youth hostel complained about the sandwich he just bought.

"I haven't found any ham in this sandwich yet," he said.

Manager: "Try another bite."

The back-packer did so. "No, nothing at all."

Manager: "Heck, you must have passed it."

&ast; &ast; &ast;

TWO professional hitch-hikers travelling through Europe were sitting by the roadside. One was poking his tongue out at passing cars. He even gave some motorists the raspberry.

"You will never get a lift doing that," said his mate.

"I know that. Who cares. I'm on my lunch break!"

&ast; &ast; &ast;

THE lad from Australia got quite a buzz walking down Fifth Avenue in the heart of the Big Apple. He was looking up at the skyscrapers when he felt somebody bump him slightly.

With a jolt he remembered he was in New York and reached for his wallet. It was gone. And the youth who bumped him was hurrying down the street.

Our lad sprinted after him, grabbed him by the shirt-front and backed him against the wall. "Okay pal. You've met your match. You're dealing with an Aussie. Hand over that wallet."

The youth produced the wallet, ducked out of the grip and ran. It wasn't until our Ocker got back to his room that he saw his wallet where he had left it beside the bed.

SOME of the famous duty-free airports of the world are Schipol at Amsterdam, Singapore and Dubai. But for the most unusual items, try Shannon Airport. Here you can get water-proof tea bags, one-piece jigsaw puzzles, inflatable dartboards for campers and solar powered torches.

*    *    *

A TRAVEL agent looked up from his desk to notice an old lady and an old gent peering in the shop window at the posters showing the glamorous destinations around the world. The agent had had a good week and the dejected couple looking in the window gave him a rare feeling of generosity.

He called them in. "I know that on your pension you could never hope to have a holiday, so I am sending you off to a fabulous resort at my expense, and I won't take no for an answer," he said.

He took them inside and asked his secretary to write two flight tickets and book a room in a five-star hotel. They gladly accepted and were off.

About a month later the little old lady came in to his shop. "And how did you like the holiday?" he asked eagerly.

"The flight was exciting and the room was lovely," she said. "I've come to thank you. But one thing has puzzled me. Who was that old bloke I had to share the room with?"

*    *    *

BACHELOR Joe had led a quiet life. But for years he had been dreaming of a cruise in the South Pacific and when he received his superannuation he had enough money to make his dream come true.

When he boarded the ship, he had no friends to wave him goodbye so he went below to look for his cabin. He went down to C-deck, then down to D-deck, then down once more where he was suddenly grabbed by

440

two burly seamen, rushed down more flights of stairs, stripped of his clothes on the way and finally thrown into a large space down in the bilge of the ship.

In darkness and confusion he was shoved onto a long bench and felt the chains go around his ankles and a rough oar was thrust into his hands.

In the dim light he could see he was one of many.

Suddenly, he heard a drum beat and could just make out a large muscular negroid man beating a drum to an ever increasing rhythm. With the crack of a whip a raucous voice yelled "Row you Scum, Row."

Shackled to the oar Joe could do nothing else. In fact, to the monotonous beat of the drum Joe did nothing else for the next two weeks until they arrived somewhere and the drummer stopped the tedious beat. The reprieve lasted only two days. The drum started again and under the crack of the whip they began to row back home.

As the ship tied up Joe slumped on his oar and turned to the emaciated figure beside him which had been his companion for the voyage.

Joe addressed him for the first time. "Excuse me," he said. "I've never been on a cruise before. How much should I tip the drummer?"

"Don't know really," said his gaunt companion. "I gave him $20 when I did this cruise last year!"

\* \* \*

KIWI tourist driving around the UK got himself lost along the south-east coast of England. He saw a local and said: "Excuse me, can you tell me where I am?"

The local said: "Great Yarmouth."

"Same to you, fish-face," was the Kiwi's retort.

\* \* \*

AN American tourist on a trip to Ayers Rock suddenly yelled "Stop the Bus" and scrambled to the front to get off. He had spotted an aboriginal with his ear to the ground on a track which turned off the main road. "He must be one of your famous black-trackers you have out here," he said as he ran back to the aboriginal.

"Can you tell me about the last people to pass this way?" enquired the Yank.

"Yeah," answered the aboriginal, and pointing to the wheel tracks he said "It was a Ford utility."

This didn't impress the Yank much. "Anything else?" he said.

"Yeah. There was ten people in it. Three in the front and seven in the back."

Now the yank was impressed. "Anything else?"

"Yeah. The three in the front were blokes with four women and three kids in the back and the truck has yellow wheel caps."

This amazed the Yank. "And you can tell all that just by putting your ear to the ground?"

"Not really," said the aboriginal. "I just fell off the plurry thing!"

*   *   *

VISITOR to the city could not decide whether to spend his last day at the football finals or at the massage parlours in the 'Red Light' district. He finally opted for the football.

"Sorry sir," said the attendant, "the only seats left are the higher priced ones at $30."

"What?" said the visitor. "I could have gone to a brothel and got a woman for that."

"Ah, yes," said the attendant, "but you wouldn't have had 100 minutes of action-packed play and a brass band at interval would you?"

*   *   *

GUIDE on a conducted tour of Rome: "And this ancient monument dates back over 2000 years."

"Don't be ridiculous," said one little old lady. "It's only 1990 now."

*   *   *

AT the airport Trevor the Traveller abused the luggage handler. His case comes up next week.

HE told the travel agent: "I want a round world ticket."

"One way?" she asked.

*    *    *

AN Australian and Irishman were waiting in the travel agent's office.

"How much to South America?" asked the Australian.

"That will cost you $1000," said the travel agent.

"But I only have $500," said the Aussie.

The agent thought for a moment.

"That's okay, just go into the next office and you will be attended to."

The Irishman said he also wanted to go to South America, and observing what happened said he also only had $500.

"Could I have the same deal?"

"Okay," said the agent. "Step inside the next office."

Paddy goes through the door and is immediately hit on the head with a club. He wakes up chained to an oar beside the Aussie and a hundred others rowing to the beat of the drum master.

"I wonder if they will fly us home?" mutters the Irishman.

"They didn't last year," replied the Australian.

# U

## UNIONS

HALF a loaf is better than no tea-break at all.

*   *   *

THE politicians were host to a United States business delegation and at the height of the dinner one of the Americans at the head table asked the waiter for some more butter.

"Sorry, just one pat of butter per person," said the waiter.

The chamber president was embarrassed to overhear this and called the waiter aside.

"Do you know who that man is?" he said angrily. "He is in charge of the American delegation."

"And do you know who I am?" said the waiter. "I am in charge of the butter."

*   *   *

WHEN Harry Bloggs arrived at the building site he was told "no ticket, no start." But Harry said it was against his principles to join the union.

They argued with him, the union organiser was called, even the boss who didn't want trouble on the site tried to cajole him to join the union. Harry wouldn't have it.

He was working on the scaffolding on the 52nd level, high over the street, when the man from the union arrived.

444

"I will only tell you once, Harry," he said. "If you don't join the union I will pick up that piece of timber, wrap it around your neck and throw you right off this platform onto the tram tracks below."

Later, when they asked Harry why he joined, he said, "I had never had it explained so succinctly before."

* * *

THE waterside workers were having a break on the wharf when a leading hand said to his boss, "Hey, that new bloke you hired this morning; he's not a spy is he?"

"No, I think he checked out okay, why?"

"Well, he just stubbed his toe on a crate of pig-iron and said, 'Oh, the perversity of inanimate objects!' "

* * *

A MOTORIST had been picked up on a traffic infringement and had given his name as Fred Shagbreak and his place of employment. When the cop arrived to deliver the brief he asked the girl at the enquiry desk: "Have you got a Shagbreak here?"

She replied: "You must be joking, the union has battled for two years just to get a coffee break."

* * *

SHOP-STEWARD: "From now on all wages are doubled, holidays extended to six months and we shall only work on Fridays."

From the back of the hall: "What, every bloody Friday?"

* * *

MANAGER to boss: "The workers are demanding shorter hours."

"Right, we'll cut their lunch hour to 30 minutes!"

* * *

THE unionist on holiday sent a postcard home: Having a lovely time-and-a-half.

# V

## VETS
See DOGS

THE German tourist dived into the river, dragged the apparently drowned dog ashore and revived it.

"Are you a vet?" asked an impressed bystander.

"Ya, I'm bloody soaking," he replied.

\* \* \*

HE entered the vet's clinic with a cat under his arm. "It's been as sick as a dog," he said.

\* \* \*

THE vet was in the middle of a tricky operation on a dog when the phone rang.

"How long should I leave a rooster in with a hen?" enquired the voice at the other end.

"Just a minute," said the busy vet.

"Thank you," said the caller, and hung up.

\* \* \*

THE elderly spinster told the vet her dog had become so old it had forgotten its house training. "I'm sorry," said the vet, "but the only thing I can suggest, is the lethal chamber."

"Yes, but will the old fleabag use it," she said.

\* \* \*

FRED the farmer told the vet that he had just purchased a very expensive prize stud bull, but it wasn't the slightest

446

bit interested in the cows. "I've done my dough," he moaned.

The vet said it wasn't a problem and gave him some tablets to include in the bull's feed. Next day the bull began performing with great passion and stamina.

Fred was telling his neighbour about the potency of the tablets. "Flamin' marvellous," he said. "What's more, they don't taste too bad either."

\* \* \*

(R) TWO women were sitting in the waiting room with their dogs, one a fox terrier, the other a Great Dane. The foxie's owner said she was there because her pooch had a shocking habit of humping anything that went past, even visitor's legs.

"I know," said the other woman. She said her Great Dane had the same embarrassing habit.

"So you are here to have him de-sexed too?"

"No," she replied, "I'm getting his toenails cut."

## WAITERS
### See RESTAURANTS

"AND what'll you have?"
Said the waiter, idly picking his nose.
"I'll have two boiled eggs, ya mongrel,
"You can't put your fingers in those!"

*     *     *

WAITER: "How did you find the meat Sir?"
"I just lifted a potato chip and there it was."

*     *     *

"WAITER! What is this fly doing in my soup?"
Waiter studies it for a while.
"Backstroke, I believe Sir."

*     *     *

"WAITER! Bring me a smaller cheque!"

*     *     *

"WAITER, what's the difference between the steak and
the hamburger?"
"About one day, sir."

*     *     *

"WAITER! This food is terrible. I demand to see the
manager."
"Sorry, sir. He is out to lunch."

"WAITER! There's a fly in my soup."

"Well, don't complain to me, mate, it's the chef that was once a tailor!"

*    *    *

"WAITER, what's with this chicken soup?"

"I dunno, what's with the chicken soup?"

"It tastes funny."

"Well, start laughing!"

*    *    *

"WAITER! Your thumb is on my steak."

"Well, you don't want it to drop on the floor again, do you?"

*    *    *

"WAITER, this plate is wet."

"That's your soup sir."

*    *    *

"WAITER, why does this chicken have one leg missing?"

"It was in a fight."

"Well take it away and bring me the winner."

*    *    *

"WAITER, what's the special on the menu today?"

"I'll call the chef."

"I don't want him. I'm not a cannibal."

*    *    *

"WAITER, this soup isn't fit for a pig."

"I will take it back sir and bring you some that is."

*    *    *

"WAITER, what's the best dish in the place?"

"That blonde sitting at table three."

*    *    *

"WAITER, can I have a salad sandwich without cucumbers?"

"Sorry, we are out of cucumbers. Can you take it without tomatoes?"

*    *    *

"WAITER, what time is it?"

"Sorry sir, this is not my table."

449

"WAITER, what's the soup du jour?"
    "It's off. We ran out if it yesterday."

* * *

"WAITER, I would like a stew that will give me indigestion immediately, instead of three o'clock in the morning."

* * *

"WAITER, is there lots of juice in this grapefruit?"
    "More than meets the eye, sir."

* * *

THE waiter approached the diner. "Why are you eating those olives on a string, sir?"
    "Because I may not like them."

* * *

"YOU are not eating your fish," said the waiter, "what's wrong with it?"
    "Long time no sea," said the diner.

* * *

"WAITER, are you sure this lobster is fresh?"
    "Yes Sir, it walked here from the beach this morning."
    The customer gave it another sniff. "Well I think it must have trodden in something on the way!"

* * *

IF you think the service is bad, wait until you taste the food.

* * *

ENGRAVED on the Maitre d's tombstone: "Bye and by, God caught his eye."

* * *

ON his first date with her he decided to impress her. He took her to a posh restaurant and ordered the whole meal in French.
    Even the waiter was surprised. It was a Chinese restaurant.

* * *

THE irate diner had complained to the waitress about the unsatisfactory pastries. She in turn got the manager.

"I don't see why you should complain about our pastrycook," said the manager, "she has been making pastry since before you were born."

"As maybe," said the diner, "but why wait until now to sell them?"

\* \* \*

THE bachelor finished his meal and placed his tip on the table as he finished his coffee. The waitress took one look at the three single cents and said. "Thank you for your generosity. You can always tell the character of a diner by the way he tips."

"Oh really," he said, "and what does that tell you about me?"

"Well you put the three cents in a row," said the waitress. "That tells me you are tidy for starters. The first cent tells me you are frugal. The second cent tells me you are a bachelor."

"That's true," he said, "but what does the third cent tell you?"

"That tells me your father was a bachelor too."

\* \* \*

THE waiter brought the cheque and the diner studied it, then sorted through his money. "By golly," he said, "I have exactly that amount, but I'm afraid I haven't got enough for a tip."

"Let me add up that bill again, sir," said the waiter.

\* \* \*

THE two women from the blue-rinse set ordered their meal. "And we will have two glasses of wine," said one. "And make sure I get a clean glass. The one you gave me last week was filthy."

After a while the waiter brought the food and wine, "And which of you ordered the clean glass?" he said.

CUSTOMER in a French restaurant. "Waiter, do you have frogs legs?"

"Oui monsieur."

"Then hop across the road and get me a packet of cigarettes."

\* \* \*

"WILL you have pie sir?"

"Is it customary?"

"No, it's apple."

\* \* \*

MOISHE settled down in his favourite kosher restaurant. "Oi waiter, do you have matzo balls?"

"No," he said, "I always walk like this!"

\* \* \*

"WHAT do you think of that brandy, sir?" said the waiter showing him the bottle. "It's 1856."

"What? Just for one bottle?"

\* \* \*

WHEN he ordered a plate of oysters he noticed that the waitress was quite pretty. When she delivered the meal he said: "How about a smile and a few kind words, darling?"

The girl obliged with a beaming smile and turned to walk away.

"Hang on," he said, "I've got the oysters and the smile, but where's the few kind words?"

She bent down, put her lips close to his ear and whispered: "Don't eat the oysters."

## WARDROBES
See INFIDELITY

HE was in bed with a married woman when he heard the back door slam. "Hell. It's my husband," she cried. "Quick, hide in that wardrobe." He gathered up his clothes and dived from the bed to the wardrobe in a flash. After a few moments another voice in the wardrobe said "It's dark as a dog's belly in here isn't it?"

The man, shivering in the nude, was shocked. "Who is it?" he whispered. It was a little boy's voice and it said: "I know who you are and it will cost you. Give me $50 or I will yell for my Dad."

He was in no position to argue, he grudgingly paid up, and when the crisis was over made a quick exit from the bedroom window. Next day the little boy and his mother were down town and he said he was going to buy a brand new skateboad. "What with?" asked his mother.

"I've got $50" said the boy.

"Where did you get that kind of money," said his mother, but the lad refused to tell. "You must have done something wrong," she persisted and after slapping him about the ears dragged him across the street to the church.

"Confession is the thing for you my lad. If you won't tell me, then you will have to tell the parish priest," and she shoved him into the confessional box and shut the door.

"Gawd. It's dark as a dog's belly in here," said the boy.

"Now don't you start that again," said the priest.

*　　*　　*

HUSBAND came home unexpectedly and found his wife in bed. But when he went to hang his suit in the wardrobe he was surprised to see a man in there, busily snatching at things in the air.

"What the heck are you doing?" asked the husband.

"I am a moth catcher," said the stranger, still snatching at imaginary insects as if they were flying around his head.

"Then why are you doing it in the nude?" asked the suspicious husband.

With that, the moth catcher looked down and noticed

his absence of clothes. "Crikey, they're worse than I thought," he said.

(Another explanation for the man in the wardrobe comes from the husband's wife: "Oh, he's just a nudist who came in to use the phone.")

*     *     *

HE arrived home from work earlier than usual and found his wife in bed. There was a long whisp of smoke coming from a cigar in the ashtray on the bedside table.

"Where did that cigar come from?" he roared.

A timid male voice from the wardrobe said, "Cuba."

*     *     *

PADDY fell into a terrible state of remorse when he discovered his wife's lover in the wardrobe. They had a frightful argument, then he reached in a drawer and pulled out a gun. He cocked the trigger and held it to his head.

"For God's sake, Paddy, put that gun down," cried Teresa.

"Shut yer mouth and say your prayers woman. You two are next," said Paddy.

*     *     *

IN the long queue waiting at the Pearly Gates were three men, all from the same town. "How come?" asked St Peter.

The first said he had suspicions his wife was having an affair so he left for the office as usual, but doubled back to their penthouse apartment in a bid to catch her. He rushed into the bedroom, sure enough, she had gone back to bed, but a search of the wardrobe revealed no trace of her lover.

But when he looked out of the kitchen window he saw a bloke putting his clothes on behind a bush in the garden. He got so angry he picked up the refrigerator with superhuman strength and hurled it down at him. "The strain gave me a heart attack and that's why I am here," he told St Peter.

454

The second man said: "That's funny, I am a landscape gardener and I was just getting changed for work, putting my overalls on, when I was hit with a fridge. That's why I'm here."

"That's funny," said the third man. "I was hiding in this fridge ...!"

*　*　*

PADDY O'Flaherty came home early one Friday afternoon and found his wife lying naked on the bed and crying.

"Whatever is the matter?" asked Paddy.

"We're invited to a wedding tomorrow," sobbed Teresa, "and I have nothing to wear."

"That's ridiculous," said Paddy. Going over to the wardrobe he said, "Look in here. Here's a red dress, a green dress, a pink dress... Hello Father, a yellow dress..."

## WEATHER

IT was so cold last week that the local flasher was spotted describing himself to a group of women.

*　*　*

IT was so cold on the Antarctic Expedition that when he returned she broke it off.

*　*　*

IT was as cold as a barmaid's heart.

*　*　*

IT was so dry the frogs were taking swimming lessons.

*　*　*

IT was so dry the Council closed two lanes of the municipal swimming pool.

*　*　*

AFTER he answered the phone yet again he said to his saucy young wife. "That's funny. We must have a number similar to the Weather Bureau. That's the third bloke to ring and ask if the coast was clear."

SITTING on the pub's verandah one farmer looked at the threatening sky and said: "D'yer think it'll rain?"

"I hope so," said the other. "Not for myself, mind you, but for the sake of my two sons. They haven't seen rain."

\* \* \*

THE farmer had a rope hanging from a dead tree at his back door.

"What's it for?" asked a visitor.

"It's my weather guide," the old farmer replied. "If its swinging back and forth, its windy, and if its wet, its been raining."

\* \* \*

IT rained cats and dogs. Poodles everywhere.

\* \* \*

THE wind blew so hard...

it blew three dogs off their chains... a chook facing east laid the same egg three times...

it blew the pricks off a barbed wire fence.

\* \* \*

"HOW did you find the weather on your holiday?"

"I just opened the door and there is was, everywhere."

\* \* \*

"THEY say London is the foggiest place in the world, but I have been to a place where the fog was much thicker."

"Where was that?"

"Don't know. It was too foggy to tell."

\* \* \*

UNCLE Fred worked in the Weather Bureau for years, but when he was promoted to the main office he only lasted a month. The weather didn't agree with him.

\* \* \*

THE BBC announcer said: Today it will be muggy, followed by Tuggy, Weggy, Thurggy and Fruggy.

\* \* \*

HE went to Mexico where the weather was more predictable: Chili today, hot-tamale.

# WEDDINGS
See MARRIAGE, MARRIEDS, NEWLY-WEDS

HAPPY is the bride that the sun of a tycoon takes a shine to today.

* * *

THERE is so much permissiveness in the world today that the only way to stop having sex is to get married.

* * *

THE relative from out of town arrived late. "Who gave the bride away?" he asked.

"Any one of us could, but we all agreed to keep our mouths shut."

* * *

SHE had turned 30 and had been difficult to unload, so when her father finally gave her away at the altar he demanded a receipt.

* * *

AFTER a few champagnes the tipsy young bride stood up to thank the guests for the presents. "... and I'd like to thank my parents-in-law for giving me such a perky copulator."

* * *

EVEN these days there are a few four-letter words which can still shock most brides, like cook, wash, dust and iron.

* * *

"DO you like big weddings or little ones?"

"Without big weddings you shouldn't have little ones."

* * *

USHER at the wedding reception: "Are you a friend of the groom's?"

Woman: "Indeed I am not. I am the bride's mother."

* * *

I WILL never forget my wedding. God knows I've tried.

THE bride wept, the bridesmaids wept, even the wedding cake was in tiers.

*     *     *

THE minister reached that part of the ceremony where the congregation is asked if anybody knows why this man and woman should not be joined together in holy matrimony.

A thin voice replied, hesitantly, "... er, yes. I'd like to say something."

The minister looked at him sternly. "Shut up. You are not part of the congregation. You're the groom!"

*     *     *

THE MC at the wedding reception stood up and roared: "Fornication!" "Fornication like this," he continued, "we should toast the happy couple in champagne."

*     *     *

A WAG who was known as a practical joker and who had played the most diabolical tricks on his friends was about to be married himself and was therefore very nervous. Would his friends get their revenge?

He was in a sweat when the vicar announced: "Is there any reason why this couple should not be joined together?" and despite his constant fear the ceremony and the wedding reception went without water pistols or rude telegrams. They even got to their hotel without incident.

Next morning the groom called room service. "This is Mr Smith in room 13, I'd like to order breakfast for two."

At this point a voice from under the bed said: "Make that five!"

*     *     *

BEN and Betty decided to get married in the Registry Office.

When filling in the appropriate forms the clerk queried Ben's name. "That's a nickname, surely," he said. "Go upstairs to the Birth, Deaths and Marriages Department and check your christened name."

Ben did so and came back to sign as Benjamin.

Betty met the same problem. "Go upstairs and check the records," said the clerk. "Betty can't be your right name."

Sure enough, she returned to sign her name as Elizabeth.

"Lucky I was here," said the clerk. "Otherwise this marriage wouldn't be legal and any kids you had would be technical bastards."

"That's funny," said Elizabeth, "that's what the bloke upstairs said about you."

\* \* \*

"CONGRATULATIONS, my boy," said the groom's uncle. "I'm sure you will look back on today as the happiest day of your life."

"But I'm not getting married until tomorrow," protested the lad.

"I know," said the uncle.

\* \* \*

THE ardent groom had exhausted his young bride on their honeymoon and one morning, while he was having a shave, she dressed and staggered down to the coffee shop. "What's the matter dear?" asked the waitress. "You look all-in. Aren't you the bride with the older husband?"

"Indeed I am," she confessed. "He is 75, but he has double-crossed me," complained the bride. "When he told me had saved up for 60 years I thought he was talking about money!"

\* \* \*

COMPLETE in her wedding gown the tearful young woman confronted her cricket-mad fiance.

"How could you do it? There I was on Saturday waiting at the church with all my relatives and where were you? Playing cricket. You left me in the lurch."

He tried to calm her down. "I distinctly said 'If it rained'."

THE Matron of Honour confided to the bride that if she wanted an unforgettable wedding night she should ensure that her groom should eat a dozen oysters at the marriage ceremony.

Next day the bride thanked her friend, but added dolefully, "Only eight of them worked!"

* * *

THE bride and groom sat up all night waiting for their sexual relations to arrive.

* * *

SHE married a sailor because she wanted to have children and rear admirals.

* * *

THE father was giving advice to his son just before his marriage. "Son, in the beginning it will be tri-weekly. After ten years it will be try weekly, and after 20 years it will be try weakly."

* * *

THE bridegroom was enjoying his last night of freedom at the buck's night when his mate confided, "Surely you can't be serious about marrying Wendy. She's been out with every bloke in town."

The bridegroom thought this over for a while. "Yeah, but it's not really a big town."

* * *

THERE was a little man
  And he had a little gun
  And his bullets were made of lead
  He stood close by
  With a fatherly eye
  While me and my girl were wed.

* * *

IT was a typical Outback Australian wedding and the reception party was in full swing by the time Jack arrived and parked his car outside the shearing shed.

460

He was about to go in when he met Fred coming out shaking his head.

"It's all over," said Fred. "Don't bother going in. It's a total disaster. They've run out of beer and the best man has just stuffed the bride."

The news was enough to turn Jack back towards his car. They were about to leave when another guest came out of the hall and began shouting: "Don't go you blokes. Everything is okay. They have found another keg and the best man has apologised."

## WEDDING TELEGRAMS

TO the groom: "Congratulations Gerald. It was better to have loved and lost, than never to have loved at all." — Mary, Terese, Wendy, Karen, Julie, Barbara, Estelle and Agatha.

      \*    \*    \*

TO the bride: "Congratulations from your loving mother. 22 years ago I sent you to bed with a dummy. Tonight history repeats itself."

      \*    \*    \*

TO the bride: "Congratulations Mabel. It was better to have loved and lost, than never to have loved at all." — Southside Football Club, and coach.

      \*    \*    \*

TO the groom: "Congratulations Gerald, and welcome to the family from the delighted father of the bride. Now that I have given the bride away, can I have a receipt?"

      \*    \*    \*

TO the groom. "Congratulations Gerald from your new in-laws. Be warned, she likes to spend money, but that's her only extravagance."

      \*    \*    \*

TO the bride: "Congratulations from all your friends at the family Planning Centre. PS: The test is positive."

TO the groom. "Congratulations from the local feminist movement. And remember, no woman has ever shot her husband while he was doing the dishes."

* * *

TO the groom: "Congratulations from the Maffioso. We have just kidnapped your new mother-in-law. If you don't pay the ransom money we will send her back."

* * *

TO the groom: "Laugh and the world laughs with you. Quarrel with Mabel and you sleep alone."

TO the groom: "Congratulations and all the best. But remember, Socrates died from an overdose of wedlock."

* * *

TO the groom: "Congratulations Gerald and all the best for the future. From all your mates at Alcoholics Anonymous.

* * *

TO the groom: "Congratulations from the best man. Can I have first option on your little black book?"

* * *

TO the groom: "Congratulations from your new family. We assure you your bride has led a sheltered life. She thinks Good Housekeeping is a women's magazine. She never uses four letter words like Work, Shop, Bake, Dust. And she believes intercourse is a ticket to the races."

## WIDOWS

WHAT would you call a woman who always knows where her husband is?

A widow!

* * *

"SO you are going to marry Widow Brown. I wouldn't like to be the second husband of a widow."

"It's better than being the first."

"WHERE did you get that black eye?"

"You know that pretty little woman who said she was a widow? Well she isn't."

\* \* \*

HER husband didn't leave her much when he died. But he left her a lot while he was living.

\* \* \*

A NOSEY neighbour chided Widow Watkins. She said she didn't think it proper for the widow to entertain the grocer boy for hours each evening.

"It's only platonic," she said.

"What do you mean, platonic?" persisted the nosey neighbour.

"It's play for him and a tonic for me," said the widow.

\* \* \*

TWO mates were leaning on the bar. "The problem is," confided Bill, "I can marry a widow with heaps of money who I don't love, or I can marry a girl on the dole who I love very much."

"Follow your heart," was Fred's advice. "True love is best."

After a few minutes' silence Bill agreed: "You're right, I will."

"Good." said Fred, "And by the way, what's the widow's address?"

## WIVES
See HUSBANDS

HERE'S to the man who takes a wife
But let him make no mistake
For it makes a lot of difference
Whose wife it is you take.

\* \* \*

WIFE, to woman next door: "I can only tell you this once, Bronwyn, I promised not to repeat it."

JAKE lamented to his mate: "How come my wife can spot a blonde hair on my shoulder, yet miss the garage doors?"

*     *     *

FRED is darn lucky. He has got a wife and a transistor, and they both work.

*     *     *

OVERHEARD at the bar: "Is it possible for a man to make a fool of himself without knowing it?"

"Not if he has a wife," counselled his wise friend.

*     *     *

"MY husband wears the pants in our family. But I tell him which pair to wear."

*     *     *

WIFE: "You certainly made a fool of yourself tonight. I only hope nobody realised you were sober."

*     *     *

"NO. I don't wake up sleepy and irritable," she said. "I let him sleep in."

*     *     *

SHE had always been a bossy wife and he had always taken the easy way out and never complained.

But when their South American tour went wrong and the bandits put them both before the firing squad he decided to make a stand.

When he was offered a blindfold he refused it and shouted, "You can stick the blindfold ya dirty rotten bastards."

"Gerald," she said. "Stop making trouble!"

*     *     *

HE reckons his wife is an outspoken woman. And having met her we would be mighty interested to know who outspoke her.

*     *     *

"WE were married in secret," she said. "Even my husband didn't know until he sobered up."

"MY husband is a man of rare gifts. I haven't received one for years."

*　　*　　*

HE introduces his missus as the awful wedded wife.

*　　*　　*

SHE was the kind of wife who spends her evenings dining and whining.

*　　*　　*

"MY mother says I should never have married you," said the young wife during a tiff. "She thinks you're effeminate."

"Well," he said, "compared to her I probably am."

*　　*　　*

A BLOKE comes home and starts to tell his wife some jokes he just heard at the pub. She interrupts and tells him to stop. "You," she says severely, "have got a dirty mind."

"Well..." he shrugged. "I suppose that's because I don't change mine as often as you do."

*　　*　　*

A COUPLE got married and the wife put a wooden box under the bed and told her husband he wasn't allowed to look inside it until after she died.

After 20 years of marriage her husband couldn't resist his curiousity any longer. While his wife was out he opened the box and found three eggs and $25,000.

He looked at it so long in puzzled amazement that his wife caught him.

"Well, what are the eggs for?" asked the husband.

"Every time I've been unfaithful to you, I put an egg in the box," she explained.

The husband said, "Only three times in 20 years, well, that's not bad. I can live with that. But what's the money for?"

The wife replied, "Every time I got a dozen I sold them!"

*　　*　　*

A COUPLE were having a heated argument about family

finances. Finally the wife exploded: "If it wasn't for my money we wouldn't have that television set. And if it wasn't for my money we wouldn't have any furniture. And if it wasn't for my money this house wouldn't be here."

"Listen," snorted her husband. "If it wasn't for your money I wouldn't be here."

*     *     *

CHAP met his ex-wife at a party and after a few drinks he suggested they go to bed.

"Over my dead body," she sneered.

He downed his drink and replied, "I see you haven't changed."

*     *     *

AS the old stockman lay dying she sat beside him wiping his fevered brow. Raising himself up on one elbow he turned to her and spoke:

"Ethel, you've been with me through it all. Remember the time when I got trampled in the stampede? You were there.

"And when I lost all that money at the cattle sale. You were at my side.

"And now I've been shot by a rustler, here you are again. You know, Ethel, I'm beginning to think you're bad luck!"

*     *     *

"HOW'S your wife?"

"Compared to what?"

*     *     *

"OUR marriage is based on trust and understanding.

She doesn't trust me, and I don't understand her."

*     *     *

"EVERY night my wife covers her face in mud and puts her hair in rollers."

"Does it help?"

"A little. But I can still tell it's her."

*     *     *

"IF you're fed up with your marriage, why don't you leave him?"

"I would, if I could find a way of doing it without making him happy."

* * *

SHE said she married one of the world's greatest lovers. "And one day I'm going to catch him at it."

* * *

TWO young housewives were having their regular cuppa but one was very depressed. "What's up?" said her friend.

"I caught my husband making love," she explained.

"So what? Don't let that bother you. I got mine the same way!"

* * *

"MY husband is an angel."

"You're lucky. Mine's still alive!"

* * *

HE got a telegram from his wife: "Harry, I missed you yesterday. Come home and let me have another shot."

* * *

HE joined the Foreign Legion to try and forget his wife, but at least six of the legionaires looked like her.

* * *

WIFE, to woman next door: "My husband has just run off with my best friend."

"Oh, gracious me, who was it?"

"Don't know, never met her."

* * *

"THERE was a phone call for you while you were out," said the wife to her husband.

"Oh, who was it?"

"It was one of those trouts you were fishing for last week."

* * *

FRED was staggering home from a bucks party when the milkman picked him up. "Where do you live?" asked the milkman.

"Robinson St," muttered Fred.

"Oh, Robinson St," said the milko. "Know it well. I have a great time on collection days in that street. Have a wonderful time with every woman except one," he laughed.

This news disturbed Fred and he woke his wife as soon as he got home and relayed the story. "Every woman except one, that's what the milkman said."

His sleepy wife thought for a while. "Oh that would be that stuck-up bitch at number 10," she said.

* * *

HARRY Henpecked stepped on the weighing machine and was about to read his horoscope when his domineering wife snatched the card from him.

"Strong leader of men, Ha," she read aloud. "Master of your own destiny." She turned the card over. "It's even got your weight wrong."

* * *

HARRY Henpecked finally had enough. He declared that he was going to commit suicide and stormed out of the house. She called after him that she had heard that story all too often before. About an hour later she went down the main street to do her shopping and saw a crowd gathered outside a very high building. The crowd was hushed and horrified, for there was Harry balancing on the highest parapet.

She screamed: "That's my husband! Save him! Somebody save him!"

A cop looked round and gave the woman a long hard stare. "Is that man really your husband?" he asked.

"Of course he is," she snapped.

"Oh, that's okay then," said the cop. "For a while we thought he was crazy and didn't know what he was doing."

* * *

HE came home in a state of utter despair and sat with his head in his hands. "I have just been sacked," he told his wife.

468

"After 40 years of doing the same job week after week I have been replaced by an electronic gadget about the size of a torch," he lamented. "What's more it can do everything I can do, and do it better and never wear out," he moaned.

But nobody was listening. She had gone out to buy one.

*　　*　　*

EIGHT kids were too many and the cost of rising prices was getting Fred down. He told his wife if they had any more kids he would go out of his mind with worry.

A week later his wife announced that she was pregnant.

"That's the end," lamented Fred. He opened the drawer beneath his desk and pulled out a revolver and held it to his head.

"Stop!" cried his wife. "You'll be killing an innocent man!"

*　　*　　*

MRS Murphy said: "Oi don't think my husband has been completely fait'ful t' me."

"Why, what makes you so suspicious?"

"My last child doesn't resemble him in the least."

*　　*　　*

CHAP watering his front garden saw a taxi leave the house next door and his neighbour waving his visitors farewell.

"Goodbye. Your wife is great in bed," he shouted as the cab drove off. "She's fantastic in the cot."

He could hardly believe it and when the cab had gone he called his neighbour over to the fence.

"Did I hear right?" he said. "Did I hear you say that bloke's wife was good in bed?"

"Well it isn't really true," said his neighbour, "but I didn't want to hurt his feelings."

*　　*　　*

SHE had been married so long she even faked the fore-play.

A MAN never knows the value of a woman's love until he pays maintenance.

* * *

IF your wife wants to learn to drive, don't stand in her way.

* * *

IF you don't like the way women drive, then get off the footpath.

* * *

MY wife has been booked so many times the cops have now given her a season ticket.

* * *

"IS your wife outspoken?"
"Not by anyone I know of."

* * *

WHEN a woman is looking for a husband she is either single or married.

* * *

MARIA Lotzabazooma has had eight husbands. Three of them were her own.

* * *

THE upkeep of a wife is often the downfall of a husband.

* * *

OLD Minnie was complaining to the doctor about the antics of her husband. "He's always looking at pretty girls and wandering off after them," she complained.

"Well, its hard to stop men admiring pretty girls," said the doctor.

"But my husband is 82 years of age," persisted Minnie.

The doctor considered this for a minute and said: "Let me put it this way. I have a little fox terrier that chases motor cars. What would happen if he ever caught one?"

* * *

THE brewery manager called around, hat in hand, to solemnly announce that her husband, Fred, had suffered a tragic and fatal accident at work. He had fallen into a vat of beer and drowned.

"Oh dear. Did he suffer much?" asked the bereaved wife.

"I don't think so," said the manager. "He got out twice to go to the loo."

*    *    *

HARRY stopped off at the pub and was soon chatting up a blonde at the bar. Near closing time she suggested going to her place. They did and after a few more drinks they had a wonderful time.

It was three in the morning when Harry got out of bed and began to dress. And with a worried frown said "How will I explain this to the wife?"

"No problem," said the blonde, "and by the way, put this bit of chalk behind your ear."

Harry was creeping up the stairs when the light was flicked on, and there was his fuming wife waiting with folded arms.

"And where the hell have you been?" she demanded.

Harry remembered the blonde's advice and told the truth. "I've been tumbling in bed with a lovely blonde I picked up in the pub," he said.

"Liar!" she roared. "You have been playing billiards all night with those hopeless mates of yours. I can tell by the chalk behind your ear."

*    *    *

THE wife was understandably annoyed when her husband came in drunk at midnight.

"I could forgive you if it was the first time," she said. "but you came home in the same condition on March 15, 1958."

*    *    *

"HOW'S your headache, Fred?"

"Out doing the shopping."

*    *    *

"YOU haven't nagged me all evening. Is there someone else?"

"ONE more word," she said, "and I'll go back to my mother."
"Taxi!"

THE doctor asked her: "Has there been any insanity in the family?"

"Yes, Doc," she said. "My husband thinks he's the boss."

\*     \*     \*

SHE has a tongue that jaywalks over every conversation.

\*     \*     \*

SHE gives me a 'Going Away Party' every time I take the garbage out.

\*     \*     \*

GOING to a party with your wife is like going fishing with a game keeper.

\*     \*     \*

IF you want your wife to listen, then talk to another woman.

# WOMEN
See WIVES

GENERALLY speaking, women are generally speaking.

\*     \*     \*

FOUR women, one English, one American, one German and one French, were all asked the same question: "What would you do if you were shipwrecked on an island with a regiment of soldiers?"

The Englishwoman said she would hide. The American said she would seek the protection of the commanding officer. The German woman said she would be out marching and it wouldn't bother her.

The French woman thought for a moment; "I understand ze question, but what seems to be ze problem?"

\*     \*     \*

WHEN a woman is looking for a husband she is either single or married.

TWO psychiatrists were in a restaurant. One said, "See that man over there, well, he claims to understand women."

"Really," said his friend, "and he's a professional colleague?"

"No. He's a patient."

# WORDS

WORDS are the means by which we confuse each other as three New Australians discovered. One was lamenting the fact that he and his wife had no children. "My wife is unbearable," he explained.

"No, you mean she is inconceivable," said the second.

"You are both wrong," said the third. "He means his wife is impregnable."

\* \* \*

THE longest word in the English language is the one following the phrase: "And now a word from our sponsor."

\* \* \*

FRED always called a spade a spade, until the night he fell over one.

\* \* \*

HE was going to have a few words with his wife, but he found she had cornered the market.

\* \* \*

ONE word of censure makes Dad hold his tongue; and Mum's the word.

\* \* \*

PROCRASTINATION is the thief of time, especially if you can't spell it.

\* \* \*

WHEN a politician says a meeting was meaningful; it means that it was meaningless.

\* \* \*

COULD-Be-Better-Put Dept: A woman on a crowded train thought she recognised her husband in the crush.

473

She pushed through, came up behind him and kissed him on the neck. When he turned round she was shocked to find it wasn't him at all.

"Terribly sorry," she blushed, "but your head looks just like my husband's behind."

* * *

TO awaken a student sleeping in his class the English professor threw a book at him.

"What hit me?" spluttered the student.

"That, my lad," replied the professor, "was a flying Chaucer."

* * *

LETTERS can be as confusing as words. Following a lesson on genetics one student asked of his colleague what DNA stood for.

"That's simple," said his friend. "It stands for the National Association of Dyslectics."

* * *

THE Maharaja of an Indian province once decreed that no wild animals were to be killed. Soon his realm was overun with tigers. When the people could stand it no longer they gave the Maharaja the heave-ho.

It was the first time on record where the reign was cancelled because of the game.

* * *

ON the anniversary of Shakespeare's birth a BBC announcer achieved this vintage spoonerism: "The usual festivities were held in Stratford today to celebrate the Bird's bathday!"

* * *

THE flying instructor had just delivered a lesson on parachute jumping. "And if it doesn't open?" asked a student.

"Well, you are jumping to a conclusion," he replied.

* * *

SHE said she had started a new diet: "No more eating my own words, swallowing my pride, or putting my foot in my mouth," she said.

WHEN Joe Bloggs scooped the agricultural show with all prizes for his vegetables he was invited on television.

"And what is the secret of growing prize vegetables?" asked the compere.

"Manure," answered Joe. "Manure for tomatoes, manure for pumpkins, manure for cabbages..." and he went on extolling the virtues of manure.

A very embarrassed daughter was watching at home. "Oh Mum, why can't Dad say fertilizer instead of manure?"

"Count your blessings," said Mrs Bloggs. "It took me 30 years to get him to call it manure!"

*　　*　　*

THE Archbishop of Canterbury was a distinguished guest at the mayoral dinner. As the first course was being served a waiter slipped and dropped a bowl of hot soup upside down in the Archbishop's lap.

The Archbishop looked depairingly around the table and said: "Is there any layman present who will be good enough to express my feelings?"

*　　*　　*

WHEN it came to writing up the log book Captain Squiggs was a stickler for accuracy, so when the first mate received news that he was the father of twins and celebrated in his cabin the captain noted in the logbook: "The first mate was drunk last night."

When the mate saw it he argued that it should be struck from the record but the pedantic captain was resolute. "You were drunk last night. I can't change that fact, so it must stay in the log."

Next day the mate was on watch and it was his duty to keep the log. In the morning the captain was aghast to read: "The captain was sober last night."

*　　*　　*

YOU have heard of the TATE family? They're everywhere.

There is Dick Tate who wants to control everybody. Ro Tate who tries to turn things around. Agi Tate who stirs up trouble and Irri Tate who helps. Hesi Tate and Vege Tate always procrastinate. Imi Tate mimics everybody. Devas Tate likes to destroy things and Poten Tate wants to be a big shot, but it's Facili Tate, Cogi Tate and Medi Tate who save the day.

*    *    *

THE Aussie had just taken up a job in the wildlife sanctuary and was explaining to some American tourists the difference between an echidna and a porcupine. "The echidnas' pricks are longer," he said.

This caused great embarrassment amongst the mixed group and later the supervisor took him aside to reprimand the Aussie on his choice of words.

"It's quills. Use a bit of decorum," he said. "It's quills."

The next group of Yanks raised the same question. "That's a doggone porcupine," said one.

"Different animal altogether," said our Aussie with authority. "The echidna is smaller, lighter in colour and its quills are longer ... but their pricks are about the same size."